CHILDREN AND SEXUALITY: PERSPECTIVES IN HEALTH CARE

Edited by

TONY HARRISON BA RN RSCN RNT

Baillière Tindall

PUBLISHED IN ASSOCIATION WITH THE RCN

LONDON   PHILADELPHIA   TORONTO   SYDNEY   TOKYO

Baillière Tindall   24–28 Oval Road
London NWI 7DX

The Curtis Center
Independence Square West
Philadelphia, PA 19106–3399, USA

Harcourt Brace & Company
55 Horner Avenue
Toronto, Ontario M8Z 4X6, Canada

Harcourt Brace & Company, Australia
30–52 Smidmore Street
Marrickville
NSW 2204, Australia

Harcourt Brace & Company, Japan
Ichibancho Central Building
22–I Ichibancho
Chiyoda-ku, Tokyo 102, Japan

A catalogue record for this book is available from the British Library

ISBN 0–7020–2208–X

Typeset by Phoenix Photosetting, Chatham, Kent
Printed and bound in Great Britain by WBC Book Manufacturers, Bridgend, Mid Glamorgan

Contents

LIST OF CONTRIBUTORS

Elizabeth Bartley BA PGCE RN RSCN RHV
Ward F8 Medical (Paediatrics), Wythenshawe Hospital, Southmoor Road, Manchester.

Peter Callery BA RN RSCN MSc PhD
School of Nursing, Midwifery and Health Visiting, University of Manchester, Gateway House, Piccadilly South, Manchester.

Grainne Graham BA MA MSc
Trafford Health Care NHS Trust, Trafford Health Promotion Unit, Trafford General Hospital, Moorside Road, Davyhulme, Manchester.

Janice Grant MSc BSc RN RSCN RM RNT
University of Salford, Department of Nursing, Peel House, Albert Street, Eccles, Manchester.

Tony Harrison BA RN RSCN RNT
School of Nursing, Midwifery and Health Visiting, University of Manchester, Gateway House, Piccadilly South, Manchester.

Sue Hooton RSCN RN RNT BSc MA
Education Officer (Children's Nursing) English National Board for Nursing, Midwifery and Health Visiting, BSP House, Station Road, Chester.

Celia Hynes RSCN RN RCNT RNT BA
University of Salford, Department of Nursing, Peel House, Albert Street, Eccles, Manchester.

Bruce Lindsay BA RSCN
Norfolk College of Nursing and Midwifery, Teaching Centre, Norfolk and Norwich Hospital, Norwich.

Steven Pryjmachuk BA MSc PGDipEd(Nursing) RMN RNT
School of Nursing, Midwifery and Health Visiting, University of Manchester, Gateway House, Piccadilly South, Manchester.

Lita Reason RN RHV MSc
Senior Nurse Advisor/Specialist Practitioner, Child Protection.

Joseph Roberts MA BSc RN RSCN RNT
University of Salford, Department of Nursing, Peel House, Albert Street, Eccles, Manchester.

Mike Thomas RMN BSc RNT Cert Ed MA
University of Salford, Peel House, Albert Street, Eccles, Manchester.

PREFACE

The aim of this text is to invigorate the perpetually closing debate which surrounds children and sexuality. This is assumed by many child care professionals to be a debate which has not only occurred, but which has been resolved. This is far from the truth. For the most part any discussion about children and sex is confined to the areas of teenage pregnancy, child sexual abuse or adolescent sexual education (normally in schools), and while these are certainly important areas, sexuality is about more than fertility, abuse and knowledge.

In order to achieve this aim I asked the contributors to write, from their experience and expertise, about a different facet of childhood sexuality. I asked specifically that they try to avoid the tryanny of balance which sees so many professional texts on varying subjects merely re-work a CD-ROM search and dictate the pros and cons dispassionately. As an educationalist I am of the firm opinion that balance can, all too often, be the enemy of debate, a debate which in this case we urgently need, if the rights of children and families to appropriate professional support in developing a healthy sexuality is to be met.

The result of such direction is a discourse of divergent and sometimes controversial views which seeks to engage the reader in intellectual debate, in the hope that the resulting 'discussion' between the authors and the reader will be fuelled with energy and passion. My hope is that through this discourse you, the reader, and we, the contributors, will make some positive contribution to improving the sexual health of children and their families, by improving our understanding of the complex issues involved.

This is not the definitive work on childhood sexuality, nor does it aim to be. This is a 'reader' which looks at some of the facets of this highly complex subject. It can be sampled or read in entirety, the latter being the more worthwhile as the reader will then be able to compare the divergent views contained in the text. Some in the professions will, I am sure, not only disagree with, but also disapprove of many of the views expressed in this text. This, I feel, can only be healthy; a chorus of approval makes a poor debate. Whether you agree or disagree, all who have contributed to this book would welcome your comments.

TONY HARRISON
1998

Chapter 1

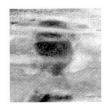

SEX AND CHILDREN IN THE PAST AND THE PRESENT

PETER CALLERY BA RN RSCN MSC PHD

MEETING POLLY

Polly is the 2-year-old sister of my daughter's friend. I collected my daughter from Polly's house for the first time on a very hot day and Polly was in the kitchen with her grandmother, who has cared for Polly since her parents died. I had a short conversation with the grandmother and also spoke to Polly. Because I am always interested in children and like their company, I set about making friends with her in my usual way — some conversation about what she was doing, a little banter and generally showing an interest. This included comments about the appropriateness of Polly's clothing for such a hot day — she was completely naked. Later I began to wonder how my interaction with Polly would have appeared to her grandmother: would my interest in a 2-year-old girl be interpreted as sinister? Did Polly's state of undress change the way that my behaviour might be interpreted?

The incident probably had little significance and I have no reason to believe that Polly's family believe that I am anything other than a slightly eccentric father. However, my responses may not be particularly unusual because adult relations with children are the subject of closer scrutiny than was the case 10 or 20 years ago, and certainly more so than in the days of Lewis Carroll and Alice. Adults, and men in particular, can expect their interactions with children to be observed and judged. The motives of adults who show interest in children are open to question. There has certainly been an increase in awareness of the extent and nature of sexual abuse of children in the past 10 to 20 years in the UK at least. Sexual abuse has been increasingly discussed in various media and its higher profile has influenced attitudes towards adult interest in children. Such scrutiny is welcome because naive trust is potentially dangerous and can be used as a tool by intending abusers. However, it also has the potential to change the nature of relations between adults and children, to introduce more uncertainty and more distance between adults, particularly men, and children. This has implications for the relationships between nurses and children in their care.

In this chapter I will draw on contemporary and historical accounts in a discussion of attitudes towards children and sex in the past and the present. The guidance offered to nurses in the UK by the Royal College of Nursing will be considered as illustrative of the difficulties faced by adult carers of children. Adult perspectives of children and sexuality and histories of childhood will be discussed. Notions of innocence and evil in childhood and problems of ambiguity and self-consciousness will be considered. The chapter will conclude with a discussion of the development of the concept of children's rights with particular emphasis on rights to information about sex, and implications for nursing practice will be considered.

Guidance for Nurses

The Royal College of Nursing (RCN) published guidance for nurses working with children in November 1996. An examination of the assumptions made in the document and the advice offered provide some insights into the anxieties that nurses have in dealing with child sexuality. The purpose of the document was

> to raise awareness among nurses and their managers of the complex issues which need to be addressed in the light of recent cases where children have been harmed by nurses and other health care staff caring for them.

The difficulty of defining the difference between the close physical contact that is part of warm, caring relationships with children and sexually inappropriate behaviour is illustrated:

> The Royal College of Nursing is aware that even flagging up this sensitive issue could contribute to fears amongst male, or even female, nurses and discourage them from touching, cuddling, or physically holding children at all. But the issue of concern is inappropriate contact. It is clearly very important not to inhibit perfectly natural therapeutic behaviour between nurses and children.

However, it must be remembered that close working relationships can never emulate close family relationships. Thus the norms for professional nursing care are different to those of mother/child and father/child.

This is a tortuous piece of writing which raises more questions than it answers. It is interesting that therapeutic behaviour is described as 'perfectly natural'. An important concern during the last 40 years has been that hospital care for children has lacked the human warmth that is described as natural here. Nurses have been criticised for providing a poor standard of psychosocial care to children and it is a commonplace to describe hospitals as psychologically unhealthy places for children to be. The expression 'perfectly natural' is particularly problematic when sexuality is discussed. One of the difficulties with discussions of sexuality is that we all regard what we ourselves do as 'perfectly natural' – it is other people whose sexual behaviour is deviant or perverted. Appeals to 'naturalness' are naive and do not help to identify the problems of sexuality and children's nursing. The campaigns of Action for Sick Children (formerly the National Association of the Welfare of Children in Hospital) to humanise the care of children in hospital would not have been necessary if care was natural. A series of studies of children's wards in the 1970s described a social world in which the care of children fell short of 'natural' standards of humanity (Stacey *et al.*, 1970; Hawthorn, 1974; Hall and Stacey, 1979). Far from being 'natural', the care provided for children is a topic of concern to central government, which has published guidelines and a Charter for children's services (Department of Health, 1991, 1996).

The distinction between 'close working relationships' and 'mother/child and father/child' norms is also interesting. The strong taboos that it is often suggested prevent sexual abuse of children by their biological parents are not present in all family relationships in a society where separation and divorce are common experiences and where children often have one parent who has no biological link with them. The RCN's reference to 'mother/child and father/child' relationships implies a naturalistic view of such relations, which is difficult to sustain when the patterns of family life are given even the most cursory examination. Children are brought up by step-parents and grandparents (as in Polly's case) and have contact with adults in many different caring relationships which are not recognised by the terms 'mother/child' or 'father/child'.

The RCN guidance lists 'strategies for minimising risk' (it appears that this refers to the risk of accusation rather than risk to children) 'where work requires care of an intimate or personal nature'. Firstly:

care of this kind should not be undertaken without appropriate training, negotiation with and explanation to the child and the child's main carer.

This raises the problem of what is 'appropriate training'? How should nurses be trained in order to provide care which will not be misinterpreted as sexual abuse? A first step is to raise awareness about the problems of children and sexuality so that nurses have some preparation for intimate care of children. This would be a useful function of this book.

The second strategy is:

> *In community settings, a parent or other carer should be present if care of an intimate nature is to be given.*

Personal privacy is an important part of sexual identity: during our physical and emotional development at puberty we become increasingly conscious that some parts of our bodies are now private. The distinction is illustrated by my daughters: the 9-year-old brings her nightwear down to the living room and gets changed in front of the family, whereas the 12-year-old will only get changed in her own bedroom, on her own. Privacy from parents as well as others is important to children at certain stages of development. Intimate procedures are by their nature an invasion of privacy and children may prefer such procedures to be private from their parents. To insist that parents observe procedures in such circumstances could be damaging to the relationship between parent and child and certainly between child and nurse.

The RCN guidance also advises nurses to be aware of the possible interpretation which might be placed on touch, particularly in a multicultural society, and recommendations are made to include such considerations in nursing assessments and to discuss care with families. It is suggested that:

> *Some children, particularly adolescent girls and those from non-Christian backgrounds, are likely to prefer a female carer. This reflects social, religious and cultural preferences and should be respected and accommodated.*

Why concentrate on girls? There appears to be an assumption throughout the document that men are potential abusers and that women are not. Although the available evidence does suggest that most sexual abusers are male, female abusers exist and the extent of this abuse is not known. It is also true that boys as well as girls are sexually abused. It must be true that some children will prefer to be cared for by a nurse of a particular sex. However, it is difficult to understand why Christians would be less concerned by the sex of their carers than Jews, Buddhists, Pagans, Muslims, Humanists, or people who consider themselves to belong to any other religion or none. Adolescent girls may well prefer female carers, but why not consider the needs of adolescent boys – do they not prefer male carers? There may not be the evidence for us to know, which is all the more reason not to rely on assumptions. The assumptions that underlie this advice are that girls are more vulnerable than boys, that religion is the important cultural dimension that affects children's desire for same-sex carers and that female nurses should always be offered to adolescent girls but that adolescent boys do not have similar needs for male carers. These assumptions illustrate the social construction of sexuality in Britain: sexual aggression is characterised as a predominantly male phenomenon and the desire for privacy as a female preoccupation. Although it is recognised that there is a range of cultural groups in the UK, the range of cultural meanings of sexuality are presented as religious differences.

These assumptions are reinforced in advice offered to male nurses, who are warned that they can be in vulnerable positions and are advised that:

> if they recognise a child they are with is distressed and wishes to be com-
> forted, they should bring the child out of a private cubicle or alert colleagues
> so that they can be observed.

The advice offered here is to make private distress public in order to avoid an accusation of sexual abuse. The actions which need to be observed are not specified – anything that is offered as comfort is open to question. Comforting a person includes a wide range of behaviours, from listening quietly, through holding a hand to close cuddling and perhaps even sexual intercourse. It is an illustration of the uncertainty that surrounds the relationships between adults and children that such a generalised warning about observation of comfort is made. The advice implies that virtually any behaviour is open to question and so must be observed. This is evidence of a loss of confidence about the nature of adult–child relations. The origins of this loss of confidence may well lie in the shock that has been experienced as evidence of the abuse of trust by adults has emerged and the disgust which is felt when details of child sex abuse are published. This loss of confidence and the warnings to nurses to be defensive and cautious in their relations with children have the potential to make the care offered by nurses colder, harsher, less caring and to make hospitals in particular less sympathetic places for children to be.

DISCUSSION POINT

What advice would you give nurses in order to ensure the safety of children and avoid accusations of abuse?

SEX AND CHILDHOOD: A DIFFICULT TOPIC FOR ADULTS

Any sentence that includes the words 'sex' and 'child' is problematic. This is a most sensitive area of discussion in which powerful emotions are aroused. It features regularly in the news media, usually in disturbing and unpleasant stories that underline the dangers of combining the ideas of sex and childhood. For example, a selection of news reports at the time of writing includes: excited comment about the transfer of pornographic images of children via the Internet; the conviction of a senior British diplomat for importing videos of child pornography into the UK by the more traditional means of carrying them on an aeroplane; a Belgian man in custody while the authorities continue to recover the bodies of children from his properties and to investigate his alleged involvement in an international paedophile ring; the launch of an investigation into the abuse of children in local authority homes in Wales.

Against this background of violence, anger and disgust it is difficult even to start to discuss children and sex. However, the horrified responses to these events also illustrate the importance of investigating adults' attitudes to sex and children. The fact that children are exploited in such disturbing ways is not comfortable for adults to face and leads to violent reactions of blame of the individuals concerned. Although it is quite right that individuals take responsibility for their actions and are brought to account for wrongdoing, it is not sufficient to dismiss the sexual abuse of children as the act of monsters and beasts. The monsters and beasts that we vilify are part of our society and it is important to understand our society's attitudes towards children and sexuality.

Adult Perspectives on Childhood

An adult is somebody who has learnt not to be a child:

> When I was a child, I spake as a child, I understood as a child, I thought as a child: but when I became a man, I put away childish things.
>
> (I Corinthians 13: 1)

Thus any view that adults have of childhood is open to the challenge that it is precisely that – an adult view which is ethnocentric – and childhood is seen through adult values, norms and mores. In childhood we see both our past and our future, the past that we have grown away from and the people who will be adults as we age and after we have gone (Jenks, 1996: 6). Thus our view of childhood is strongly coloured by our view of ourselves as we contemplate our past and our future. What we see when we look at children can therefore be an image generated as much by the adult viewer as the child actor.

Histories of Childhood

The development of childhood is a controversial historical topic. The seminal work in the history of childhood is by Ariès (1962) in which it is argued that childhood is a modern invention and that the status of childhood only started to be acknowledged in the fifteenth century as education grew in importance. Prior to then:

> In the Middle Ages, at the beginning of modern times and for a long time after that in the lower classes, children were mixed with adults as soon as they were considered capable of doing without their mothers or nannies, not long after a tardy weaning (in other words at about the age of seven). They immediately went straight into the great community of men, sharing in the work and play of their companions, old and young alike.
>
> (Ariès, 1962: 395)

The reference to the world of men implies the different status of girls, who were not regarded as in need of education and whose adult lives were not delayed by schooling:

> *The concept of childhood developed as an adjunct to the modern family ...*
> *childhood did not apply to women. The female child went from swaddling*
> *clothes right into adult female dress. She did not go to school, which, ... was*
> *the institution that structured childhood. At the age of nine or ten she acted,*
> *literally, like a 'little lady'; her activity did not differ from that of an adult*
> *woman. As soon as she reached puberty, as early as ten or twelve, she was*
> *married off to a much older male.*
>
> *(Firestone, 1972: 43–44, cited in Jenks, 1996: 48)*

Expectations about the sexual behaviour of children are fundamental to our idea of childhood. The extension of childhood beyond the development of adult sexual characteristics defines when childhood ceases to be determined by physical immaturity and becomes entirely a matter of social construction. Education is the social force that extends childhood and as educational demands become more complex childhood is extended through the relatively recent notions of 'youth', 'adolescent' or 'teenager' (Jenks, 1996).

An alternative view of childhood to that offered by Ariès was dramatically presented by deMause:

> *The history of childhood is a nightmare from which we have only recently*
> *begun to awaken. The further back in history one goes, the lower the level of*
> *child care, and the more likely children are to be killed, abandoned, terrorized,*
> *and sexually abused.*
>
> *(deMause, 1974: 1)*

deMause described the sexual treatment of children in ancient Greece in uncompromising terms:

> *The child in antiquity lived his earliest years in an atmosphere of sexual abuse.*
> *Growing up in Greece and Rome often included being used sexually by older*
> *men. The exact form and frequency of the abuse varied by area and date ...*
> *Boy brothels flourished in every city, and one could even contract for the use*
> *of a 'rent-a-boy' service in Athens.*
>
> *(deMause, 1974: 43)*

The history of childhood sexuality took a turn for the better with the development of Christian concepts about the moral status of children:

> *Christians throughout the Middle Ages began to stress the idea that children*
> *were totally innocent of all notions of pleasure and pain.*
>
> *(deMause, 1974: 47)*

deMause suggested that Christ's comment that people should 'become like children' in order to enter heaven indicated that the Christian view was that children were innocent. The development of the idea of childhood innocence was an innovation introduced by Christianity. However, this did not mean that children were not abused and the idea of childhood innocence could actually provide justification for those who claim that sexual activity with children is not corrupting for the child.

The idea of childhood innocence was followed by its contradiction, that innate desires and behaviours are vicious and must be suppressed, so that in the eighteenth century:

> parents began severely punishing their children for masturbation, and doctors began to spread the myth that it would cause insanity, epilepsy, blindness, and death. By the nineteenth century, this campaign reached an unbelievable frenzy, doctors and parents sometimes appeared before the child armed with knives and scissors, threatening to cut off the child's genitals; circumcision, clitoridectomy, and infibulation were sometimes used as punishment; and all sorts of restraint devices, including plaster casts and cages with spikes, were prescribed.
>
> (deMause, 1974: 48)

deMause certainly has a vivid turn of phrase and has presented some dramatic evidence about the way that children have been treated by adults in the past. However, his central argument, which implies that children are better treated in modern times than ever before, would be treated with more scepticism today than when it was published in 1974. Today there is uncertainty and concern about children and childhood, with considerable public debate about the behaviour of children, political interest in the development of programmes to support parenting, and scrutiny of the moral climate of schools. Sexuality is a particular area of concern. There is anxiety about the level and nature of child sexual abuse as a result of a series of court cases. There is also concern about sexual awareness and behaviour during the teenage years, partly because of concerns about sexually transmitted diseases and HIV infection in particular and partly because of the numbers of teenage pregnancies.

CHILDHOOD INNOCENCE OR ORIGINAL SIN?

There are essentially two ways of interpreting childhood which underlie our attitudes towards children and child-rearing. Children can be seen as essentially innocent and virtuous, with qualities that adults can nurture and encourage in order for a child to grow into a person naturally and uncorrupted. Alternatively the child can be seen as essentially savage and in need of taming, in which case child-rearing is concerned with the subjugation of the child to the will of more wise adults who have learnt to overcome the wickedness of the world. The latter form of child-rearing is exemplified by the Quakers of the sixteenth and seventeenth centuries who went to great efforts to control children and it is from this era that the famous saying endorsing physical punishment arises:

> Love is a boy, by poets styled,
> Then spare the rod, and spoil the child.

Ηυδιβρασπτ. 2(1664), χαντο Ι, λ. 843
Samuel 'Hudibras' Butler, 1612–80

This principle did not expire in the sixteenth century; I am not alone in recalling my father's tales about being beaten for not having learnt his Latin to the satisfaction of his Jesuit teachers. The alternative principle of viewing the child as uncorrupted and essentially worthy also has a long history which can be traced at least as far as Rousseau (Jenks, 1996). The child is to be valued and nurtured and the role of adults is to allow the full expression of the child's natural abilities and strengths.

To present these two approaches in this way is to imply that they are entirely contradictory and mutually exclusive. While the fundamental logic of the view of childhood upon which each rests is entirely different and inconsistent, this does not prevent us approaching children and child-rearing with an ambiguous mixture of the two views. In the area of sexuality our deepest prejudices and fears about childhood are exposed and our responses to children and sexuality include a confusing mixture of both of these contradictory approaches to childhood. Thus newspaper accounts of child abuse will emphasise the child's innocence, vulnerability and lack of responsibility for the events. This is in contrast to accounts of murders of women, whose behaviour and occupations are open to enquiry. For example, a newspaper account of the murder of a woman who has worked as a prostitute is likely to include this information and to imply less sympathy than an account of a woman whose occupation was 'blameless'. However, when the subject of media coverage is child crime or misbehaviour in some other way, then the child is presented as fully responsible and as having traits of wickedness and evil. In the UK the most notable recent case is the death of the child Jamie Bulger, whose child murderers received a hostile press. I am not suggesting that either of these views of childhood is wrong, or right for that matter, but merely observing that we are able to apply attitudes quite inconsistently when considering children's behaviour. The ambiguity of our attitudes towards children is nowhere more evident than in the area of sexuality.

AMBIGUITY AND SELF-CONSCIOUSNESS

Children are usually presented as the unwilling victims of sexual abuse. However, this is not always the case. In his humorous column in the *New Statesman* of July 1996, Laurie Taylor described the visits of a priest to his school dormitory during which the priest would fondle the genitals of certain boys. Far from suffering traumas and fear about these experiences, the boys regarded the events with some interest and amusement. Apparently they quite enjoyed the attention and swapped beds to give each other a turn and thwart the priest's intention to concentrate on the slimmer and more attractive boys. Taylor's experience of camaraderie and amusement is very different to the experiences of isolated children who cannot share their experiences, which can be far more unpleasant and even violent. It would be wrong to minimise the horror of experience of child abuse because one author has written about his experiences in an amusing way. However, Taylor's description does challenge assumptions about abuse and the place of children in such encounters and illustrates that children can be left with ambiguous feelings, knowing that something is regarded as wrong but also having collaborated in some small way. This does not make abuse better but it does make the responses of children and adults more complex. One of the features of Taylor's experience was of the innocent and un-self-conscious way in which he viewed what was happening to him at the time.

Children's lack of self-consciousness can present adults with difficulties when attempting to define what is and what is not a sexual crime against a child. A newspaper report headlined 'Innocent fun. Or a paedophile's dream' (Rayner, 1996) described the conviction of an American postman who had travelled to Bournemouth on the English south coast to take video pictures of naked children.

> Morgan, a 44 year old postman from southern California, was convicted last week by Bournemouth magistrates of taking indecent pictures of young children. He had been seen by a beach inspector, apparently videoing nothing in particular for hours on end. Police found his camcorder had been fitted with a mirror and false lens to record naked children playing to one side.

The article is headed by a photograph of a group of young girls and a boy in swim suits jumping into the sea and the relevant law is considered:

> 'Usually we can't get it as an offence because the child has no knowledge that anything was going on,' says Ray Wyre, an independent consultant on sexual crime to the police. 'The Children Act is designed to protect children, but it is deemed not to cover the taking of pictures where nothing untoward is pictured happening to the child.'
>
> Likewise the indecency statutes can be ineffectual, because there is no firm definition. In criminal trials it is up to the jury. 'And what is considered indecent in London may not be indecent in, say, Birmingham.' Where pictures concentrate on the genital area the law is clear; otherwise it is less so.
>
> Finally, there are the laws on material designed to deprave and corrupt. 'That is totally useless,' Mr Wyre says. 'If you do not have the mind-set of a paedophile, then you are not going to find anything of a sexually provocative nature in pictures of naked children on beaches.'
>
> The solution is legislation to make it an offence to take photographs without the child's knowledge.
>
> (Rayner, 1996)

The difficulty that is grappled with here is that children are unconscious of their sexuality and it is the process of adolescence that makes them self-conscious and aware. Adults are faced with a dilemma. Children can be allowed to behave in the spontaneous and uninhibited way which characterises pre-pubescent children and is regarded as socially acceptable. However, allowing children to run around naked in public makes it possible for adults to observe them as sexual objects. Yet, if children are prevented from behaving in an uninhibited way it requires that adults teach children to be self-conscious about the sexuality of their bodies and so to deny them their 'childish' view of themselves.

DISCUSSION POINT

Should legislation make it an offence to take photographs without a child's knowledge?

ADULTS' AMBIGUITY IN THEIR RELATIONS WITH CHILDREN

Adults who spend time with children are open to accusations of sexual motives. For example, Lewis Carroll's relations with young girls have been the cause of much comment. The Alice of his most famous stories, *Alice in Wonderland* and *Alice Through the Looking Glass*, was a special friend called Alice Liddell. The ambiguity of the relationship is suggested by a famous photograph that Carroll took of her. In the photograph Alice is dishevelled and her pose can be interpreted as implying an alluring presentation to an adult viewer – she appears to be conscious of her own sexuality. Apparently Carroll had friendships with 'hundreds of little girls' (Gardner, 1962: 36). 'The Hunting of the Snark', a strange and sometimes disturbing nonsense poem, was dedicated to Gertrude Chataway who Carroll met on the beach at Sandown in the Isle of Wight when she was seven. She recalled as an adult that

> We used to sit for hours on the wooden steps which led from our garden on to the beach, whilst he told me the most lovely tales that could possibly be imagined.
>
> (Gardner, 1962: 36)

Carroll's relationships with little girls present the modern reader with some difficulty because such relations between adults and children are open to suspicion. Gertrude Chataway's account has the quality of innocent explanation that we associate with childhood but can tell us nothing about the motives of the adult she describes. In the ingenious acrostic with which he dedicated the Snark to Gertrude, Carroll spelt out her name with the initial letters of the lines and with the initial word of each stanza. The first stanza can add to a sense of ambiguity about the relationship:

Girt with a boyish garb for boyish task,
Eager she wields her spade: yet loves as well
Rest on a friendly knee, intent to ask
The tale he loves to tell

The reference to the child's clothes and the emphasis on the sexual identity of the clothes demonstrates that the child is not seen as asexual. The reference to resting on the man's knee is discomforting because such intimacy can have sexual connotations. However, the poem can also be read as being without any sense of sexual interest. It is the ambiguity of adults' motives in their relations with children that is so troubling and so difficult to determine.

AN INNOCENT PHOTOGRAPH?

The contemporary sense of uncertainty about how children should be viewed was highlighted by the case of the Mapplethorpe exhibition at the Hayward Gallery in September 1996. Mapplethorpe was an American photographer who produced many homoerotic images. The Hayward Gallery in London staged an exhibition which included explicit images of men having sex with each other, featuring photographs of erect penises and various sexual acts, including fisting and watersports. However, the most controversial picture was one that was excluded from the exhibition. The *New Statesman*, an established and respected weekly journal of politics and the arts, was refused permission to reproduce the photograph, entitled 'Rosie'. It reported that

> *Rosie is a photograph taken in 1976 of three year old Rosie Bowden, the grand-daughter of Lord Lambton. She is pictured sitting on a garden bench, wearing a summer dress. One knee is raised, revealing her bottom ... Ms Bowden, who now runs a restaurant in Notting Hill, is entirely happy with the photograph; indeed, she intends to hang a copy on her restaurant wall. 'It is a very, very sweet picture, taken on a hot day spent running around naked', she told the* Independent on Sunday. *'The only unnatural thing about that photo was that I was wearing a dress.' Her family has testified previously that it was taken with permission.*

This is the sort of photograph that many of us take of our children and treasure. I have photographs of my daughters as nude babies and toddlers, indeed I regularly illustrate teaching about normal childhood development with these photographs. The *New Statesman* summarised the law:

> *In Britain, the Protection of Children Act 1978 (along with more recent amendments) makes it illegal to possess or to publish an indecent photograph of a child below the age of 16. The courts have defined this to mean any picture of*

*a partly unclothed child in an immodest or unbecoming pose ... It is the Child
Protection Act which can be used by Boots the Chemist to justify reporting
you to the police for taking pictures of your kids in the nude, as happened to
the ITN newsreader Julia Somerville.*

How does nudity, surely our 'natural' condition, become regarded as unnatural and dangerous? Children are naturally uninhibited and unconcerned with their bodies. The first recog-
nisable pictures that children draw of themselves and others are potato people, characterised
by disproportionately large heads from which stick limbs protrude without any recognition
of the form of the body. A toddler will feel dressed up to play in a hat, sunglasses and shoes
and nothing else. It is almost as if the space between head and feet does not exist, it is certainly of little importance. As we grow older, bigger and develop sexual characteristics our
body image changes and we become more self-conscious and private. Young children's lack of
inhibition is problematic for adults rather than for children: it challenges us with an openness
that we have lost as we have become more sophisticated.

The *New Statesman* editorial concluded that:

*a world in which you cannot own or show a picture of a naked child because
of fears about child abuse and pornography is a world that has lost its sense
of proportion and self-confidence to a degree that will damage, not protect,
children.*

Although the picture of Rosie might have gone unnoticed in another exhibition that had not
also included explicit images of sexual activity, the mention of lost confidence is justified.
There is great uncertainty about the dividing line between the 'natural' and the 'unnatural'. In
our society we now feel concern that our responses to images of children cannot be trusted
because we are liable to corruption which will allow a dark, submerged and untrustworthy
sexuality to emerge in a depraved form. Freud has unnerved us about what is going on in our
subconscious and we are not convinced that we own and control our sexual desires. However, we also crave the natural. The back cover of the edition of the *New Statesman* discussed
here is taken up by a photograph of a naked man holding a child naked except for a nappy.
This is an advertisement for Scope, the charity for people with cerebral palsy. Images of naked
adults and children are used frequently by advertisers, presumably because they appeal to an
ideal of natural caring relationships with children. Nudity is used here as a symbol of close,
loving and safe relationships between adults and children.

CHILDREN'S SOCIAL STATUS AND SEXUALITY

It has been suggested that a pattern of change can be traced in children's social status over
the last few hundreds of years. It is argued that children have emerged from the social status of private property through a period of status as public property to a more recent

development of a status carrying the rights and responsibilities of person-hood (Hart, 1991). There is certainly historical evidence that children have been regarded as personal sexual property. According to deMause the Romans mutilated infants in order to improve the product:

> *Intercourse with castrated children was often spoken of as being especially arousing, castrated boys were favorite 'voluptates' in imperial Rome, and infants were castrated 'in the cradle' to be used in brothels by men who liked buggering castrated boys.*
>
> *(deMause, 1974: 46)*

The use of children as sexual commodities was not restricted to ancient Rome. In times of economic hardship children are vulnerable to exploitation. A description of China in the 1940s during the disruption of civil war between the Kuomintang and the advancing Communist revolutionaries includes this graphic illustration of the use of children for economic purposes:

> *One trade was prospering: trafficking in young girls for brothels and as slave-servants to rich men. The city was littered with beggars offering their children in exchange for food. For days outside her school my mother saw a desperate-looking woman in rags slumped on the frozen ground. Next to her stood a girl of about ten with an expression of numb misery on her face. A stick was poking out of the back of her collar and on it was a poorly written sign saying 'Daughter for sale for 10 kilos of rice'.*
>
> *(Chang, 1991)*

Children have traditionally been regarded as the property of parents or guardians. The status of child as property is epitomised by the origin of the concept of wardship in child protection legislation which survived even the major overhaul of legislation that resulted in The Children Act, 1989. Originally, wardship proceedings were designed to protect the property of a family where the line of succession was a minor. Wardship was a device to ensure that the family property was maintained in trust until a child came of age. Wardship could be the subject of political dispute, for example article 24 of 'Ketts' demands being in rebellion of 1549' was:

> *We pray that no person of what estate degre or condicion he be shall from hensforth sell the adwardshyppe of eny chyld but that the same chyld if he lyve to his full age shall be at his owne chosyn concernyng his marriage the Kyngs ward only except.*
>
> *(Fletcher, 1973: 144)*

Thus children were the property of parents until they reached an age of majority. The development of children's status went through a phase of children as public property, where a value was placed on children as potential for the future. During the Boer War there was a moral panic in Britain which arose from the quality of men available for military service and attention was given to child care in order to produce a better crop of young men for future military service. Thus the emphasis was on the protection of children from harm and Hart characterised this as a period of 'child saving'. More recently it is suggested that children have rights as persons in their own right, rather than as the property of their fathers or as the potential valuable property of a community. This new view of childhood is exemplified by the United Nations Convention on the Rights of the Child and by the emphasis on children's representation in the Children Act, 1989.

SEXUALITY AND CHILDREN'S RIGHTS

Because sexuality Is such a sensitive topic and children's sexuality is particularly sensitive, it is an area in which questions of children's rights are fought over very strongly. The notion of 'Gillick competence' which can apply in judgements about a child's right to consent to treatment in health care arose out of the Gillick case, which concerned the rights of children to consult their General Practitioner about contraception without obtaining parental consent. Although subsequent case law has limited a child's right to refuse treatment, it was in this area of consenting to treatment (in this case concerning contraception) that principles of the rights of children were established:

> In 1970, Lord Denning spoke of parents' 'dwindling right which the courts will hesitate to enforce against the wishes of the child. It starts with a right of control and ends with little more than advice.'
> Lord Scarman echoed this view:

> '... as a matter of law the parental right to determine whether or not their minor child below the age of 16 will have medical treatment terminates if and when the child achieves a sufficient understanding and intelligence to understand fully what is proposed.' [Gillick v West Norfolk and Wisbech AHA (1985) 3 All ER 423.]

> It is the doctor's duty to decide when a child patient is competent and, if a competent child wishes to exclude the parents, always to advise that the parents should be involved, but not to enforce this.
>
> (Alderson, 1993: 45)

The rights of children to consent to sexual intercourse and their protection from the responsibility of consent are controversial political issues. A radical proposal that 14 years should be the age of consent for both heterosexual and homosexual activity (Tatchell, 1996) is unlikely to gain much political support in a climate of apprehension and concern about the protection of children. However, the judgement in the Gillick case tacitly acknowledged that the current age of heterosexual consent of 16 years is not an effective chastity belt.

The question of the age of consent to sexual activity is certainly a thorny one. However, even the right of children to information about sex is a challenging area for adults. Sex education is unique in that primary schools must explain their programme of sexual education to parents before teaching children and parents are entitled to withdraw their children from such lessons, as they are from religious education or worship. However, early education of children has also been promoted, for example a book of dramatic photographs of embryos with text designed to provide clear explanations to children (Kitzinger and Nilsson, 1986). Favourable reviews by *Nursery World* and *Mother and Baby* appear on the cover and parents are invited to read the book with their children. The text gave a clear explanation of the process of conception:

> *Millions of sperm, much smaller than the ovum, were in the testicles underneath your father's penis. When your mother and father felt very loving and kissed and cuddled each other, your father's penis became hard so that it could slide into your mother's vagina, the soft opening between her legs which leads to her uterus. As they held each other in their arms a liquid called semen spurted out from his penis into her vagina.*
>
> (Kitzinger and Nilsson, 1986)

Another example is a hilarious sex education picture book by Babette Cole (1993). As the title *Mummy Laid an Egg* suggests, this is both intended to inform about reproduction and about the extraordinary stories that adults invent in order to avoid telling children the truth. A series of outlandish pictures illustrate the unlikely explanations of parents, including storks, seeds, bushes and other myths. The children set about giving their parents a lesson in which they outline the details of sexual intercourse in a clear way illustrated by explicit diagrams, which always amuse and sometimes shock nursing students.

The message of these books is that children have a right to know about sex from an early age. However, this is a point of political contention. Sex education is the only subject about which schools must consult parents about the content and method of teaching before it is delivered. Parents can opt for their children to be removed from lessons. An unfortunate school nurse was given a great deal of publicity when her answers to a child's questions about the use of chocolate bars and oral sex were leaked to the press. Moral outrage followed in which her answers to a child's questions were presented as an incitement to explore the potential uses of confectionery in exotic sexual acts. As anyone who has spent any time in a playground can testify, children are interested in the details of sexual activity which adults choose to keep hidden. How adults should respond to this interest is a highly contentious question. The explicit and factual approach of Babette Cole and Sheila Kitzinger treats information as helpful and presents details about sexuality in an open way. However, adults can feel uncomfortable with this open approach. Magazines which have presented detailed information about sex to girl readers have also received publicity and threats of censorship from Members of Parliament. One of these magazines had published an answer to a girl's question about oral sex. The message of the public response would appear to be that there are some things which it is best that children do not know. Why is ignorance regarded so favourably by British public opinion? The image of childhood that is expressed by the public response to cases where children are given information about sexual behaviours suggests that sexuality is something which can contaminate children and that they are vulnerable to corruption by adults. An alternative view is that children are less vulnerable if they have information, less likely to be abused and more likely to delay the start of sexual activity or at least to protect themselves more effectively from pregnancy and hazards. The passion with which these topics are discussed suggests that empirical evidence plays a much smaller part in this debate than emotion and anxiety.

DISCUSSION POINT

When should sex education start and what should it include?

IMPLICATIONS FOR NURSING

Children's sexuality is an important and problematic area for children's nurses. There are some conclusions that can be drawn from this discussion of historical and contemporary sources. This is not a new problem. Just as every generation of teenagers believes that it is the first to have discovered sex, there is a danger that the current discourse can treat the problems presented by children's sexuality as novel. However, sexual abuse of children is certainly not new, although there may have been a recent re-discovery of the phenomenon. It is also the case that while sexuality is a particularly sensitive aspect of childhood, our attitudes towards children and sexuality are exemplifications of our attitudes towards children generally. It is in sexuality that the question of the degree to which children are to be understood as innocents in danger of corruption or animals in need of taming is most acute. Our attitudes towards sexuality are also important indicators of attitudes towards the rights of children as decision-makers in life and in health care.

All professionals who work with children – nurses, doctors, teachers, social workers – will have to address themselves to the question of childhood sexuality in their careers. As the Royal College of Nursing (1996) guidelines indicate, it is very difficult to define terms clearly and to provide generalised guidance for those who care for children. What is important is for practitioners to be have an understanding and awareness of features and issues in children's sexuality. The conclusion is then a justification for this book.

REFERENCES

Alderson P (1993) *Children's Consent to Surgery*. Buckingham: Open University Press.
Anonymous (1996) Siding with Rosie. *New Statesman* 125(4301), 5.

Ariès P (1962) *Centuries of Childhood.* London: Jonathan Cape.

Chang J (1991) *Wild Swans: Three Daughters of China.* London: Harper Collins.

Cole B (1993) *Mummy Laid an Egg.* London: Jonathan Cape.

deMause L (1974) *The History of Childhood.* London: Bellew.

Department of Health (1991) *Welfare of Children and Young People in Hospital.* London: HMSO.

Department of Health (1996) *The Patient's Charter: Services for Children and Young People.* London: Department of Health.

Fletcher A (1973) *Tudor Rebellions.* London: Longman.

Gardner M (1962) *The Annotated Snark.* Harmondsworth: Penguin.

Hall D, Stacey M (1979) *Beyond Separation: Further Studies of Children in Hospital.* London: Routledge & Kegan Paul.

Hart S (1991) From property to person status – historical perspectives on children's rights. *American Psychologist* **46**(1) 53–59.

Hawthorn PJ (1974) *Nurse – I Want My Mummy.* London: Royal College of Nursing.

Jenks C (1996) *Childhood.* London: Routledge.

Kitzinger S, Nilsson L (1986) *Being Born.* London: Dorling Kindersley.

Rayner J (1996) Innocent fun. Or a paedophile's dream. *The Observer,* 18 August.

Royal College of Nursing (1996) *Protection of Nurses Working with Children and Young People.* Issues in Nursing and Health no. 39. London: Royal College of Nursing.

Stacey M, Dearden R, Pill R, Robinson D (1970) *Hospitals, Children and their Families.* London: Routledge & Kegan Paul.

Tatchell P (1996) Recognise your age. *Tribune* **60**(50), 6, 13 December.

FURTHER READING

Ariès P (1962) *Centuries of Childhood.* London: Jonathan Cape.
    A seminal work in the history of childhood.

deMause L (1974) *The History of Childhood.* London: Bellew.
    A colourful and provocative history of child abuse.

Jenks C (1996) *Childhood.* London: Routledge.
    An important contribution to the sociology of childhood.

Royal College of Nursing (1996) *Protection of Nurses Working with Children and Young People.* Issues in Nursing and Health no. 39. London: Royal College of Nursing.
    Important because it is RCN guidance and because it is revealing about attitudes in nursing.

Chapter 2

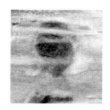

CONTEMPORARY CULTURAL INFLUENCES UPON DEVELOPMENT OF SEXUALITY, SEXUAL EXPRESSION AND MORALITY OF CHILDREN LIVING IN THE UK

SUE HOOTON RSCN RN RNT BSC MA

KEY POINTS

- THE SOCIAL CONSTRUCTION OF CHILDHOOD; EFFECTS OF SOCIAL CONTROL

- THEORIES OF MORAL AND SEXUAL DEVELOPMENT

- EFFECTS OF RELIGION, ETHNICITY AND CULTURE UPON SEXUAL AND MORAL DEVELOPMENT

- CULTURE AS A DETERMINANT OF SEXUAL AND MORAL IDENTITY

- SEXUAL PROGRAMMING THROUGH MARKET AND MEDIA INFLUENCES

- CHILDHOOD UNDER THREAT

- CHILDHOOD AS A SUBCULTURE

- MEDIA VICTIMS

- IMPLICATIONS FOR PRACTITIONERS

'SUGAR, SPICE AND ALL THINGS NICE'?

The Spice Girls reached number one in the British record charts, proving to be a major hit with the younger age range of the record market. Their latest top-selling CD is marketed in a way most likely to appeal to primary school children and young people. It is unusual to have an all-girl band and perhaps this is the secret of their phenomenal success. It might also be something to do with the youthful 'streetwise' image portrayed by their clothes, hairstyles and manner as they smile teasingly out of children's TV, pages of pop magazines and pop posters. Whatever the winning formula, it seems to appeal to young girls and boys, few of whom won't recognise the following lyrics from their number one single:

> *I need some love like I never needed love before,*
> *(Wanna make love to ya baby)*
> *I had a little love, now I'm back for more,*
> *(Wanna make love to ya baby)*
> *Cause tonight is the night when two become one.*

Although these lyrics may seem typical of many other love songs, the thought of young children memorizing such lyrics and singing along in full 'Spice Girl' mode can prove disturbing. Such feelings of discomfort arise from a growing realisation that childhood is changing. As the safe, controlled and protected childhood that adults have tended to manipulate for children slips away, a new experience of childhood is emerging, one which exposes children directly to the less protective values and influences of the adult world. The success of the sophisticated 'Spice Girls' marketing serves to illustrate how children can become just another consumer group and may be at risk of becoming 'socially sexualised' at a very young age. And it would appear that parents can do very little about it.

The intention of this chapter is to consider the ways in which societal influences impact upon and shape the moral and sexual growth of children in Western multifaith and multicultural society. The range of possible social influences is immense and this chapter can only provide a snapshot of some of today's issues. As such, readers are encouraged to read further around points of interest, to draw upon their own thoughts and experiences *en route*, and most importantly to talk to young people who very often have much to say! The chapter presents issues and ideas in a way that is intended to encourage reflection upon individual experiences and in some cases challenge existing beliefs and values in an attempt to make better sense of issues that may affect the development of others.

It is with some unease that I set out to explore issues relating to childhood sexual development as my own childhood seems ever distant. Therefore to avoid some of the obvious dangers inherent within adult interpretations of childhood experiences, I have asked children and young people to contribute directly to this work and, where appropriate, interview material and dialogue have been used to help illustrate the major issues. All of these interview/dialogue extracts are included with the consent of the young people concerned.

Each section is used to reflect upon the interplay of cultural influences that are the building blocks of socially constructed notions of childhood and ideals of socially acceptable moral and sexual behaviour. It is argued within each section that the societal expectations placed upon children and young people are unrealistic and that our social systems are failing to support children at a time when 'childhood' can be seen to be at its most vulnerable.

Sexual and Moral Development – A Dynamic Concept

Historically, literature relating to moral and sexual development has predominantly been written from a biological perspective. Webb (1994: 41) considers such issues and discusses the concept of 'living sexuality' – regarding moral and sexual expression as being reflected in the personality of the whole person. In this respect, self-presentation, body language, dress and self-concept are all felt to be expressions to the outside world of an individual's sexual identity.

Webb considers issues pertaining to adult sexuality, however, this dynamic concept of a living sexuality, which changes and adapts over time, appears to have particular relevance to moral and sexual development throughout childhood. It is therefore used as a fundamental concept underpinning the terms sexuality and sexual expression throughout the text.

The range of factors that affect sexual and moral development will vary in nature and complexity from person to person. Although this chapter concentrates on social factors, the need to consider the interrelationship of biological and emotional influences upon the developing individual cannot be overemphasised and will be reinforced throughout the chapter.

Moral Development

Taylor and Muller (1995: 35) suggest that any discussion relating to sexual development of young people is 'incomplete without reference to moral development'. There are varying theories of moral development, but that of Kohlberg (1976) offers a fundamental theory which is commonly used to explore the interrelationship of cognitive development with moral understanding and moral behaviour.

Kohlberg identifies three levels of moral development, the first level being 'pre-conventional', which describes the ways that young children learn basic ideas of right and wrong behaviour. Level two, 'conventional morality', involves moving from an egocentric viewpoint to consider the opinions of others. It also involves a growing awareness of the rules of wider society, as the older child learns through increasingly complex social experiences. 'Postconventional morality' is the third and final level, an advanced stage characterised by the formulation of personal values and moral behaviour which reflects the rules and laws of society. Kohlberg relates individual cognitive development directly to the growth of moral and sexual awareness as a natural learning process.

Kohlberg's theory is founded upon a developmental framework and acknowledges the importance of psychosocial experiences upon cognitive growth throughout childhood and into adolescence. Therefore, children who establish early friendships and encounter experiences outside of the home will be more likely to benefit in terms of developing a sense of social and moral value (Hobsbaum, 1995). Such issues become more complex through adolescence as young people form more permanent relationships and are faced with the many moral dilemmas associated with sexual relationships and sexual experimentation which is a feature of adolescent behaviour (Avert, 1992). At this stage it could be argued that young people most need opportunities for open discussion about relationship issues. It is through such discourse that moral awareness is heightened and reasoned moral decision-making develops. The opportunities for such discussion will be greatly influenced by differing cultural attitudes towards childhood morality and sexuality.

CULTURE AS A DETERMINANT OF SEXUAL AND MORAL DEVELOPMENT

Sexual Programming Within Society

The range and nature of social experiences that children and young people encounter will be culturally determined from birth. Cultural interpretation and expectation will influence the moral and sexual messages that children will receive throughout childhood and will be fundamental to their own developing sexual expression and sexual behaviour. In this way, young people acquire 'culturally programmed' attitudes to morality and sexuality which become central to the growing person's sense of 'individuality'. By its very nature, individuality is a difficult concept to define, but it is clearly something that differentiates us from those around us, yet is something that is achieved within socially defined parameters.

REFLECTION POINT

Consider the following extract from a conversation about 'being an individual' with Elizabeth, aged eleven.

> I think this is about the way I behave. Sometimes I act mad, sometimes I am sensible, but this depends on my mood – and that's about being me as a person. I decide how I want to behave.
>
> When I'm with my friends I am always happy, not like when I'm with my brother – that's when I'm most mad and angry. I have lots of friends and now most of my friends are boys. I really like this because we talk a lot and I learn about what it's like to be a boy and that helps me to understand more about things. This is important to me.
>
> I don't see anyone on the TV who I want to be like but sometimes I see pop singers and would like to dress more like them. I don't want to be like anyone else, I just want to be me.

To achieve individuality appears to be a central task of childhood (Bee, 1995) and as a particular feature of adolescence it is reflected in a young person's choice of friends, opinions, recreational activity and sexual expression. Dunn (1985) states that cultural influences

---

throughout childhood will direct the way that children are viewed and treated within the family unit, the way that they learn to interact with others, and the way that they start to interpret the world around them. In this sense it could be argued that culture is the major determinant affecting the moral and sexual development of young people.

It is no easy task, and probably rather unwise, to attempt to draw comparisons between early childhood experiences and their direct impact upon moral and sexual development.

Lindsay (1994: 98) attributes culture to the development of the patterned, repetitive, ways of thinking, feeling, acting and behaving within society; all factors that affect the growing sense of self-worth and self-identity from an early age (Sieving and Zirbel Donisch, 1990). Generative theories of culture (such as that indicated by Lindsay's account above) infer that cultural norms are 'inherited' through family generations. This is in contrast with 'interactive' theories of culture where individuals actively make cultural changes and re-interpret cultural themes as circumstances change through time. Clearly, children are exposed to cultural norms throughout childhood as they pervade every aspect of daily life, teaching us early lessons about the acceptability of our own behaviour as well as the behaviours of others.

Although theories of child development abound to inform us of particular aspects of behavioural and emotional development, they may be criticised for being decontextualised from the child's cultural experience. As such, the experiences of each child will result in very different outcomes depending upon individual emotional and social circumstances.

REFLECTION POINT

Reflecting upon your own experiences, can you identify the sources of the 'cultural norms' in our society which serve to 'shape' children's sexual behaviour and sexual expression?

You might have considered issues relating to:

○ family values
○ local customs
○ gender attitudes
○ legal issues
○ ethnicity
○ religion
○ peer behaviour
○ education.

Some of these issues can be related to Elizabeth's account, given above. Clearly, Elizabeth values the friendship of boys of her own age and in the past has been able to invite them to her house for birthday parties, etc. Mixed-sex friendships have appeared to be acceptable for Elizabeth. However, during our conversation, Elizabeth expressed concern that her parents would prefer her to attend a single-sex secondary school. This conflicted with her own strong wishes to attend a coeducational school and maintain the friendships she had established. Her parents had both attended single-sex schools and from their own experience felt that Elizabeth should 'concentrate on her work, not on boyfriends'. In this instance the norms that were important to Elizabeth's sense of individuality were about to be compromised by the 'norms' underpinning Elizabeth's parents' opinions, attitudes and fears. Understandably, Elizabeth felt let down by her parents 'switch in attitude' towards her friendships with boys and their apparent lack of trust in her motives for wanting to attend a coeducational school. Whilst Elizabeth could articulate the rationale for her choice of school in a reasoned way that was important to her sense of individuality, Elizabeth's parents seemed dogged by cultural 'instincts and fears' that this was wrong.

Frameworks and Boundaries

The above example helps to illustrate the interplay of the many complex factors that serve to 'shape' children into socially acceptable patterns of behaviour. Such influences may be regarded as positive features which offer guidance and structure for sexual behaviour within society, however, these mechanisms may also be regarded as subtle 'mechanisms of control'. It could be suggested that this is particularly so when considering moral and sexual behaviour. In this context, such fundamental cultural influences can serve to restrain and confine human behaviour within socially acceptable boundaries.

REFLECTION POINT

Consider the following extract from a newspaper article which describes sexual activity and sex education for Dutch school children:

> Let's Talk About Sex
> *Dutch girls and boys can have sex at 12, they are bombarded with sex education. Sex is not actually legal at 12, but it is officially 'tolerated'.*
>
> *Teachers state: 'We will talk about sex to groups of children from four years up ... We have special books and picture material for the very young ones, so we can jump in when the moment arises.'*
>
> *(Henley and Mihill, 1993)*

How does this compare with sex education for British primary school children?

This extract serves in a small way to illustrate differing cultural attitudes and practices towards sexual development and sexual expression of young people. The Dutch children described in the article are supported and educated through their natural sexual inquisitiveness from a very early age and enter into a society more readily prepared for sexual activity. It would also appear that societies that foster open sexual attitudes, such as Holland, reap the

---

benefits of a more sexually responsible youth (Henley and Mihill, 1993). Such examples explode societal myths about sexual freedom leading to promiscuous behaviour and expose the injustices experienced by young people in societies which still regard sex as the great 'taboo' topic.

It can be an interesting and informative exercise to compare differing national and international social frameworks which serve to contain and direct human sexual behaviour. Exploration of such socially constructed frameworks reveals much about the inherent historical, political, ethnic and religious values which serve to determine the moral and sexual behaviour of young people.

Subcultures

It would appear that society has always created frameworks that serve to separate and distance childhood from adulthood. In the past such frameworks have been modelled on the 'bedrocks' of society such as the family and the church and have served as barriers, distancing adult sexual behaviours from childhood. These frameworks remain today but almost appear to have stood still in time whilst all around is changing at a dizzy pace. Holland (1996: 155) considers the effects of contemporary change upon childhood and proposes that the 1990s are leading to a new construct of childhood. She describes 'the shifting relationships between adults and children' as today's dramatic pace of technological change leaves adults confused and inadequate and children find a new mastery as they latch onto the future in a significantly new way. There appears to be an emerging subculture of the 1990s in which children are seen to be using their new mastery to shape their own future. Children are finding their own ways to access the adult world, redefining the artificial and antiquated social structures which fail to represent the reality of today's children.

Historically, the degree to which such frameworks have served to shape children's sexual behaviour has been dependent upon the role of the family within society.

Acquiring Sexual Identity Through Primary Socialisation

Early Childhood Experiences

The functional role of the family in transmitting the wider values and norms of society to its children should not be underestimated. Bee (1995) considers such 'family function theories' along with the subtle ways in which family roles convey social messages of morality and 'normality'.

Family life is changing for many children in Britain in line with changing sociopolitical and religious beliefs. Many children will be raised in lone parent families or in reconfigured

---

families as family structures move away from the more typical Western nuclear family. These changes are discussed at length by Wilson (1995: 79), who provides an in-depth account of the causes of family breakdown and the effects upon child development.

The Office of Population Censuses and Surveys (1991) shows that 10% of children within the UK come from ethnic origins outside of the UK, and Thomson (1993) describes the features of 'normal family life' for children from Sikh, Hindu and Muslim families, which is more likely to be experienced within extended family networks.

Irrespective of the type of family structure, childhood can be seen to offer rich experiences through which even the youngest of children learn about feelings, friendships and gender differences. Such everyday experiences provide insights into family roles and the obligations and expectations underpinning relationships from which a growing sense of identity is established. Primary socialisation can therefore be seen to be fundamental to the child's subsequent growth of sexual and moral development.

Early Experiences and Relationship Development

Close physical contact has been shown to be an essential factor affecting relationship formation from a very early age. Theories of infant/maternal attachment (Bowlby, 1969; Bradley, 1989) describe attachment processes in infancy and the possible adverse psychological effects caused by attachment disruption. Hobsbaum (1995: 152) compares intimacy within the maternal/infant relationship across different cultures and concludes that regardless of the rituals and practicalities that become part of child-rearing experience within individual cultures, it is the wider construction of cultural values that influence 'what it means to be a child and what the goals of adulthood are'.

Bruner (1975) suggests that children will learn the goals and acts of adulthood through 'social learning theory', implying that young children rehearse what they see happening about them. This of course Includes responding to gender roles within the family (Hobsbaum, 1995: 140), recognising and mimicking behaviours as a natural learning process. Such early socialisation is fundamental to identity development of the developing child (Bee, 1995) and play will dominate in these early learning experiences. By acting out experiences and events within the family the young child will learn much about self-expression and the limits of acceptable behaviour.

Play is universal to children of all cultures; however, cultural differences will be evident in the way that the child plays. Daily worship may be a regular feature for children from Hindu and Muslim families, and may become symbolic in the play of such children, whilst children from orthodox faiths may act out more traditional gender roles which might prove contradictory to the beliefs of the wider group. Likewise, some Muslim parents might not encourage mixed-sex friendships for their older children, as the Islamic religious codes strictly forbid close contact with non-family members of the opposite sex and uphold very strict modesty values in relation to body cover (Noibi, 1993). Children will also symbolise religious dress codes, for example Sikh children may draw men wearing turbans.

The ways in which children from differing ethnic cultures socialise and are accepted by other children can be largely dependent upon the sensitivity and knowledge of those who have responsibility for caring for children. Even from the earliest age, young children need to be supported in relationship development in a way that is acceptable to the child's ethnic and religious background. Wong (1989) describes the ways in which early experiences of 'feeling different' can be damaging to the child's developing self-esteem, suggesting that friendships which foster positive feelings of security and social value promote self-esteem and provide the basis for future stable and loving relationships.

It has been established therefore that the young child's self-esteem is derived from the sense of value that the child gains from interactions with family and close friends in social groups. Table 1 outlines the ways in which the family can function to foster positive relationships and to engender positive attitudes towards sexual and moral development.

Table 1   The role of the family in developing self-esteem and self-identity in the young child

Role modelling	Sexual behaviour
	Language
	Parenting rules
	Cultural and religious practices
Interactions	Giving and receiving criticism
	Expressing opinions
	Respecting others' views
	Testing ground for ideas/values
Socialisation	Relationship formation
	Nurturing behaviour
	Discipline and authority
	Regarding family values
	Sexual expression

REFLECTION POINT

Consider Table 1 and identify the 'hidden' assumptions relating to adult/child relationships within its contents.

The following assumptions relate to the role of children and the rights of children within the family unit:

○ children have respect and value within the family unit
○ children are encouraged to formulate and express opinions
○ discussion around 'sensitive issues' takes place.

Such entitlements would appear to be the right of every child and have been shown to be fundamental to the subsequent development of sexual attitudes and sexual behaviours.

However, there is evidence that many children will be deprived of such 'nurturing' opportunities and some may find themselves victims within abusive relationships within their own families. Such children are known to be more likely to abuse their own children in the future as 'generative' cycles of sexual abuse unfold (White and Woollett, 1990). It is also known that children bear the legacy of such abuse within future relationships by experiencing difficulty in establishing relationships and confusion about their sexual identity throughout adolescence and adulthood (Watkins and Bentovim, 1992).

There is also growing evidence relating to the difficulties that children from split marriages experience in forming future relationships (Wilson, 1995: 82). It is difficult to know how such children's perceptions of parenting are affected by such potentially damaging experiences. Many children will feel let down by their families and a society which continues to promote moral and sexual ideals through the political promotion of traditional 'family values', a concept which will contrast sharply with the reality experienced by many children in Britain today.

Deprivation and Moral and Sexual Development

The effects of low income and social disadvantage upon children's moral and sexual development has been poorly researched. However, the relationship between low income, poor housing and child-rearing practice has been established. Conway (1988) and Bradshaw (1990) describe the effects of low income upon family life where insufficient money or space fails to ensure individual sleeping arrangements and privacy for children. There may, for example, be a lack of adequate washing facilities resulting in children wearing dirty clothes which might attract ridicule and be damaging to the child's self-esteem. Conway (1988) describes the experiences of children growing up in bed and breakfast accommodation in Britain and suggests these children are amongst the most vulnerable in society. Such deprivation often results in cramped living conditions where adults and children may have to sleep together and children are exposed to adult sexual behaviours. The higher incidence of domestic violence and childhood prostitution for children from socially deprived families is also well documented (Conway, 1988; Bradshaw, 1990). The effects of such experiences upon the developing moral and sexual understanding and behaviours of children is unknown.

Social deprivation has been cited as a major factor for 'moral breakdown' within society and press reporting following the murder of Jamie Bulger exemplified and projected such attitudes. Franklin and Petley (1996: 134) provide a comprehensive analysis of the reporting of the murder, giving a detailed account of the emotionally and economically deprived childhoods of the two young child murderers. They further explore the 'vitriolic' reporting of these children as 'evil', 'monsters', 'freaks' and 'animals'. It would appear that the press were more comfortable with the image of the 'children who were born evil', as opposed to the children who might have been let down by society. Although these are extreme cases, they serve to expose the need for further scrutiny of the links between deprivation and moral and sexual behaviour.

RELIGIOUS INFLUENCES UPON SEXUAL IDENTITY

Religion will play a major role within any society, determining social attitudes towards morality and sexuality (Thomson, 1993). The degree to which this religious influence is exerted will be dependent upon the state of religious affairs within any given society. The demise of the church within British society is well documented and well discussed; however, this does not necessarily mean that religion is not a fundamental part of British life.

REFLECTION POINT

Think of the usual social occasions when families 'get together' in British society.

The more usual gatherings are for celebrations — occasions such as weddings, christenings, funerals, which are often centred around a religious ceremony. Public holidays continue to follow the significant religious events such as Easter and Christmas. Although church attendance generally is falling, the religious frameworks can be seen to remain as being inextricably woven into the very fabric of society through the religious ceremonies and social gatherings that are associated with significant life events. This is so across the many different religions that are part of British multicultural and multifaith society.

For many families religion will play a dominant role in determining cultural norms, especially those from more orthodox religions. Religious practice is difficult to categorise in any absolute way, as all religions can be seen to vary from liberal forms to those more extreme and orthodox in nature. For many children religious identity will form an important and central aspect of self-identity and religious writings and practices will offer guidance in terms of moral and sexual values.

Young children receive exposure to multicultural and multifaith issues through the National Curriculum (Department of Education and Science, 1991) which serves to provide sex education directly to children from all backgrounds, as well as promoting awareness of multicultural issues, for all children. The National Children's Bureau (NCB) promotes the following principles to underpin delivery of sex education within the National Curriculum across different ethnic and religious groups as follows.

○ Sex education should be made accessible to all children through school.
○ The moral framework for sex education should be inclusive of all religions.
○ Young people should be made aware of the range of moral and cultural frameworks within society.
○ Schools must ensure that there is a gender dimension for all sex education work.
○ Young people should be supported, not undermined, in their cultural identities.

The Search for Cultural Identity

School attendance takes the child from the immediacy and the protection of the family, extending the social exposure and range of experiences for children. Such experiences are out of the control of the family and may expose the child to friendships and experiences that may offer stark contrast from the family norms. This may be particularly so for children who may not have been exposed to wider social contacts in early childhood. Children who appear to be particularly vulnerable in this respect are young disabled children (Hooton, 1995) and children from some ethnic minority backgrounds (Cohen, 1991). Such restricted social contact may arise from cultural or religious preference or might reflect the lack of good quality, affordable childcare facilities (David, 1990; Moss, 1990). Limited contact with children outside of the dominant culture restricts the range of social learning experiences essential for relationship and identity formation. The NCB guidance is useful for teachers and other professionals who have direct responsibility for ensuring that children are supported and not undermined in their cultural identities.

Such issues are central to the development of sexuality for young people, as a firm sense of cultural identity will be fundamental to moral and sexual development. These issues are explored in some depth through the following personal account.

Ambi's Story

Ambi is a young Asian woman from a Sikh religious background. She was born in Birmingham and now lives in London where she is employed in a professional capacity.

Identity development

I haven't really thought about this much – you don't do you? I remember very little about the early days at school but when I was young I wanted to be like everyone else. I didn't want to be different in any way and tried hard not to stand out. Now I'm older I want to be seen as an individual, it's very important to me to be seen as an Asian person and I want my background to be understood. I am very proud of my identity – this started at about 15 years old when I started to develop my identity as an Asian person. I started to wear the metal bracelet (Kara) which is symbolic of the Sikh religion; this differentiates me from other Asian castes. This is important to me as it relates my ethnicity to my religion in a way that is obvious to the outside world. I also enjoy Bangra music – this mixes Asian music with modern dance and it is very popular with young Asian people. I think that it is very important to maintain a sense of cultural identity.

Religious influences on identity

Religion played a major part in my childhood – it is a way of life. When I look back on my upbringing, I feel that it was very strict. My parents did not let me stay out late and I was not allowed to wear fashionable clothes. This was typical of other Sikh families but I felt that it was overprotective. A particular issue was the religious restriction on my having my hair cut. This became a real issue with my parents and my strongest form of rebellion was to have a friend cut an inch off my hair at regular intervals without my parents knowing. This was very daring for me.

However, my Mum was only very young and I always understood the pressure on my parents from other family members (aunts particularly), so I usually conformed — that's how it works in Sikh families. Now my family is much more relaxed about everything and my younger sisters have far more freedom than I did.

Identity and role models

I didn't really have any role models when I was growing up. Certainly not on the TV. I saw much more negative stereotyping than positive role models. However, I would probably say that female Asian newsreaders inspired me most. This is because I recognise the struggle that they might have faced to have made it against the odds. Enormous pressures can be put on people from families, religion, and wider society and this is especially so for Asian women. But I always admire ability and achievement for its own sake — not because of the colour of people's skins.

Love and marriage

I always knew that sex before marriage was not tolerated in Sikh families and I grew up to expect an arranged marriage, although that didn't actually happen. You see, it was always my choice. Today, things are becoming much more relaxed as the Sikh community recognises that unhappiness can result from arranged marriages too — our culture is becoming very Westernised as is the Hindu community. We talk a great deal in our family about marriage — maybe more so than Western families because this is an important issue for young Sikh women who want to explore their options.

I always knew that I wanted to marry someone from my own background — someone like me. I can remember being aware of this from an early age.

The above account is extremely frank and informative about the ways in which religion can impact upon a young person's developing sense of cultural and personal identity. Certain themes have emerged as being particularly important in influencing childhood experiences and moral and sexual identity. As such they have been used as a template to proceed to explore broader moral and sexual transcultural issues.

Family Honour and Attitudes to Sex and Marriage

Family honour features particularly strongly in Ambi's account and can be seen to be a central feature of the other Asian and Eastern religions. It is a well respected aspect of Jewish,

Hindu and Islamic religious codes and consequently has direct cultural impact on the everyday social experiences of young people from such religions. Family honour is most often reflected in the behaviour of its young people, which is required to be modest and respectful. This is particularly the case within arranged marriages, which are still common for many young people from Eastern cultures. For such young people, boyfriends and girlfriends will not be tolerated; first sexual experiences will be expected to occur following marriage, within which an unblemished sexual reputation will be a fundamental aspect of the marriage contract.

In the Sikh community emphasis is placed upon family honour, where the wider community itself is viewed as 'family' and is charged with looking after its young — almost as second parents. Community life takes precedence within social events where generations will be expected to celebrate and worship together (Singh, 1993). Ambi discusses the ways in which her aunts were always on hand to guide her mother in parenting issues. Although this felt repressive in some aspects, the respect and obligations evident within this cultural practice reflect fundamental aspects of family honour and its implicit roles.

There may be harsh consequences in cases where family honour is tarnished and severe penalties may result in individuals being cast out of the family — this is particularly so for young women as there are varying cultural attitudes towards responsibility for non-married women within Asian communities (Thomson, 1993).

Religious Attitudes Towards the Body

It is a requirement of the Hindu, Sikh and Jewish religions that modest dress codes are observed following puberty. Islamic requirements can be far more strict, forbidding revealing of private body parts for men and allowing only exposure of the face and hands for women. Such practices aim to protect against sexual provocation and send out very clear messages to young people about sexual codes and the 'temptations of the flesh'. Consequently, there is a religious requirement that touching, hugging, and kissing is forbidden with non-family members of the opposite sex within Islamic teachings. Such religious codes may serve to suppress sexual expression and confine sexual activity to relationships within marriage and consequently will strongly influence young people's growing sexual and moral identity.

Thomson (1993: 9) suggests that moral development is enhanced by social relationships and through engaging young people in discussion and exploration of their own moral understandings. The development of self-esteem and moral autonomy is as being more to do with the development of a set of personal values as opposed to 'being told what is right or wrong', as might appear to be the religious message.

The need for open discussion of such issues would appear to be particularly relevant for children and young people from different religious backgrounds who are faced with strict cultural and religious behavioural expectations. One can only guess at the difficulties and confusion encountered by young people expected to follow strict codes of morality and modesty, whilst living in a Western culture which promotes starkly contrasting sexual images through advertising and the media. Thomson (1993) suggests that discussion within appropriate religious and cultural moral frameworks may help children facing such dilemmas. However, within many orthodox religions discussion of sexual matters is regarded as a deeply private affair, not for open discussion. Therefore young people may find themselves unable to discuss such sensitive matters with those who are close to them. Indeed, religious influences may work to discourage parents from undertaking this educational role, as religious or cultural beliefs may inhibit such open sexual discussion.

At such times, young people may experience identity crises associated with conflicting religious and cultural moral and sexual ideals. Children may turn to professionals for help and advice. School may be the obvious source for such advice, where it is important for children from varying backgrounds to be able to relate to teachers from similar cultures and religions who should be able to offer culturally sensitive counselling.

Menstruation

Many young people have difficulties coming to terms with emotional and bodily changes associated with puberty (Bee, 1995). This situation may prove particularly difficult for young people who enter puberty unprepared for the practical reality of such changes (Conger, 1991). Within society generally there appears to be a reluctance and an associated embarrassment around issues such as masturbation and menstruation. Children are sophisticated receivers of social messages and will be aware of the social 'taboos' from an early age. In this way a cultural distancing and prohibition of discussion around sexually related matters commences.

Lenderyou and Porter (1993) suggest that there are few clear rites of passage in British culture and few 'signposts' against which young people can be prepared for their sexual development. Across different cultures, menstruation is often regarded as one such rite of passage, signifying physiological maturity, and may be seen to represent the onset of adulthood. Within British society, Lenderyou and Porter call for more positive attitudes towards sexual matters generally and propose that menstruation is probably the most 'secretive' and least discussed aspect of development. As a result many young find themselves unprepared for the onset of periods and understand little about their own physiology.

Difficult enough within Western society, these ideals appear particularly troublesome when applied to those cultures where sexual discussion is particularly limited and attitudes towards menstruation are inextricably linked with religious practice. Within some religions, menstruating women are prohibited from certain religious activities, leaving young girls particularly vulnerable to negative feelings and attitudes towards normal body changes.

Victims of Religion

Many religious codes offer moral and sexual guidance for the 'mainstream' population, so that individuals who find themselves outside of the religious 'norm' will face particular difficulties. This may apply to victims of rape and domestic violence, and a particularly contentious area is that of homosexuality, which is strictly forbidden by most orthodox religions. Consequently, many young homosexual people may find themselves ostracised by their families and their communities, who refuse to acknowledge and accept homosexuality on religious grounds. The effects of such religious and cultural rejection upon young people is poorly researched; however, it is clear that many young people exposed to contrasting societal norms and expectations become victims within society, as reflected by parasuicide attempts within these groups.

It is clear how religious frameworks serve to offer moral and sexual guidance for individuals within communities and become integral to the local culture. However, the tensions experienced by young people who have to adjust and adapt to meet their cultural and religious obligations whilst experiencing directly contrasting moral and sexual social messages are far less clearly understood.

MEDIA

The increasing exposure of children to media influences is well documented (Fishbein, 1987; Lewis and Volkmar, 1990; Gunter and McAleer, 1990). Much of this literature relates to the changing nature of the media and issues of social control in the light of technological advancement, with concern around children's exposure to TV viewing dominating the literature.

Gunter and McAleer (1990) state that 98% of British homes have at least one TV set and it has been estimated that some young children will spend up to 19 hours viewing per week (Huston *et al.*, 1990). Video watching and cartoon networks have become a common everyday experience for many young children, often freeing parents to do other tasks and reducing the usual amount of direct contact and attention demanded by younger children.

The effects of extensive TV viewing upon child development remain largely unknown, but children are known to act out violent behaviours that they have seen on TV (Meltzoff, 1988). This study by Meltzoff has been central to the ongoing debate concerning TV viewing and moral decline, which often focuses upon the behaviours and attitudes of children.

The effect of TV upon children's moral and sexual development is far less researched. It is generally agreed that children should not be exposed to 'adult material' and the 9 o'clock watershed is meant to protect children from unsuitable viewing. However, the content of programmes scheduled before 9 o'clock appear to expose children to many 'sensitive' issues and the ever popular 'soap operas' have received particular criticism for pushing boundaries too far.

Children and young people appear to be great lovers of TV 'soaps'. The degree of interest the central characters hold for young people is indisputable and warrants some exploration. Soap operas dominate British TV and may be accused of straddling the usual child and adult boundaries as they often address socially sensitive issues. In an attempt to establish young people's own ideas about 'soaps', a conversation with two 13-year-old boys revealed the following:

Themes in Current Soap Operas

Eastenders is currently covering gay relationships and all of the problems associated with that. It is also featuring a girl who isn't sure who the father of her baby is. Recently, Joe has had a mental breakdown and that's unusual for a young person so that was interesting. I don't like the threats and violence and everyone is always in the pub drinking.

Coronation Street is covering young people in prison and a suicide attempt and everyone is having affairs at the moment, but it is usually very mild and doesn't show too much.

Brookside is the soap that takes things too far – especially the violence – there was even a murder because a girl was being sexually abused by her father. There is a lot of swearing in it and it's always full of drug issues.

These soaps just aren't like real life at all; they are way over the top. You can see right through them but I don't like to miss them.

This account shows how these two young people are able to provide a résumé of current issues in just about any 'soap'. They were able to analyse the social relevance of the issues involved and displayed clear selectivity and personal preference in TV viewing. Rice and Woodsmall (1988) propose that children are active processors of the media, being selective and involved rather than being passive in their viewing. Although the topics identified by the boys were clearly sensitive in nature and are often regarded as 'taboo' topics for children, the boys had no difficulty in discussing them openly, as contextualised within the world of the soaps.

Following Postman's (1983) warnings that the 'undifferentiated accessibility' of TV is responsible for eroding the barriers between childhood and adulthood, it is becoming increasingly fashionable to regard TV viewing in a more positive light.

REFLECTION POINT

Consider the ways in which TV viewing might be a positive experience for children and young people in developing moral and sexual awareness.

The potential for using TV as a positive medium for discussing social issues in a joint watching capacity remains relatively unexplored, but would appear to offer 'opportunistic' possibilities for parents to talk about moral and sexual issues with children and vice versa. It could also be argued that the exposure of children to moral and sexual issues through TV may make them more aware of related dangers within society. Issues such as safe sex, personal protection and wider health promotion messages could be delivered to young people in an appropriate media-friendly format. Nutbeam *et al.* (1989) encourage professionals to exploit this medium to optimise the effectiveness of health promotion messages.

The media has long been and continues to be widely attacked for negative stereotyping. However, certain children's programmes receive praise for breaking away from stereotyping and promoting positive racial and gender images. *Grange Hill* is one such programme, being popular with children whilst actively attempting to portray positive social images to young people. Story lines show that it is OK for boys to show emotions and girls can be strong, able and career-minded, breaking long-established stereotypical images. Holland (1996) suggests that such long-running programmes remain popular because they take children and childhood issues seriously and often involve young people in writing and editing. Buckingham (1996) warns of the 'impossibility of children's programmes' which rely on adults for writing and editing due to the occurrence of 'paedocracy' (Holland, 1996: 157) which draws on adult perceptions and fantasies of childness.

Perhaps of more concern than TV viewing is the increased access to computers and to information systems such as the Internet, which are far more difficult to control. Holland (1996: 157) suggests that when it comes to information technology, children's knowledge has far outstripped that of adults and they are able to bypass adults and teachers to access a culture which facilitates contact with less responsible adults. This is a culture where the retrieval of sexually explicit material is relatively simple for children who display mastery over adults within the sphere of information technology.

However, it would appear that there is a degree of overanxiety about accessing technological provision of sexually explicit material when many young people have access to such material in the high street.

Teenage Magazines

Many young people will gain their early education through images and story lines featured in magazines aimed at the younger person. This medium is far more 'private' than TV viewing, which might be censored or may feel uncomfortable within the home, and is accessible to all young people. Such magazines sell well and appear equally popular with boys and girls. Those aimed at boys are presented more as music magazines but tend to hold the same interest in issues related to sexual relationships, problem pages, music features and fashion.

The Teenage Magazine Arbitration Panel has been established to review the content of such publications which have been described as 'lurid' (Poulter, 1996). A recent review of the articles in three of the weekly bestsellers revealed the following topics:

○ The ultimate flirting guide
○ Sex questions pages
○ What boys find attractive about girls' bodies
○ How to pull at parties.

REFLECTION POINT

How might such magazines prove to have a positive influence on young people?

Although sexually focused, these articles also promote girls as fun-loving and able to make decisions rather than passively awaiting the attention of boys. They promote the concept of sexual pleasure and sexual gratification for both partners, issues which might prove difficult for adults with less liberal attitudes. They also promote and advise upon matters of 'safe sex'. McRobbie (1991) suggests a 'new realism' is appearing within such magazines where gender issues are being addressed and career issues are taken seriously.

Such magazines are most criticised for their increasingly sexually explicit material. However, this material should be considered against the fact that the first sexual experiences of young people are occuring earlier and earlier. Cumulative results of studies by Currie (1990) and Ford (1990) suggest that between a third and a half of 16-year-olds (the legal age of consent for heterosexual intercourse) have experienced sexual intercourse before their sixteenth birthday (Table 2). It could be argued that it is the content of such magazines that helps to contextualise the unreliable 'playground' chatter that continues to suffice as the major source of sexual information for many young people.

Table 2   Reported sexual activities among young people aged 16–18

Activity	Age 16–17		Age 17–18	
	M	F	M	F
Deep kissing with a female	86.9	1.9	91.1	1.2
Deep kissing with a male	0.9	88.9	2.8	93.4
Massaging a female's breasts	80.1	0.5	86.1	1.2
Massaging a man's upper body	–	76.5	2.8	84.2
Stimulating a woman's vagina/clitoris by hand	68.5	0.5	78.6	1.2
Stimulating a man's penis by hand	2.2	68.3	6.5	73.2
Vaginal sex	53.8	54.8	65.6	66.1
Passive oral sex with a female	43.4	0.5	57.9	0.9
Passive oral sex with a male	0.4	48.6	4.2	58.8
Active oral sex with a female	39.8	0.8	53.0	1.2
Active oral sex with a male	0.9	47.8	3.3	55.2
Active anal sex with a female	4.3	–	9.0	–
Active anal sex with a male	–	–	1.4	–
Passive anal sex with a male	–	3.9	1.4	6.7
Bases:	240	398	225	350

Figures are percentages of each sex reporting the activity based on all those providing non-missing data.
Bases are sex by cohort totals and include cases who may have had missing data on one or more sex act items.
Reproduced from Breakwell and Fife-Schaw (1991) cited in AVERT (1992).

Media Victims

Young people are constantly exposed to subtle media images that promote ideals of 'beautiful people'. Such images are falsely constructed, largely to suit the needs of the fashion world, and usually portray women as being tall and excessively thin. In contrast, men are portrayed as being tall, handsome and muscular. The usual image is that of the white, wealthy middle class, an image which becomes synonymous with success and happiness. These images are unrepresentative of the population at large and particularly so for young people from non-white backgrounds. However, for adolescents who are searching for identity at a time of profound emotional and physical change, they might serve to magnify the differences between actual body image and the vision of perfection presented by the media.

Adolescence also marks the need for peer and group acceptance which is often established through adopting a group image (Atkinson *et al.*, 1996). Group images will also be formulated by media portrayal of fashion models in magazines or by certain pop groups as they appear on TV or on pop posters, leaving many young people unhappy as they strive to achieve the unachievable.

Self-esteem and self-identity are linked to physical appearance, especially in adolescence, and Fontaine (1991) suggests that the 'contemporary cultural ideal of thinness' is responsible for much of the misery experienced in adolescence. In more severe cases such low self-esteem can manifest in eating disorders such as anorexia nervosa and bulimia. Taylor and Muller (1995: 92) offer a comprehensive account of the psychosocial causes and effects of 'culture-bound' eating disorders in childhood and adolescence.

Anorexia nervosa and bulimia are conditions found predominantly in females who experience a disordered perception of the 'perfect body'. However, there is increasing evidence that young men also respond to media images of 'lean, muscular' men and they, too, are prone to eating disorders. There is also an increase in the numbers of young men who work out in gyms and exercise to gain the desired physique; evidence suggests that significant numbers may resort to abuse of anabolic steroids in pursuit of the perfect physique. The short- and longer-term effects of steroid therapy can severely damage health and more rigorous campaigning is needed to make young people aware of the dangers.

CONCLUSION

This presentation of key issues and reflection points has been used as a basis from which to explore the range of societal and cultural influences upon childhood sexuality and morality. Much attention has been given to the ways in which the experience of childhood itself is changing due to the significant impact of societal change and technological advancement.

It is proposed that children are at risk in society today as they are increasingly exposed to adult sexual images, behaviours and values through the media. TV soap operas, teen magazines and access to the Internet have been used as examples to analyse the nature of this exposure. It is asserted that it is not necessarily the exposure itself that is harmful to children and young people, but the apparent reluctance of adults to acknowledge the ways in which the childhood experience of sexuality is changing. Historically, adults have colluded to create and uphold social frameworks that provide artificial divisions between childhood and adulthood, in many respects to provide protection for children against the 'evils' of society. The ways in which these frameworks are failing many children today have been critically analysed, presenting an argument for change.

Clearly, such change would challenge the underpinning concepts and values upon which the present social construction of childhood is founded, requiring a 're-engineering' of the social frameworks to represent more accurately and support children through their own defined 'reality'. Failure to change unrealistic adult expectations about the nature of childhood leaves adults poorly prepared in helping children and young people to cope with the considerable sexual and moral dilemmas they encounter.

Reference has been made to the growth of a childhood 'subculture' as children find themselves marginalised in a society largely unwilling to acknowledge and respond to their needs. Perhaps adults should take time to reflect upon this situation, which could be interpreted as an attempt by children and young people to take control in creating the supportive social frameworks that they themselves feel are more appropriate and supportive in facing today's challenges.

REFERENCES

Atkinson RL, Atkinson RC, Smith EE, Ben DJ, Nolen-Hoeksema S (1996) *Hilgard's Introduction to Psychology*, 12th edn. London: Harcourt Brace.

AVERT (1992) *AIDS: The Secondary Scene. A Guide to Issues, Approaches and Resources*. London: AVERT.

Bee H (1995) *The Developing Child*, 7th edn. New York: Harper Collins.

Bowlby J (1969) *Attachment and Loss*, vol. 1. Harmondsworth: Penguin.

Bradley BS (1989) *Visions of Infancy: A Critical Introduction to Child Psychology*. Cambridge: Polity Press.

Bradshaw J (1990) *Child Poverty and Deprivation in the UK*. London: National Children's Bureau.

Breakwell GM and Ford N (1991) Sexual activities and preference in a UK sample of 16–20 years olds. *Social Behaviour* (in press).

Bruner J (1974) *Beyond the information given: studies in the psychology of knowing*. London: Allen Unwin.

Bruner J (1975) From communication to language: a psychological perspective. *Journal of Child Language*, 1–19.

Buckingham D (1996) *Moving Images: Understanding Children's Emotional Response to Television*. Manchester: Manchester University Press.

Children's Act (1989) London: HMSO.

Cohen B (1991) *Children in a Modern System: Towards a New National Policy*. London: Institute for Public Policy Research.

Conger J (1991) *Adolescence and Youth: Psychological Development in a Changing World*. New York: Harper Collins.

Conway J (1988) *Prescription for Poor Health: The Crisis for Homeless Families*. London: Shelter.

Currie C (1990) Young people in independent schools, sexual behaviour and AIDS. In: Aggleton P *et al.* (eds) *AIDS: Individual, Cultural and Policy Dimensions*. London: Falmer Press.

David T (1990) *Under Fives – Under-educated?* Milton Keynes: Open University Press.

Department of Education and Science (1991) *National Curriculum Council 'Personal and social development'* News issue No. 6 p. 2. London: HMSO.

Dunn J (1985) *Sisters and Brothers.* Harvard: Harvard University Press.

Fishbein H (1987) Socialisation and television. In: Boyd-Barratt O and Braham P (eds) *Media, Knowledge and Power.* London: Croom Helm.

Fontaine KL (1991) The conspiracy of culture: Women's issues in body size. In: Taylor J and Muller D (eds) *Nursing Adolescents.* Oxford: Blackwell Scientific.

Ford N (1990) *Psycho-active drug use, sexual activity and AIDS awareness of young people in Somerset.* Institute of Population Studies, Somerset Health Authority and SW Regional Drug Advisory Service.

Franklin B, Petley J (1996) Newspaper reporting of the death of James Bulger. In: Pilcher J and Wagg S, *Thatcher's Children? Politics, Childhood and Society in the 1980s and 1990s.* London: Falmer Press.

Gunter B, McAleer J (1990) *Children and Television: The One-eyed Monster?* London: Routledge.

Henley J, Mihill C (1993) Let's talk about sex. *The Guardian,* Friday 19 November.

Hobsbaum A (1995) Children's development. In: Carter B and Dearmun A (eds) *Child Health Care Nursing.* Oxford: Blackwell Scientific.

Holland P (1996) Barrier! children, childishness and the media in the ruins of the twentieth century. In: Pilcher J and Wagg S, *Thatcher's Children? Politics, Childhood and Society in the 1980s and 1990s.* London: Falmer Press.

Hooton S (1995) Learning disabilities: children and their families. In: Carter B and Dearmun A (eds) *Child Health Care Nursing.* Oxford: Blackwell Scientific.

Huston *et al.* (1990) Development of television viewing patterns in early childhood: a longitudinal investigation. *Developmental Psychology* 25(3), 409.

Kohlberg L (1976) Moral stages and moralization: the cognitive developmental approach. In: Lickona T (ed.) *Moral Development and Behaviour.* New York: Holt, Rinehart & Winston.

Lenderyou G, Porter M (1993) *Sex Education, Values and Morality.* London: Health Education Authority

Lewis M, Volkmar F (1990) *Clinical Aspects of Child and Adolescent Development,* 3rd edn. Philadelphia: Lea & Febiger.

Lindsay B (1994) *The Child and the Family: Contemporary Nursing Issues in Child Health and Care.* London: Baillière Tindall.

McRobbie A (1991) *Feminism and Youth Culture: From 'Jackie' to 'Just Seventeen'.* Basingstoke: Macmillan.

Meltzoff AN (1988) Imitation of televised models by children. *Child Development* 59, 1221.

Moss P (1990) Work, family and the care of children: equality and responsibility. *Children and Society* 4(2), 145–165.

Noibi D (1993) An Islamic perspective. In: Thomson R (ed.) *Religion, Ethnicity and Sex Education – Exploring the Issues.* Sex Education Forum, London: National Children's Bureau.

Nutbeam D, Aar L, Catford J (1989) Understanding children's health behaviour: the implications for health behaviour of young people. *Social Science and Medicine* 29(3), 317.

Office of Population Censuses and Surveys (1991) *Population Trends.* London: HMSO.

Postman N (1983) *The Disappearance of Childhood.* London: WH Allen.

Poulter S (1996) Teen magazines target innocence. *Daily Mail,* 21 December, p. 18.

Rice ML, Woodsmall L (1988) Lessons from television: children's word learning when viewing. *Child Development* 59, 420.

Sieving R, Zirbel-Donisch S (1990) Development and enhancement of self-esteem in children. *Journal of Paediatric Health Care* 4(6), 290–296.

Singh K (1993) A sikh perspective. In: Thomson R (ed.) *Religion, Ethnicity and Sex Education – Exploring the Issues.* Sex Education Forum, London: National Children's Bureau.

Taylor J, Muller D (1995) *Nursing Adolescents: Research and Psychological Perspectives.* London: Blackwell Scientific.

Thomson R (ed.) (1993) *Religion, Ethnicity and Sex Education – Exploring the Issues.* Sex Education Forum, London: National Children's Bureau.

Watkins B, Bentovim A (1992) The sexual abuse of male children and adolescents: a review of current research. *Journal of Child Psychology and Psychiatry* 33(1), 107–151.

Webb C (1994) *Living Sexuality.* London: Scutari Press.

White D, Woollett A (1990) *Families: A Context for Development.* London: Falmer Press.

Wilson M (1995) Children, health and families. In: Carter B and Dearmun A (eds) *Child Health Care Nursing.* Oxford: Blackwell Scientific.

Wong D (1989) *Essentials of Paediatric Nursing* (4th edn). Missouri, USA: Mosby.

FURTHER READING

Clift S, Sears D (1992) *AIDS: The Secondary Scene. A Guide to Issues, Approaches and Resources.* Sussex: AVERT.

This text contains much factual information relating to sexual beliefs and practices of young people. It presents important issues around sexual health promotion for young people.

Lindsay B (1994) *The Child and the Family: Contemporary Nursing Issues in Child Health Care.* London: Baillière Tindall.

This text explores the changing attitudes towards childhood in light of changes in family structures and child-rearing practices. It uses a thorough and logical approach to explore the application of sociological and psychological theories to the care of children.

Pilcher J, Wagg S (eds) (1996) *Thatcher's Children? Politics, Childhood and Society in the 1980s and 1990s.* London: Falmer Press.

This is a collection of chapters which cover many contemporary political and social issues which directly affect the experience of childhood in the 1980s and 1990s.

Thomson R (ed.) (1993) *Religion, Ethnicity and Sex Education – Exploring the Issues.* Compiled and Edited by R Thomson on behalf of the Sex Education Forum. London: National Children's Bureau.

This is an excellent text covering a wide range of sensitive issues relating to sex education for children from different ethnic, religious and cultural backgrounds. The chapters are written by individuals from different religious backgrounds and it contains a lot of practical information as well as guidance around moral and ethical sex education issues.

Chapter 3

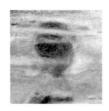

SEXUOEROTIC DEVELOPMENT IN CHILDREN AND YOUNG PEOPLE

STEVEN PRYJMACHUK BA(HONS) MSC PGDIPED(NURSING) RMN RNT

KEY POINTS

- ○ THE ARBITRARY NATURE OF 'CHILDHOOD' AND 'ADOLESCENCE'

- ○ SEXUOEROTIC ASPECTS OF CHILDHOOD; CHILDREN AS SEXUAL BEINGS

- ○ WHAT THE POPULAR DEVELOPMENTAL THEORISTS – PSYCHOANALYTICAL, BEHAVIOURAL AND COGNITIVE – HAVE TO SAY ABOUT SEXUOEROTIC DEVELOPMENT IN CHILDREN AND YOUNG PEOPLE

- ○ APPLICATION OF THE POPULAR THEORIES TO CHILD CARE PRACTICES

- ○ THEORIES OF MORAL DEVELOPMENT AND THEIR RELEVANCE TO CHILDHOOD SEXUOEROTIC FUNCTIONING

- ○ ADOLESCENCE, IDENTITY CRISIS, SEX AND SEXUALITY

- ○ MONEY'S 'LOVEMAPS' AS A THEORY OF SEXUOEROTIC DEVELOPMENT

- ○ THE IRONY OF CHILD PROTECTION

- ○ IMPLICATIONS FOR PRACTICE

This chapter is concerned with how the erotic and sexual – *sexuoerotic* – aspects of our personalities develop from birth onwards. In particular, it focuses on the period of our lives known as 'childhood'. The chapter examines the position of several major developmental theories with regard to sexuoerotic development and, in the course of the discussion, the issue of childhood sexuoerotic functioning is explored, as is the issue of childhood itself.

The developmental theories discussed are considered within the particular school of psychology in which they lie: within the psychoanalytical school, the theories of Freud and, to a lesser extent, Jung and Erikson are considered; in the behavioural school, the theories of Watson and Skinner are considered; and in the cognitive school the theories of Piaget and, to a lesser extent, Kohlberg are considered.

Apart from Freud, most of the major developmental theorists have completely ignored childhood sexuoerotic functioning. On the surface this observation is not surprising, given society's views on children and sex; but given that academics are rarely afraid of controversy, it is also rather curious. There is, however, a recent developmental theory that concerns itself solely with the sexuoerotic aspects of human development. The theory of 'lovemaps', formulated by the American sexologist John Money, is radical in many respects but has the advantage of being supported by a sound scientific basis and rational argument. Money's theory is explored in some detail.

Child care practices are examined in the light of the various theoretical perspectives discussed, with the conclusion that there is little validity in any of the child care practices considered when it comes to dealing with childhood sexuoerotic functioning. This, ironically, includes some current child protection practices. The work of Money and other researchers, however, has led to a number of recommendations for changes in practice which, though contentious, may ultimately prove to be of greater validity where the sexual health of children is concerned.

INTRODUCTION

The title of this chapter – 'Sexuoerotic Development in Children and Young People' – includes a term that you may not be familiar with, namely 'sexuoerotic'. I have deliberately chosen this term in preference to other terms such as 'psychosexual' and 'sexual' in order to reflect the central issue under discussion in this chapter. The chapter is not concerned with the development of the genitals and other physical sex characteristics; it is not, as such, a consideration of sexual development in children. I could have chosen to title the chapter 'The Development of Sexuality in Children'. In the truest sense of the meaning of 'sexuality' (as a noun meaning 'sexual behaviour'), this title may well have reflected the contents of the chapter. However, sexuality is frequently (and, it could be argued, erroneously) used to describe one's position on the heterosexual–homosexual continuum and I felt that, had I used this particular title, some confusion may have arisen. 'Psychosexual', though an appropriate term, was rejected because it is a rather clinical term, used most often when *abnormalities* or *dysfunctions* are being discussed.

The term 'sexuoerotic' is taken from the work of John Money (see Money, 1986), an American sexologist ('sexology' is the scientific study of sex) whose writings I will refer to in some detail later on in the chapter. It is a useful term because it implies that the imagery, thoughts and feelings of sexual love (the 'erotic' aspects of ourselves) are inseparable from sexual behaviour. In other words, it is a term that encompasses both the psychological and physical aspects of sex.

Few would doubt that normal, healthy adult functioning has both erotic and sexual elements. Indeed, many would argue that these elements are *essential*. The picture is, however, somewhat different where children are concerned. Is sexual behaviour and erotic thought a normal and essential part of healthy child functioning? Put to the average person in the street, the response to this question would be a resounding 'no'. This response, however, is more likely to stem from society's view that children and sex are two issues that should only be discussed together within highly specific contexts (such as child protection), than from a real desire to find an answer to the question. If sexual behaviour and erotic thought are, indeed, essential for healthy child functioning (and there is, as we shall see, some evidence to back up this position), then society's denial of a sexuoerotic component to childhood has important implications for the future health of our children. Ironically, we may be doing more harm than good by protecting our children from exposure to sexual matters.

Demarcating 'Adulthood'

Discussions of sex and sexual functioning, particularly where children and young people are concerned, almost always impinge on the wider concepts of 'childhood' and 'adulthood'. Put simply, sex only becomes permissible once adulthood is attained. On the surface, this seems a sensible, rational approach. However, difficulties arise when we attempt to establish when adulthood begins and childhood ends. One solution to these difficulties is to enshrine the demarcation between childhood and adulthood in law, by arbitrarily setting an age at which an individual becomes adult. This 'solution', however, creates further difficulties. Our own laws regarding 'adult' behaviour illustrate this point: at the age of 16, you can purchase cigarettes and enter into heterosexual sexual relationship, driving a car is permissible at age 17 and full social and political adulthood (in that you can vote and freely drink alcohol) begins at 18. These laws take no account of those in their 20s, or even 30s, who cannot be trusted behind the wheel of a car, nor of the many adults who are incapable of drinking alcohol sensibly.

The arbitrary nature of the law is all the more apparent when sex is considered. Despite the fact that from a *biological* perspective some individuals are capable of sex and, indeed, reproduction at ages as young as 10 or 12, the law assumes that those under 16 are devoid of sexual feelings. Yet, at the same time, it openly condones 'mature' sexual relationships, despite the fact that many adults are immature when it comes to forming and sustaining close relationships, let alone sexual relationships.

Historical and cross-cultural perspectives also illustrate the arbitrariness of demarcation between childhood and adulthood. As Humphries *et al.* (1988) remark, prior to the First World War, childhood ended abruptly at 12, the age at which many could legally begin work. And there are still many cultures within the world where adulthood begins at 12 or 14 (Bee, 1995).

If you were a legislator, at what age would you set adulthood? What are your reasons for choosing this particular age?

Society's insistence that childhood and adulthood be rigidly demarcated has led to the assumption that childhood is somehow 'special'. We have children's stories, children's television, children's meals, children's shops and so on. And society widely holds the view that childhood is '... an age of innocence and purity to be guarded at all costs from adult corruption' (Weeks, 1985: 223). Academics, too, are guilty of treating childhood as something special: for example, it is interesting to note that many developmental theorists have limited their research efforts to a specific and relatively small part of life in spite of the fact that development is really a lifelong process.

As we shall see, the assumption that childhood is somehow special is not without question.

The Age of Innocence?

Innocence has not always been associated with childhood. As Weeks (1985) points out, childhood has only begun to be more sharply demarcated as an age of innocence and purity since around the eighteenth century. Even in more recent times, what we now see as childhood was for many a time of exposure to the harsh realities of adult life. Humphries et al. (1988) report the recollections of man in his 80s who, at 13, was initiated into the world of work by having his trousers pulled down and his penis massaged with grease and horse manure. 'Sexual abuse' would ring in the ears of many child care professionals nowadays, but at the time activities such as these were considered part of the norms and social practices of work: '... when the next new boy came you were doing it with the rest of them' (Humphries et al., 1988: 160).

There is an inherent contradiction in the notion of childhood innocence. In its truest sense, 'innocence' means untainted by evil or sin; in its less formal sense, and when applied to children, it means protection from the harsh realities and unpleasant aspects of adult life. Yet what exactly is harsh and unpleasant in adult life is open to debate. Would you describe sex as unpleasant? Yet within this framework of innocence, unpleasant aspects of life are overtly condoned. As Money (1986) points out, most children with a Christian upbringing are exposed to the intimate details of a man's violent execution – Christ's crucifixion – yet few question whether this is appropriate material for a young child to be exposed to. Aggression is also condoned, albeit in a more covert form, in comic books, cartoons and daily television schedules.

The fact that, as far as children are concerned, society appears to condone aggression and condemn sex has more to do with what *adults* think children should be exposed to than to any objective measure of what really is harmful.

The Reality of Children as Sexual Beings

Many in society still hold the view that we somehow metamorphose into sexual beings overnight (during adolescence), just like caterpillars turn into moths. However, most aspects of human functioning, psychological and physical alike, arise not as a result of metamorphosis, which implies a rapid transformation, but as a result of *development* and there is no logical reason why the same should not apply to sexuoerotic functioning. If we assume that sexuoerotic functioning arises from a developmental process, then we should be able to find evidence of its early manifestations during the earlier parts of our lives. And, as you will see, there is no shortage of this evidence.

For instance, intimate discussions with parents will yield admissions that children are indeed sexual beings. Most parents are aware that children play with their own genitals and are naturally curious about other people's bodies (Aquilino and Ely, 1985). Children frequently ask questions about the differences between boys and girls and seem to be fascinated with where babies come from. Most mothers are all too aware that pre-pubertal boys get erections, and there is even evidence of penile erection in male fetuses (Money, 1986).

Empirical studies also put the sexuoerotic functioning of children into perspective. Finkelhor (1979), for example, reports that well over half of all children have childhood sexual experiences with other children, and Money (1986) reports that rhythmic pelvic thrusting is often observed in children as young as three or four when in close contact with one another.

The work of Kinsey *et al.* (1948) — work that is almost 50 years old — first opened the world's eyes to the reality of childhood sexuoeroticism, though the world, on the whole, chose to ignore it. Though dated, this work remains a benchmark in the study of sexual behaviour given the large sample it employed (though it should be added that Kinsey and his colleagues only dealt with males in their 1948 volume). Indeed, Kinsey *et al.* dedicated a whole chapter to the study of childhood sexual behaviour though, surprisingly, this chapter is infrequently cited when the work is discussed, perhaps because he gleaned a substantial proportion of his data from practising paedophiles (though from a *scientific* point of view, this chapter is as valid as the others).

Despite these observations, expressions of sexuoerotic functioning in children are frequently taken out of a sexual context and seen merely as natural inquisitiveness or as a normal part of growing up. Benjamin Spock, in his world-renowned manual *Baby & Child Care* (1955), attempted to address this issue by acknowledging that young children do indeed handle their genitals. Spock's attempts to enlighten the world about childhood sexuoeroticism are rather half-hearted, however: Spock, too, falls prey to society's antipathy towards childhood sexuoeroticism by suggesting that it is fears that something might happen to the genitals, not sexuoerotic feelings, that underlie this behaviour. He then, with some irony, goes on to speculate that many parents chose to deny the existence of sexuoeroticism in children because '… they themselves had been brought up so frightened of sex, they wanted to avoid recognizing it as long as possible in their children' (p. 279).

Though Spock attempted to make parents face the truth in the 1950s, and though there has been a whole generation of parents brought up during the 'swinging 60s', attitudes to childhood sexuoeroticism have subsequently changed little. Some 20 years later, Penelope Leach, another child care guru, wrote:

> If you walk in and find the child red faced and panting, you will probably be shocked, but that is because adults prefer to believe that small children have no sexual feelings, not because they either do not or should not have any.
>
> (Leach, 1977: 477)

Even today, in the more enlightened 1990s, many parents still find sexuoerotic expressions sinful, shocking or disturbing, to be discouraged or, at the very least, ignored.

REFLECTION POINT

Think about your own children or your own childhood. Would you accept that children are sexual beings? At what age did you become aware of your own sexuoerotic feelings?

That discussions of childhood sexuoerotic functioning still create controversy today is all the more surprising, considering that the debate began almost a century ago with the thoughts of Sigmund Freud.

AHEAD OF HIS TIME: SIGMUND FREUD

In 1905, the publication of Freud's *Three Essays on the Theory of Sexuality* (see Freud, 1949) shook the Western world. Not only was Freud brave enough to consider the issue of sex in an era that had been dominated by a philosophy of anti-sex and anti-sexualism, he was brazen enough to speak the unspeakable, namely that contrary to society's widely held beliefs, children did, indeed, have a sexuoerotic aspect to their lives. Moreover, and more controversially, Freud's *psychoanalytical* theory postulated that these sexuoerotic aspects were the driving force behind the developing personality and that interference with these aspects, be it wilful or accidental, could lead to problems in later life.

Not surprisingly, given its controversial nature, Freud's theory had little impact on society at the time. Hardyment (1983: 109) writes:

> The world was not ready for the complication of the unconscious and subconscious minds of their children — parents had barely got used to the idea that their babies had nervous systems ... They were appalled at the idea that infants were born with sexual urges ...

It was not until the 1940s — some 30 years later — that Freud's ideas began to gain mainstream credibility, even to the point of pervading child care practices. For example, much of Spock's *Baby & Child Care* (1955) owes its allegiance to Freud, as does the work of the child

---

care specialists John Bowlby, Margaret Ribble and Edith Buxbaum. Though psychoanalytical theories fell out of favour in Britain and, to a lesser extent, the USA during the 1960s, there is still a significant proportion of those working in certain aspects of child care (e.g. some child psychotherapists) who have a psychoanalytical bias, though more so in the USA. Still, Freud has to be applauded for '… opening our eyes to the existence of childhood sexuality' (Martin, 1980: 51), for launching the issue of childhood sexuoeroticism into the public arena and for forcing society to accept, whether it likes it or not, that the concepts of 'childhood' and 'innocence' are not necessarily congruous.

An Overview of Freudian Theory

Three concepts are central to Freud's model of the mind:

○ the ego
○ the id
○ the superego.

At birth, according to Freudian theory, our personalities consist of nothing more than a seething mass of powerful and instinctual needs, known collectively as the *id*. These needs include, for example, the need to eat and drink, eliminate, avoid pain and obtain sexual pleasure. All of these *unconscious* needs are fuelled by a 'sexual energy', which Freud termed *libido* (but, see the discussion of Jung later). The id itself is amoral, pleasure-seeking and predominantly sexual in nature.

As we grow, however, we realise that we have to live by the restraining demands of external reality (which includes demands placed upon us by our parents, by those in authority and by society as a whole). As awareness of external reality unfolds, so does the *ego* (the part of us that others see; the 'self'). The ego is, to all intents and purposes, a mediator; it is the part of the mind that, to a significant extent, *consciously* balances the instinctual demands of the *id* against the demands of external reality. Throughout life, the *ego* attempts to reach an ideal, the *ego-ideal*, a mental representation of the person we really want to be, based on those who have influenced our lives.

At a later stage, the *superego* develops. The *superego* is an internal representation of parental controls and societal demands, supplemented by the influence of the ego-ideal. It is roughly equivalent to the concept of 'conscience' and has the ability to punish us with guilt whenever we transgress its moral authority and to reward us with euphoria and satisfaction whenever we comply. A schematic diagram of Freud's model of the mind can be found in Figure 1.

Ego development is achieved via progression through various psychosexual stages (see Figure 2), of which there are five.

○ The first stage, the *oral* stage, lasts from birth to around the age of two. During this stage, food is the primary focus and pleasure is derived from sucking, be it a nipple, thumb, bottle or any other object.

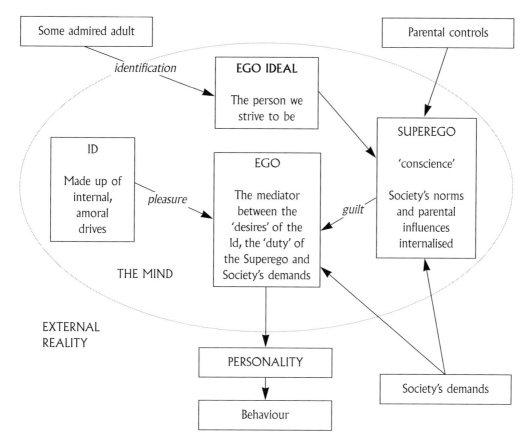

Figure 1 The Freudian model of the mind.

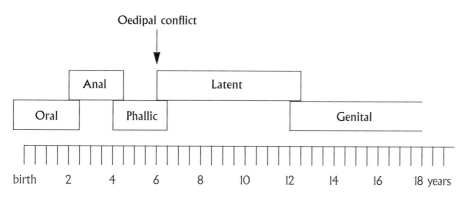

Figure 2 Freud's psychosexual stages.

○ The second stage, the *anal* stage, lasts to around the age of 4. During this stage, the focus is on the expulsion (or, indeed, retention) of faeces. Voluntary control of bowels develops and the child realises that both the retention and expulsion of faeces can be pleasurable.

○ The third stage, the *phallic* stage, lasts to around the age of 6. Here, the genitals become the focus of pleasure. During this stage, satisfactory resolution of the 'Oedipus complex' (a situation where the child is attracted to the parent of the opposite sex and views the same-sex parent as a rival) leads to development of the superego.

○ From the age of 6 until puberty, there is a period of latency (the *latent* stage) during which the libido retreats. Children become less interested in their bodies and more in their environment. Sexuoerotic expression rarely occurs during this stage (though, as we will see, there is evidence to the contrary), possibly because the establishment of the superego suddenly instills a moral sense into children.

○ Finally, the resurgence of sexual interest brought about by puberty brings about the *genital* stage, where the libido finds expression in a mature, adult sexual relationship.

Thus, according to Freud, sexuoeroticism is intrinsically linked to psychological development, though because most sexuoerotic expression is *unconscious*, the sexuoerotic demands of the libido manifest in more subtle ways, e.g. Freud postulated that slips and lapses of the tongue have a sexuoerotic underpinning, hence the so-called 'Freudian slip'.

During any of the stages, wilful or accidental interference with the libido's demands could arrest healthy personality development. The child might become 'fixated' at any one of the stages. For example, a child weaned early might become 'orally fixated' and in later life find they are excessively dependent on oral pleasures such as food or smoking. Similarly, problems with resolution of the Oedipus complex could lead to poor superego development and a lack of any real moral sense.

REFLECTION POINT

From your own experiences of dealing with children, would you say there was much evidence to support Freud's stage theory?

Jung and the Libido

Not all psychoanalytical theorists and practitioners accept that sexuoeroticism is the driving force behind personality development. In particular, Carl Gustav Jung, an early disciple of Freud's, had a well-publicised disagreement on the issue, which ultimately led to Jung and Freud's disassociation. Jung's major point of contention (see, for example, Jung, 1983) was Freud's overemphasis on sexuoeroticism; in particular, he argued that the libido was not synonymous with sexual energy. Instead, Jung saw the libido as mere 'psychic' energy.

TRAINING CHILDREN: BEHAVIOURISM

The traditional opponent of the psychoanalytical school has been the behavioural school, founded by John Broadus Watson during the 1920s. The central focus of the behavioural psychologists, as you might expect, is the individual's observable behaviour. Unlike the psychoanalytical school of thought, behaviourism has no interest in internal, mental processes; it is, as such, not interested in concepts such as consciousness and unconsciousness. In its most extreme form, behaviourism considers only the individual's *responses* to various environmental *stimuli* (hence the so-called '*stimulus–response*' paradigm).

According to the behaviourists, patterns of behaviour (including sexuoerotic patterns of behaviour) are acquired via *conditioning*. There are two main conditioning mechanisms: *classical* conditioning and *operant* conditioning.

Classical Conditioning

Classical conditioning has its roots in the work of the Russian physiologist, Ivan Pavlov. Pavlov's well-known work with dogs led to the observation that the pairing of certain stimuli could induce an unanticipated response, a response that has come to be known as a *conditioned* response. Dogs salivating at the smell of food could be conditioned to salivate to the sound of a bell which had previously been presented alongside the food. Watson advocated the classical conditioning model as an explanation of all human learning and claimed to be able to shape any child's future using this technique (see, for example, *Behaviorism*, 1930). His ideas also had much in common with those of Sir Frederick Truby King, founder of the 'Mothercraft' movement popular in the 1920s and 1930s.

Whilst discussing classical conditioning, it is worth briefly mentioning 'aversion therapy', a treatment approach that has its roots in the classical conditioning paradigm and which gained some popularity in the 1960s and 1970s as a 'cure' for the paraphilias (the more correct term for what most people call 'sexual deviations'). Here, attempts are made to associate the stimuli underlying the paraphilia with some nauseous stimuli (like electric shocks or nausea-inducing drugs). Thus, in an attempt to rid a man of homosexual feelings, pictures of naked men might be presented shortly after a nausea-inducing drug has been given.

The efficacy of aversion therapy is questionable, though there is some evidence that those truly motivated to change might derive some benefit (a review of the efficacy of behavioural approaches involving punishment can be found in Axelrod and Apsche, 1983). Aversion therapy, like classical conditioning, has fallen out of fashion in recent years.

Operant Conditioning

Of much greater interest to a discussion of sexuoeroticism is operant conditioning, an approach to learning proposed by B. F. Skinner in the 1930s (see, for example, Skinner, 1953). Underlying operant conditioning is the notion that we are more likely to perform behaviours that result in some sort of reward than those which hurt or cause us pain. We are, by and large, *hedonistic* (pleasure-seeking) creatures. Within an operant conditioning framework, it is easy to understand why humans participate in sexuoerotic acts, and why children explore their genitals – quite simply because these acts are *pleasurable*.

In a nutshell, operant conditioning theory implies that behaviour can be modified by the use of rewards and punishments. In a sense, operant conditioning suggests that humans can be *trained* in much the same way as animals. Operant conditioning principles have dominated child-rearing practices for many years, though in recent years there has been less emphasis on punishment and more on its fairly benign cousin, the sanction. Any parent who sends a child to their room for swearing, or buys the child an ice-cream for being good, is essentially using operant conditioning principles. So, too, are parents who scold, or even smack, their children for expressions of sexuoeroticism. Operant conditioning principles do work to some extent in that their use may produce the desired behavioural change (for example, the child may stop masturbating); on the other hand, critics of behavioural approaches (again, see Axelrod and Apsche, 1983) claim that at best behavioural techniques merely drive the 'undesirable' behaviour underground, whilst at worst they produce entirely unanticipated and even damaging consequences.

DISCUSSION POINT

Have you ever used behavioural principles with children of your own or children you have worked with in a professional capacity? Have they been successful, i.e. was the anticipated change in behaviour evident?

COGNITIVE DEVELOPMENT: JEAN PIAGET

During the 1950s, a third force entered a child care arena that had traditionally been dominated by the behaviourists and psychoanalysts – 'cognitive' psychology. Cognitive psychology arose as a result of the advances in computer technology made during the 1950s and from a belief that humans, like computers, are nothing more than mere information processors.

As far as child development is concerned, the most well-known cognitive psychologist is Jean Piaget (though Piaget was, in fact, a biologist and philosopher by training). Most child care professionals have heard of Piaget and are all too aware of his influence on child development. However, what many child care professionals fail to realise is that Piaget was merely concerned with *one* aspect of child development, namely *cognitive* development. Consequently, Piaget had little, if anything, to say about sexuoerotic development (given Piaget's training as a biologist, this statement is perhaps more surprising than it might at first seem). However, as I pointed out earlier, sexuoeroticism has a cognitive aspect to it and it is, as such, worth asking whether any of Piaget's observations have any relevance to sexuoerotic development. To consider this question, we need to briefly explore Piaget's theory, but before doing so I need to digress a little and consider the 'schema' notion.

The Schema Notion

Of central importance to the cognitive psychologists is the notion of a schema (plural *schemata* or *schemas*). Schemata are mental 'templates' that guide both behaviour and thought (schemata actually guide *action*: external action being observable behaviour; internal action being thought), in a similar way that a recipe is a template for creating an exotic dish. Any action, internal or external, will have a schema underpinning it. Thus, there are schemata for skilled tasks, like driving or typing, schemata for making judgements about people, schemata for language, schemata for perceiving, and so on. Some aspects of certain schemata may be inherited (indeed, the simplest schemata are mere reflex actions), but the vast majority are acquired. To those familiar with computers, a schema is little more than the software that drives our action. However, unlike computer software, schemata can replicate, change and become redundant as we experience the world.

Schemata help us process the vast amount of information in the world. They serve us well for the majority of the time; however, they are not always applicable to a particular situation and when we misapply them, errors occur. For example, when we misapply a 'braking' schema whilst driving, we might be involved in an accident. Similarly, the misapplication of 'judgemental' schemata can lead to the creation of stereotypes.

An Overview of Piaget's Theory

Piaget's theory (see, for example, Donaldson, 1978; Atkinson *et al.*, 1996) is an *adaptation* theory. Adaptation theories are concerned with how we interact with, and adapt to, the environment and Piaget's theory postulates that intellectual (cognitive) development results as a consequence of our interaction with, and adaptation to, the environment. And as we interact with and adapt to our environment, so the schemata underlying our cognitive processes change.

Though cognitive development is, to all intents and purposes, continuous throughout life, Piaget claims that there are marked stages. Note that though ages are given for these stages, some individuals move through the stages at a greater speed than others; the ages given, as such, are averages:

○ *Sensorimotor stage* (birth–18 months, approximately)
A baby is born only with a limited number of reflexes (these innate reflexes being little more than simple schemata). To begin with, the child is profoundly 'egocentric', i.e. the child literally sees everything from their own perspective; he or she is unable to distinguish between itself and the environment. During the first stage, the egocentric child begins to differentiate itself from the environment, and begins to realise that the world consists of objects that are independent of him or herself. It is during this stage that 'object permanence' (the realisation that objects still exist when removed from the child's immediate perception) develops.

- ○ *Pre-operational stage* (18 months–7 years, approximately)

  During this stage, the child starts to internally represent objects by the use of images or words. However, though the child has the ability to internally represent certain aspects of the world (as schemata), these internal representations are not yet organised in a coherent manner.

- ○ *Concrete operational stage* (7–12 years, approximately)

  During this stage, the child becomes capable of operational thought. This means that the child develops the ability to use 'operations' on his or her internal representations: the child can mentally combine, order and separate objects. The child also develops the ability to classify objects, and during this stage, 'conservation' develops. With the acquisition of conservation, the child realises that certain qualities of objects (height, weight, length, etc.) are conserved whenever those objects are moved or modified in some way.

- ○ *Formal operational stage* (12 years onwards, approximately)

  This stage begins when the child begins to think abstractly rather than concretely, and, as such, can follow logical propositions and reason by hypothesis. Essentially, once the child reaches this stage, he or she thinks like an adult.

Piaget's theory is not without its critics; in particular, Piaget's conclusions are based on small and biased samples of children and larger-scale studies have not always confirmed his findings (Taylor *et al.*, 1982). Nevertheless, it is an important theory to consider because of the impact it has made on Western society over the last three decades. Its impact on education, in particular, has been immense.

Moral Development

One concept that is often discussed in the same breath as sex is morality. Piaget also had an interest in moral development and argued that, as morality has its foundations in reasoning, a child's sense of morality is ultimately dependent upon his or her degree of cognitive development. According to Piaget, there is a distinct shift in moral thinking at around the age of 7, when the child moves from the pre-operational to the concrete operational stage. 'Heteronomous' morality is typical in children under the age of 7; 'autonomous' morality is typical of older children. Heteronomous morality, which has its roots in egocentrism, is typified by the belief that rules are universal and sacred and that to transgress ultimately results in some severe punishment, whether there is a real threat of punishment or not. Autonomous morality is typified by the realisation that rules are made by others and that they are (sometimes) negotiable. Autonomous morality further develops as the child reaches the formal operational stage at around the age of 12 to the point that the child starts to look at moral issues wider than those that relate to his or her own personal and interpersonal situations. This, to some extent, explains why teenagers often have an interest in social and environmental concerns.

Kohlberg (see, for example, Kohlberg, 1969) has developed the work of Piaget into his own theory of moral development. Using 'moral dilemmas' (short stories where a judgement on a moral issue is required), Kohlberg identified six stages of moral development within three levels. These stages are summarised in Table 1.

Table 1   Kohlberg's stages of moral reasoning

Level I	Pre-conventional morality
Stage 1	*Punishment orientation* – the individual obeys rules simply to avoid punishment
Stage 2	*Reward orientation* – the individual conforms to obtain rewards and to have favours returned
Level II	Conventional morality
Stage 3	*Good-boy/good-girl orientation* – the individual conforms to avoid the disapproval of others
Stage 4	*Authority orientation* – the individual upholds laws and social rules to avoid condemnation by those in authority and guilt feelings associated with not doing one's duty
Level III	Post-conventional morality
Stage 5	*Social-contract orientation* – the individual's actions are guided by principles commonly agreed on as essential to the public welfare; principles are upheld to retain the respect of peers and, thus, self-respect
Stage 6	*Ethical principle orientation* – the individual's actions are guided by self-chosen ethical principles, which usually value justice, dignity and equality; principles are upheld to avoid *self*-condemnation

Adapted from Atkinson *et al.* (1996).

Unlike Piaget, Kohlberg does not concede that moral development is complete during childhood; instead, the development of morality is seen as something that lasts a lifetime. Though Kohlberg's stages are sequential (each successive stage builds upon its predecessor), transition through the stages is not absolute. Some individuals never progress beyond Level I, though Kohlberg argues that *most* of us will attain Level II by the age of 13. Level III, if it develops, can develop at any time during adulthood, though Kohlberg argues that fewer than 10% of us actually attain Stage 6.

Given that most of us rarely progress beyond Level II (or Stage 5 at the very least), then there is an argument that Level II moral thinking is typical of most of society. As most children attain this stage by the age of 13, it could be said that the moral thinking of most teenagers is in tune with society as a whole.

Cognitive Theories and Sexuoerotic Development

It is clear from the overview of Piaget's theory that there is no *direct* applicability to sexuo-erotic development. However, the very fact that children appear to think differently as they grow older has some implications regarding what children of different ages *understand* about sex.

Implicit in adult sexuoerotic functioning is an assumption that the individual understands certain basic, abstract concepts: consent, body ownership, intuition, assertiveness, choice and responsibility, for example. For most young children, an understanding of these concepts is beyond their cognitive ability. According to the cognitive theorists, only at around the age of 12 do children sufficiently develop a level of cognitive and moral functioning capable of dealing with these abstract concepts. This observation has important implications for the notion of 'innocence', especially in cases of child sexual abuse, in that it could be argued – and remember that this is only speculation based on one *theoretical* perspective – that older children, to some extent, know exactly what they are doing when engaging in sexuoerotic behaviour, whereas younger children do not.

There are also some implications for sex education too, in that the cognitive theories imply that older children are more able to deal with the concepts inherent in sexual behaviour – that is, the realities of sex – than are younger children. Smith (1993) supplies a framework for providing sex education in children, based on the intellectual abilities of the child at a given age.

DISCUSSION POINT

If children are biologically capable of sex and have the cognitive ability to understand its ramifications (including its moral ramifications) from the age of around 12 or 13 as the cognitive theorists imply, is there an argument for lowering the age of consent? What are the advantages/disadvantages of the current age of consent?

ADOLESCENCE AND SEXUOEROTICISM

Whilst society generally feels that it is not legitimate to discuss the issues of sex and childhood in tandem, society begins to relax when adolescence is considered.

A definition of adolescence is difficult. There are arguments that adolescence is merely a social invention confined to technological societies. It does not exist in all societies (in some 'primitive' societies, children become adults almost overnight through some rite of passage), and it did not exist in modern-day society until the turn of the century (Burns, 1986). One of the most basic problems surrounding adolescence is determining the age at which it begins and, like childhood, the age at which it ends. In addition, there are many other factors that influence our conceptualisation of what adolescence actually is. These factors are summarised in Figure 3.

Burns (1986) suggests that adolescence starts with puberty and ends with the assumption of adult social, legal, economic, political and sexual rights and duties. However, as we have seen when I earlier discussed the demarcation of childhood and adulthood, there is no clear-cut

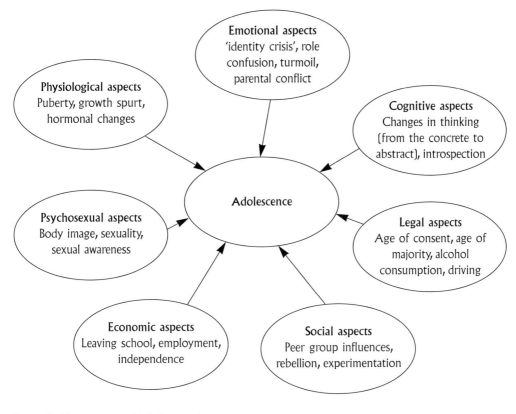

Figure 3 The concept of 'adolescence'.

age at which these rights and duties are adopted, both within our culture and between other cultures.

Sex and sexuality are issues that are often associated with adolescence, primarily because of its correlation with puberty, '… the period of sexual maturation that transforms a child into a biologically mature adult capable of sexual reproduction …' (Atkinson *et al.*, 1996: 105). Driving puberty are the major hormonal changes that occur within the body, and it has long been supposed that these hormonal changes play a significant part in the turmoil that is often associated with adolescence. Indeed, this turmoil is the central focus of a developmental model that perhaps has the most to say about adolescence – that of Erik Erikson.

Erikson and Adolescence

Erikson (see, for example, Erikson, 1963) combined a psychoanalytical perspective with sociological observations to produce a *psychosocial* model of personality development. There are eight stages to Erikson's model (Erikson called these stages the eight 'ages of man'), the focus of each being a 'psychosocial crisis'. Successful resolution of each successive psychosocial crisis leads to the acquisition of 'virtues' necessary for healthy psychosocial functioning. Erikson's stages are summarised in Table 2.

Table 2 Erikson's eight 'ages of man'

'Age of man'	Psychosocial crisis	Favourable outcome (*virtue acquired*)
1. First year of life	Trust–mistrust	Trust and optimism. *Hope.*
2. Second year	Autonomy–doubt	Sense of self-control and adequacy. *Willpower.*
3. Third–fifth years	Initiative–guilt	Purpose and direction; ability to initiate one's own activities. *Purpose.*
4. Sixth year–puberty	Industry–inferiority	Competence in intellectual, social and physical skills. *Competence.*
5. Adolescence	Identity–confusion	An integrated image of oneself as a unique person. *Fidelity.*
6. Early adulthood	Intimacy–isolation	Ability to form close and lasting relationships; to make career commitments. *Love.*
7. Middle adulthood	Generativity–self-absorption	Concern for family, society and future generations. *Care.*
8. The ageing years	Integrity–despair	A sense of fulfilment and satisfaction with one's life; willingness to face death. *Wisdom.*

Adapted from Atkinson *et al.* (1996).

The psychosocial crisis affecting adolescence is one of 'identity versus confusion'. According to Erikson, there is an upsurge, at puberty, of instinctual id forces (remember that id forces are, in Freuds's eyes, primarily *sexual*) that generates great emotional upheaval. This upheaval is coupled by the marginalisation of the young person in society – the adolescent is neither child nor adult – and the adolescent has to reconcile conflicting demands from society to survive. In order to resolve these demands the young person becomes deeply introspective and, both consciously and unconsciously, ponders the question 'who am I?'. Satisfactory resolution of this 'identity crisis' produces an integrated image of the self. The virtue acquired following resolution of the identity crisis – *fidelity* – is necessary for the move into early adulthood (the next stage) as individuals without it are, according to Erikson, incapable of forming deep and loving relationships.

However, as with most other developmental theorists, Erikson's approach shies away from any direct discussion of sex and sexuality; these issues are only incidental to Erikson's theory in that they are factors contributing to the turmoil being experienced. Erikson's avoidance of a sexuoerotic component is surprising given his psychoanalytical influences and the fact that, of all periods in life, adolescence is perhaps the time when we become most aware, at least physically, of our sexual selves.

Though the issues surrounding sex and sexuality are only important within Erikson's framework because they contribute to turmoil, the widely accepted view of adolescent turmoil is not backed up by research. Adolescence does have its problems, but it appears that these problems are no greater than at any other developmental stage. Rutter *et al.* (1976) studied adolescents in the Isle of Wight and reported that though adolescent turmoil was evident in *deviant* groups, the majority of young people were reasonably well-balanced emotionally. The 'myth' of adolescent turmoil is perpetuated by a variety of influences, including sensationalist media reporting and the fact that those studying young people – psychiatrists and psychologists in particular – often study unrepresentative subgroups, such as those habitually in trouble or early/late maturers. Rutter *et al.*'s work is backed by Coleman's studies of adolescent boys (Coleman, 1980; Coleman and Hendry, 1990), which found that adolescence is a period of stability and normality for most, and by Petersen (1988), who found that most Americans get through adolescence without any major turmoil.

Whilst it is easy to understand why society feels that sex is not an issue for pre-pubescent children (on the grounds that younger children are not ready *biologically*), it is difficult to understand why society shies away from discussing these issues with adolescents. Maybe it is because we do not want to add any further turmoil to our already troubled teenagers. However, should adolescence generally be a time of relative stability, as the evidence seems to suggest, then we have little to fear by confronting sexuoerotic issues during adolescence. Indeed, as Bee (1995) points out: 'In cultures in which 12- or 14-year olds are considered adults ready to take on adult tasks and responsibilities, to marry and bear children, adolescent sexuality is handled very differently' (p. 117).

DISCUSSION POINT

Are you comfortable discussing sexual issues with adolescents? If not, what anxieties do you have? Do you think sexual issues need to be dealt with in a different way when adolescents, rather than younger children, are considered?

Though the anecdotal, scientific and empirical evidence points strongly to there being a sexuoerotic aspect to childhood, the developmental theorists have generally failed to gauge its significance or incorporate this aspect into their theories. There are mavericks, however. We have already seen how Freud was bold enough to confront the issue at the turn of the century. Let us now turn to another.

A THEORY OF SEXUOEROTIC DEVELOPMENT: MONEY'S 'LOVEMAPS'

Towards the beginning of this chapter, in explaining why I had chosen to employ the term 'sexuoerotic', I made reference to the American sexologist, John Money. Like Freud, Money argues that it is the *sexuoerotic* aspects of childhood that contribute to our future development. However, whilst Freud views sexuoeroticism on a predominantly *unconscious* level, Money would claim that the individual is all too aware of his sexuoerotic thoughts and feelings. And although Freud suggests that sexuoerotic functioning manifests, by and large, in rather subtle ways, the sexuoerotic aspects that Money describes are of a more concrete and overt nature.

At the centre of Money's approach is the notion of a 'lovemap'. According to Money (1986), a lovemap is '... a developmental representation or template in the mind and in the brain depicting the idealized lover and the idealized program of sexuoerotic activity projected in imagery or actually engaged in with that lover' (p. 290). This 'template' that Money describes is essentially a schema. Using the computer analogy I referred to when earlier discussing the schema notion, lovemaps are the software programs that dictate our sexual thoughts and our sexual behaviour. To this end, Money's approach has more in common with Piaget and the cognitive psychologists than Freud.

Lovemaps are specific to each individual and have both a genetic aspect and an environmental (experiential) aspect to them. Built into the lovemap are aspects such as *gender status* – a term which embraces the twin concepts of 'gender identity' (how you view your own gender) and 'gender role' (the ways in which your gender is manifested to others) – as well as other aspects such as sexual orientation, sexual preferences and specific representations of the 'ideal' lover.

| REFLECTION POINT |

Think about your ideal partner. What aspects come to mind? Have you specific criteria regarding, for example, physical characteristics, race, gender and temperament? Do you have any likes/dislikes regarding specific sexual activities? Money would claim that by thinking about your ideal partner, you are invoking elements of your lovemap.

The Development of Lovemaps

Lovemaps are not present at birth. However, the foundations of a lovemap are laid as the developing brain is exposed, *in utero*, to the sex hormones, the hormones that masculinise or feminise the fetus. To this end, there is a biological (genetic) aspect to a lovemap.

As the child develops, so does its lovemap. As the child interacts with its environment, so the lovemap begins to change. As the child absorbs new experiences, certain experiences, whether they are of an overtly sexuoerotic nature or not, are incorporated into the developing lovemap.

Money conjectures that the incorporation of experiences into the lovemap is at its most intense between the ages of 5 and 8. By the age of 8, lovemaps are pretty well established. Up until puberty, there is not a period of latency as argued by Freud, but a period where

---

consolidation of the lovemap takes place. By the time the individual reaches puberty, if not before, the lovemap that has developed is extremely resistant to change.

Money stresses the importance of 'sexuoerotic rehearsal play' in the development of lovemaps. During sexuoerotic rehearsal play, children imitate the motions and positions characteristic of adult sexuoerotic behaviour, such as pelvic thrusting and coital positioning. Crucial to the development of a *healthy* lovemap is 'age-synchrony' during sexuoerotic rehearsal play. This means that children who engage in sexual play with children of a similar age (children whose lovemaps are developing in synchrony) tend to have few sexuoerotic problems in adult life.

The 'Vandalism' of Lovemaps

Money asserts that, under optimum conditions, normal lovemap development results in 'heterosexual differentiation without complexities'. The optimum conditions to which Money refers includes the endorsement of sexuoerotic rehearsal play within a framework which views sex as positive and healthy, rather than degenerate and unhealthy.

Money argues that adults frequently 'vandalise' (albeit with good intentions) the lovemaps of children, particularly in the most vulnerable years of lovemap development (ages 5–8). As you might expect, this vandalism occurs when children are exposed abruptly to socially tabooed expressions of sexuoeroticism; however, it also occurs when children are denied the opportunity to engage in, or are punished or reprimanded for engaging in, sexuoerotic rehearsal play.

Money cites some evidence to back up this hypothesis: he reports that males in sex therapy tended to have negative feelings surrounding their first ejaculation (e.g. thinking it was wrong, dirty or shameful), whereas the feelings of a control group tended to be more positive. Similarly, he cites reports that the situational components of women's first experiences of intercourse tended to determine whether it would be viewed negatively or positively.

Vandalism of the lovemap ultimately distorts it in adulthood. Money argues that the sexual activities that we term 'kinky' or 'perverted' (the paraphilias), which can range from the playful and harmless to the bizarre and deadly, occur as a result of lovemap distortion. The latter statement has important implications in that, if Money is right, then a change in society's attitude to sex could well eliminate many of the sexual problems society has to deal with today. Indeed, Money *et al.* (1970) claim that the paraphilias are nonexistent in the aborigines of Arnhem Land, where childhood sexuoerotic rehearsal play is traditionally endorsed.

Homosexuality and Other 'Gender Transpositions'

It is worth mentioning briefly that, although Money claims that healthy lovemap development leads to 'heterosexual differentiation without complexities', he also suggests that homosexuality should not be viewed as a paraphilia, but rather as a characteristic much like left-handedness.

Money refers to homosexuality as a 'gender transposition'. Transvestitism and transsexualism are also examples of gender transposition. Gender transpositions differ from paraphilias in that, unlike the paraphilias, the lovemap is not distorted during its development. Rather, aspects of one component of the lovemap – gender status – become transposed. Remember that gender status is not merely concerned with whether we are 'male' or 'female', it reflects the sexuoerotic, occupational and social aspects of gender as well as other gender-related factors such as mannerisms and dress. Any, or indeed all, of these aspects can be transposed. However, despite these transpositions, the lovemaps of the gender-transposed still develop normally, that is heterosexual differentiation. On first sight, there appears to be some ambiguity here. How can 'normal heterosexual differentiation' lead to homosexuality? Money explains it in the following way. If, for example, only the sexuoerotic aspect of gender status in a male becomes transposed, then to all intents and purposes, this aspect becomes female rather than male. Normal development then occurs from a female starting point: 'heterosexual' differentiation here means sexual attraction towards men. If no other aspects of gender status are transposed, then the homosexual male remains male in every other aspect: he will dress like a man, act like a man, undertake work in typically male-dominated occupations, and so on. If other aspects of gender status become transposed as well, then the picture will be different. For example, if mannerisms and social role also become transposed, then the homosexual is likely to be effeminate. Contrary to popular belief, however, effeminacy does not necessarily equate with homosexuality. There are, after all, many heterosexual, effeminate men: Money would suggest that in these men, only the mannerisms associated with their gender status have become transposed.

With transvestites ('cross-dressers'), it is the dress aspect of gender status that becomes transposed. With transsexuals, the entire gender status is transposed. Normal heterosexual development of the lovemap means that the transsexual develops a lovemap as if he were female. It is only the fact that he has the wrong physical make-up that leads to problems.

Gender transpositions occur, according to Money, as a result of the hormonal influences in the womb (the extent to which each of us are masculinised and feminised, bearing in mind that 'male' and 'female' sex hormones are present in both sexes), supplemented by our subsequent experiences of life.

THE IRONY OF CHILD PROTECTION

Acknowledging that children have a sexuoerotic aspect to their lives raises some difficult issues for society. In particular, the notion that we are protecting our children by shielding them from sex is open to question. My review of Money's work has already illustrated how our well-intentioned attempts to 'protect' children from sex may ultimately damage them in later life. Krivacska (1992) supports Money's view, but is even more specific. He argues that approaches designed, with the full backing of society, to prevent child sexual abuse may ultimately — and ironically — encourage it. The crux of Krivacska's argument is that sexuo-erotic experiences which might otherwise be insignificant to the child (such as masturbation or peer group sex play) become enshrouded with a negativistic, punitive quality. This kind of approach, as we have seen, does not help with healthy lovemap development.

Krivacska also challenges the validity of some assumptions regarding sexually abused children. The first is that sexually abused children are always damaged by the abuse. This is not to deny that sexual abuse can damage some children, but that sometimes it is exposure to the legal system and the guilt surrounding involvement in acts seen as wrong that creates the damage. Bear in mind that many sexually abused children have strong affiliative bonds with their abusers. In essence, the child is in a 'lose–lose' situation: should he or she keep quiet, then the child risks being damaged by the secrecy and guilt of the actions; should the child tell, he or she risks the humiliation of exposure and, possibly, separation from a person that society sees as a 'perpetrator', but which the child may well see as a loved one.

These comments are backed up by Sandfort (1982, cited by Weeks, 1985), who studied 25 boys engaged in paedophilic homosexual relationships. Sandfort reported that many of these boys viewed their experiences *positively* and that, more often than not, negative feelings arose from the anxiety surrounding others' reactions to the relationship (anxiety about police involvement and parental exposure, for example) rather than the trauma of sex itself.

Another assumption that Krivacska challenges concerns the appropriateness of models used in the prevention of child sexual abuse. Most of the models used are based on adult analogies (such as rape crisis models) and require understanding of abstract concepts such as body ownership, rights, empowerment and responsibility. As we have seen, these requirements may well be beyond the intellectual capabilities of most young children. Krivacska writes: '… theories of cognitive and moral development … suggest that they [young children] lack the cognitive skills, conceptual schemas and experiences to accurately process such abstract concepts …' (p. 90).

Money (1986, 1988) adds a further dimension to the argument. Those working in child protection, he claims, are guilty of subscribing to a number of myths. In particular, he cites the myth that children never tell lies about sex. Moreover, he claims, the myth that those working with 'victims' are most flagrantly guilty of perpetuating lies in a failure '… to differentiate the statistical norm of what people *actually* do from the ideological norm of what they *should* do' (1988, p. 9, my emphasis). This point is reinforced by Krivacska (1992), who suggests that the notion of child sexual abuse has its foundations in political ideology (which has at its centre an abhorrence of sex) rather than in scientific rigour.

It is extremely important to note that none of the authors referred to in this section specifically condone adult–child sexual relationships. As Weeks (1985) argues, accepting childhood sexual play (which Money and Krivacska advocate) is not the same as tolerating adult–child sexual relationships. At the same time, however, they also refuse to condemn outright all such relationships, particularly where older children or adolescents are concerned, not because there are issues surrounding the morality of such relationships, but because they believe that a kneejerk condemnation of such relationships on the grounds that the child has been damaged, is a victim, or does not know what he or she has been doing does little, if anything, to truly protect the child.

Money, in particular, believes that the establishment of a true 'sexual democracy' within society may do more to protect children (and, indeed, adults). He adds, however, that '... sexual democracy is not synonymous with sexual licentiousness' (p. 4). Sexual democracy creates a situation where sexual diversity and individual eccentricity are tolerated whilst, at the same time, no individual's sexual rights are violated. As such, those advocating society's acceptance of adult–child sexual relationships lose their argument, not on the grounds that adult–child sexual relationships are necessarily traumatic, but on the grounds that there can be no democracy when the sexual freedom of one party (the adult) violates the sexual rights of the other (the child).

What is needed, according to Money and to Krivacska, is a society that embraces sex positively; a society that acknowledges that we all, regardless of age, have a sexuoerotic aspect to our lives; a society that accepts sexuoerotic rehearsal play and age-synchronous sexual relationships during childhood; ultimately, a society that is less hypocritical. Within this framework, it is possible to develop the sexual health of us all, including that of our children, to its fullest potential.

CONCLUSION: IMPLICATIONS FOR PRACTICE

When working with children, child care professionals have to be aware that there is much evidence to support a sexuoerotic aspect to childhood and that, with this acceptance, children must be given the freedom to explore their sexual selves in an environment that does not condemn or disapprove. To this end, child care professionals need to accept that:

○ Children, like adults, have a sexuoerotic aspect to their lives and that this sexuoerotic aspect is not only a normal part of the developmental process, it is an *essential* part.
○ Sexual activity is pleasurable: children, just like adults, can gain pleasure from sex.
○ Genital exploration, masturbation and age-synchronous sexuoerotic rehearsal play are normal; moreover, these activities are *healthy*.
○ Children are not necessarily victims in adult–child sexual relationships. Some children know exactly what they are doing when they enter such relationships; on the other hand, there are many who do not understand. Likewise, the same could apply to many adults.
○ Overzealous intervention in some cases of sexual abuse may, ironically, damage rather than protect the child.
○ Sex education should emphasise the positive aspects of sex (its warm, pleasant and loving aspects), rather than warn about its dangers.
○ The prevention of child sexual abuse should be seen from the perspective of the child, rather than the adult, and should take into account such factors as the child's level of intellectual development.

Above all, child care professionals need to be aware of the need to remain objective. This is not easy in a society that is generally anti-sex, and may require a considerable degree of self-analysis and reflection on the behalf of practitioners so as to ensure that our own negative views on sex are not transmitted onto our children.

It is worth ending with a quote from Smith (1993): 'As a child's sexuality unfolds, there are several basic guidelines that may aid ... children develop healthy sexual attitudes. The first is, simply, that sex is good.' (p. 37).

REFERENCES

Atkinson RL, Atkinson RC, Smith EE, Bem DJ, Nolen-Hoeksema S (1996) *Hilgard's Introduction to Psychology*, 12th edn. London: Harcourt Brace.

Aquilino ML, Ely J (1985) Parents and the sexuality of preschool children. *Pediatric Nursing* 11, 41–46.

Axelrod S, Apsche J (1983) *The Effects of Punishment on Human Behavior*. London: Academic Press.

Bee H (1995) *The Developing Child*, 7th edn. New York: Harper Collins.

Burns RB (1986) *Child Development: A Text for the Caring Professions*. London: Croom Helm.

Coleman JC (1980) *The Nature of Adolescence*. London: Methuen.

Coleman JC, Hendry L (1990) *The Nature of Adolescence*, 2nd edn. London: Routledge.

Donaldson M (1978) *Children's Minds*. Glasgow: Fontana/Collins.

Erikson EH (1963) *Childhood and Society*. Harmondsworth: Pelican.

Finkelhor D (1979) *Sexually Victimized Children*. New York: Free Press.

Freud S (1949) *Three Essays on the Theory of Sexuality* (translated by J Strachell). London: Imago.

Hardyment C (1983) *Dream Babies: Child Care from Locke to Spock*. London: Jonathan Cape.

Humphries S, Mack J, Perks R (1988) *A Century of Childhood*. London: Sidgwick & Jackson/Channel 4.

Jung CG (1983) *Selected Writings* (selected and introduced by A Storr). London: Fontana.

Kinsey AC, Pomeroy WB, Martin CE (1948) *Sexual Behavior in the Human Male*. London: WB Saunders.

Kohlberg L (1969) Stage and sequence: The cognitive–developmental approach to socialization. In: Goslin DA (ed.) *Handbook of Socialization Theory and Research*. Chicago: Rand McNally.

Krivacska JJ (1992) Child sexual abuse prevention programs: the prevention of childhood sexuality? *Journal of Child Sexual Abuse* 1(4), 83–112.

Leach P (1977) *Baby & Child*. London: Dorling Kindersley.

Martin B (1980) *Abnormal Psychology: Clinical and Scientific Perspectives*, 2nd edn. London: Holt, Rinehart & Winston.

Money J (1986) *Lovemaps: Clinical Concepts of Sexual/Erotic Health and Pathology, Paraphilia, and Gender Transposition in Childhood, Adolescence and Maturity*. New York: Irvington.

Money J (1988) Commentary: Current status of sex research. *Journal of Psychology and Human Sexuality* 1(1), 5–15.

Money J, Cawte JE, Bianchi GN, Nurcombe B (1970) Sex training and traditions in Arnhem Land. *British Journal of Medical Psychology* 43, 383–399.

Petersen AC (1988) Adolescent development. *Annual Review of Psychology* 39, 583–607.

Rutter M, Graham P, Chadwick OFD, Yule W (1976) Adolescent turmoil: fact or fiction? *Journal of Child Psychology and Psychiatry* 17, 35–36.

Skinner BF (1953) *Science and Human Behaviour*. London: Macmillan.

Smith M (1993) Pediatric sexuality: promoting normal sexual development in children. *Nurse Practitioner* 18(8), 37–44.

Spock B (1955) *Baby & Child Care.* London: The Bodley Head.

Taylor A, Sluckin W, Davies DR, Reason JT, Thomson R, Colman AM (1982) *Introducing Psychology,* 2nd edn. Harmondsworth: Penguin.

Watson JB (1930) *Behaviorism,* 2nd edn (reprinted 1959). Chicago: University of Chicago Press.

Weeks J (1985) *Sexuality and its Discontents: Meanings, Myths and Modern Sexualities.* London: Routledge.

FURTHER READING

Appignanesi R, Zarate O (1992) *Freud for Beginners.* Cambridge: Icon.
Excellent introduction to Freudian theory, written in a fun, cartoon style.

Atkinson RL, Atkinson RC, Smith EE, Bem DJ, Nolen-Hoeksema S (1996) *Hilgard's Introduction to Psychology,* 12th edn. London: Harcourt Brace.
Excellent introductory general psychology text.

Bee H (1995) *The Developing Child,* 7th edn. New York: Harper Collins.
The foremost text on child development. A must for any child care practitioner.

Finkelhor D (1984) *Child Sexual Abuse: New Theory and Research.* New York: Free Press.
Objective, research-based text on child sexual abuse.

Hardyment C (1983) *Dream Babies: Child Care from Locke to Spock.* London: Jonathan Cape.
An excellent discussion of the history of child care practices, well written and easy to read.

Money J (1986) *Lovemaps: Clinical Concepts of Sexual/Erotic Health and Pathology, Paraphilia, and Gender Transposition in Childhood, Adolescence and Maturity.* New York: Irvington.
A radical theory of sex, written by America's foremost authority on sexual behaviour. Not all of the book is relevant to childhood sexuoeroticism, though Money raises many important points about morality and sex.

Weeks J (1985) *Sexuality and its Discontents: Meanings, Myths and Modern Sexualities.* London: Routledge.
Weeks examines the 'moral panic' surrounding sex and offers an alternative view based on the acceptance of diversity and choice. Some discussion of childhood sexuoeroticism.

Chapter 4

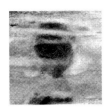

PSYCHOLOGICAL DEVELOPMENT: SEX AND SEXUALITY IN ADOLESCENCE

JANICE M GRANT MSC BSC RN RSCN RM RNT
JOSEPH ROBERTS MA BSC RN RSCN RNT

KEY POINTS

- PSYCHOSEXUAL DEVELOPMENT
- PERSONALITY AND DEVELOPMENT OF THE SEXUAL SELF, GENDER IDENTITY
- DIFFICULTIES ASSOCIATED WITH ADOLESCENT SEXUAL/RELATIONSHIP DEVELOPMENT
- ASSESSMENT OF TWO MODELS OF SEXUAL HEALTH PROMOTION/EDUCATION FOR ADOLESCENTS
- ROLE OF CHILD HEALTH PROFESSIONALS IN FACILITATING HEALTHY SEXUAL DEVELOPMENT

The personal, psychological, social and emotional experiences that occur in adolescence may have great significance to the adult who finally emerges.

Development of sexuality is affected by a number of factors. Perhaps the most critical of these is the degree of self-esteem that a child acquires before adolescence, which is to a great extent determined by the nature and outcomes of childhood interpersonal reactions. The level of the adolescent's self-esteem profoundly affects his or her ability to grow, work through conflicts and change.

During adolescence, the parent–child relationship changes from one of protection–dependency to one of mutual affection and equality. The process of achieving independence often involves turmoil and ambiguity as both parent and adolescent learn to work through the process and learn to play new roles.

What follows is an attempt to consider a range of psychological, emotional and interpersonal factors that appear to impact upon the development of sexuality and contemporary sexual behaviour. Case studies are used to relate theoretical constructs to real-life scenarios.

RÉSUMÉ OF NORMAL PRE-ADOLESCENT AND ADOLESCENT SEXUAL/RELATIONSHIP DEVELOPMENT

The sequential process of sexual maturation leading to puberty and adolescence appears to be a linear, straightforward, biological process. However, there are corresponding changes on psychological, emotional and social levels. In combination, these components of sexual maturation relate very clearly to the central issues of individuality and sense of identity. It has been suggested by Erikson (1968) that there is a natural tension between the biological and the psychological phenomena. Despite the fact that, as human beings, we experience exactly the same biological developmental processes, becoming mature demands the development of unashamedly individualistic qualities. This is essential if we are to 'find' ourselves irrespective of how much we have in common with others in our peer group. These changes require time to be integrated into a positive, self-confident personal identity, and the feeling of self-consistency may come under threat or challenge at any time (Shaffer, 1989; Conger, 1991). The struggle for consistency of identity in adolescence may well be manifested in adulthood by anxiety-provoking memories of needs, desires and fears associated with a problematic adolescence.

The tension between developmental changes and the need for adjustment in making the transition from youth to adult very often results in adolescents focusing upon their physical attributes. This focus is undoubtedly influenced by other factors, such as peer groups and cultural conformity to masculine and feminine stereotypes for both physical appearance and 'pro-social' behaviour (Faust, 1983; Striegel-Moore et al. 1986; Brooks-Gunn, 1988).

Once the adolescent experiences puberty and becomes sexually mature, sexuality assumes far greater importance in his or her life. At this point, adolescents must incorporate concepts of themselves as sexual beings into their male or female gender identities. In addition, they also have to discover how to express their sexuality within the context of interpersonal relationships. At best these tasks are never easy, but they can be made even more difficult by the prevailing cultural norms and morality relating to sexual behaviour (Shaffer, 1989).

It is apparent that adolescents have become comparatively liberal in their views about sex in present-day society. This is manifested by a greater tolerance of deviations from what their parents would regard as the 'norm'. In a review of the literature on teenage sexuality, Dreyer (1982) identified three major changes in teenagers' sexual attitudes which reflected their views on sexuality at that time. The main points are summarised below:

○ Premarital sex is acceptable if the people concerned are in a loving relationship but casual or exploitative sex is wrong.

○ The 'double standard' that allowed men to have premarital and extramarital sex without censure, while women who behaved in a similar fashion were vilified, was becoming less prevalent. Respondents advocated equality for both sexes.

○ Although adolescents ostensibly have more freedom to decide on their own sexual norms, they are confused by mixed messages from parents, school and religious groups. This creates a gulf between the adult and adolescent worlds which prevents development and integration of experiences into sexual identities in a supportive, empowering and liberating environment. This schism has been commercially exploited and created a lucrative market for business. Unfortunately this threatens the delicate balance in the development of the adolescent's cultural norms, values and freedoms which can be cynically manipulated commercially with the possibility of causing polarisation away from parents.

Adolescents are in a potentially fragile psychological and emotional state as they move from total dependence on their parents or carers to a state of relative independence in society with its accompanying responsibilities. It is desirable that young people should have the input of mentors and role models to assist them in their quest for self-determination. It is suggested that the use of mentors and role models could help to dispel myths and misconceptions about sex and sexuality.

Lamke (1982a,b) suggests that for both adolescent boys and girls, sex role and self-concept are inextricably linked. But even more interestingly, the expression of masculine or androgynous sex roles and self-concepts is associated with higher self-esteem than expression of feminine ones. This finding, in twentieth century Western society is, to say the least, surprising — particularly as it is often the assumption that feminism exerts fairly strong pressure on women in today's society. Nevertheless, this finding appears to be based on the assumption that both boys and girls place high value on traditionally male stereotypical values such as independence and competence. The corollary of this is that the traditional feminine role may engender the development of lower self-esteem and make the formation of good peer relationships with both sexes difficult (Massad, 1981). This possibly indicates that, in comparison with the young child, for whom developing schemata for sex role is a vital process, for the adolescent an androgynous self-concept may be important because of its association with more positive sex-role outcomes. Furthermore, young people have the unenviable task of integrating their search for identity, self-esteem and sex roles with their burgeoning sexual interest during the adolescent years.

Sexuality is seen by some writers as a dimension of an individual's personality (Katchadourian, 1980; Greydanus, 1982). As the adolescent searches for identity and self-esteem, it may be that their sex role also becomes more clear and refined, enabling them to express themselves sexually in the long term.

Sexual urges experienced by adolescents are usually attributed to hormonal changes in puberty, but there is a very powerful argument that psychosocial factors are equally important in the awakening of libido (Foster *et al.*, 1993). This upsurge of feelings results in experimentation with sex roles that make adolescents feel 'manly' or 'womanly'. The expectation of self-discovery through themselves and significant others is pivotal to the establishment of romantic or sexual relationships. Sexual experimentation helps adolescents not only to recognise the experience of being sexual beings, but also to answer questions about the normality of their feelings and behaviours.

Odiorne and Tenerowicz (1980) suggest that the normal experiences of attachment to same-sex friends, crushes, masturbation and fantasies are the forerunners of early adolescent sexual interest. It is felt that these behaviours help the young person to prepare mentally and physically for sexual activity in adulthood. If the significant influences on adolescents' sexual health are both external and internal, then the literature currently aimed at the adolescent market needs to be carefully monitored. Some teenage magazines seem to be extremely reliant on the language of overt sexuality as the underpinning marketing ploy. For many parents this calls into question their ideas about what adolescents of different ages should be reading. Nevertheless, for those parents who find it difficult to discuss sexual issues with their adolescent these magazines would probably be seen as a welcome development. For the child, the transition from childhood to adolescence is a time when ideas and practices acquired from parents and other influential adults are examined and often rejected, so these magazines may help towards the direction they desire.

For adolescents the urge to become independent from their parents propels them in the direction of their peers in order to find a reference point for support, help and security. As well as being a major component of personal identity, sexuality during adolescence may be a part of this search for identity (Erikson, 1963). Sexuality therefore has a very strong relationship to self-esteem as the young person's ability to evoke desire in another individual results from his or her personality or physical appearance. This can have a profound effect upon the adolescent's psyche, as acceptance and rejection are taken with deadly seriousness (Katchadourian, 1980). Adolescents exhibit increased dependence upon their peers for approval and the maintenance of a sense of belonging within their group. In order to maintain the status quo, this sometimes leads adolescents to conform to the mores and wants of that group irrespective of the personal cost. Pressure to conform to the group norms can be intense and the adolescent will only take the risk of peer group disapproval in limited circumstances (Roberts, 1987). Nevertheless, despite their apparent conformity to the often outrageous fashion codes of the day, adolescents usually choose their friends and their own 'crowd'. They are likely to choose to associate with a group of companions who share their own values and attitudes. In addition, it is also noticeable that in early adolescence the groups or cliques are almost entirely same-sex, but by late adolescence these very cliques have assumed a different configuration and become mixed-gender groups (Schofield, 1973).

Whatever clique or crowd an adolescent may identify with, psychological theorists agree that the peer group performs the highly important function of helping adolescents with making the adjustment from exclusive unisexual to heterosexual social relationships. Heterosexual relationships seen in early and middle adolescence are part of the preparation for assuming a full adult sexual identity (Brown, 1990). Expressing sexuality physically is part of realising sex-role identity, but so is the learning of the skills of personal intimacy with the opposite sex. These include flirting, communicating and reading the social cues used by members of the opposite sex.

The young person can therefore begin to experiment with newly developed relationship skills in the ostensibly protected environment of his or her clique. Only after some degree of confidence is developed will dating begin to take place, and this is superseded later by more committed heterosexual pair relationships (Dunphy, 1972).

Psychosexual Development

Cognitive Theory

Kohlberg (1966) provides a three-stage framework through which it is suggested that all children pass:

○ *Basic gender identity*: the child recognises him or herself as being a boy or a girl
○ *Gender stability*: the child recognises that boys remain boys and girls remain girls (present from age 3 onwards)
○ *Gender constancy*: the child recognises that superficial changes in appearance do not alter gender (develops at around 5–7 years of age).

Social Learning Theory

Social learning theorists argue that gender identity is a consequence of socialisation. They suggest that there are cultural norms and expectations regarding the interests and values that members of each sex should exhibit.

Social learning theory advocates believe that differential treatment of boys and girls begins early in life with the apparel of young babies and the expectations of young children's behaviour. According to Weitzman *et al.* (1972) this is also reinforced by the media. For example, textbooks and reading books for children still portray women as passive and supportive and men as intelligent and active, despite the social and cultural changes that have moved this situation forward in recent years. Social learning also underpins the acquisition of an adolescent's gender identity.

It is apparent that the experience of becoming an adult varies in different societies, cultures and from one generation to the next. In many ways, it is not the same process for our children as it was for us or our predecessors (Demos and Demos, 1979). Nevertheless, children or adolescents have little say in formulating the rules of moral or social behaviour, or indeed the content and context of education about sexuality. This is regrettable, as adults can only use retrospective information based on their own experiences as adolescents or use an idealised view of adolescent behaviour to inform their perspective on social and sexual norms.

Adolescence is a search for and redefinition of identity as an independent social and sexual being. Young people may feel under strong parental pressure and societal demands in addition to the physical and psychological changes that accompany puberty. The timing of these pressures to change may cause the adolescent to feel vulnerable as he or she vacillates between demanding independence and wanting the protection of parents. Adolescents often begin to question their identity, normality, how they compare with others and their personal worth. Questions on normality are usually associated with the wide variations in the appearance of pubertal changes and development of sexual characteristics. Penis size and breast development, for example, are aspects of development that come for comparative critical evaluation. At this time of emotional fragility the influence of celebrity role models and prominent icons of society becomes paramount. Dissatisfaction with weight, size or discomfort with the bodily changes associated with sexual maturity may result in disorders of self-perception such as anorexia nervosa or bulimia in both sexes. In severe cases even clinical depression may result. Moreover, the development of adolescent sexuality is shaped not only by an individual's self-esteem and the ability to form and maintain intimate relationships, but also by the formulation of short- and long-term goals.

It is apparent, therefore, that parents and child health professionals need to be cognisant of these factors in order to help adolescents to achieve healthy psychosexual development and behaviour.

SEX-ROLE DEVELOPMENT

Acquisition of sex or gender roles is not purely dependent upon biological factors; learnt behaviours from the environment in the formative years play a very significant part. The preparation for gender role, according to Bandura (1986), starts in childhood. It could be argued that this influence may begin even before the child is born. At this time parents begin to discuss their preference for the sex of the child, decide on names, and may even have future aspirations for a child of a particular sex.

As the child gets older, adults have been observed to adopt different strategies for playing with girls and boys. Children are therefore being treated consistently in a specific way even before they develop any understanding of the meaning of gender. As they grow and develop young children learn gender roles by punishment and reward. They are rewarded for behaving in a way that adults feel is appropriate for their sex. For example, little girls are given attention and praise when they are adorned in pretty dresses or when they display 'mothering' attitudes towards dolls or younger children. Boisterousness is approved of in boys and parents often gaze proudly on the 'manly' behaviour of their sons. On the contrary, when children behave in ways that parents believe fall outside these expected parameters for their gender, they are scolded or ignored in the hope that the behaviour will become extinct. For example, it is often perceived as a weakness if boys cry. This behaviour may be either ignored or dismissed by parents or ridiculed by siblings and peers.

The behaviour of adult members of both sexes is carefully observed and boys and girls in families with two parents soon learn that their mothers in particular, and women in general, usually look after the house, the cleaning, the shopping, the cooking and care for the children, whether they have paid employment outside the home or not. The male adult is regarded as the master of the household, the breadwinner, and much store is put by his ability to sustain a job, irrespective of the fact that his partner may have the same earning capacity. This stereotypical view is reinforced by the existing double standards relating to men's sexual behaviour in adolescence and in adulthood.

GENDER IDENTITY

Gender identity is described by Hyde (1979: 57) as:

> *the person's private internal sense of maleness or femaleness which is expressed in personality and behaviour – and the integration of this sense with the rest of the personality and with the gender roles prescribed by society.*

An adolescent's perception of his or her gender identity will predict power and responsibility in future relationships. Issues arise such as who is in control and who decides? Who is responsible for whom, in what ways and to what extent? These will need to be clarified at the outset. Adolescents establish the parameters surrounding these and similar areas through a process of experimentation or, in other words, by trial and error. Adults in general, and parents in particular, are the primary role models until adolescents' own personalised modes of interaction emerge. Interpersonal issues such as dominance and responsibility will therefore have implications for heterosexual relationships. Take, for example, the decision to become sexually active and responsibility for contraception. These may be left to the young male partner if the girl involved has an external locus of control and thinks the man should have this responsibility. Conversely, the adolescent boy may have the view that his partner has the responsibility to avoid pregnancy and is therefore unlikely to use contraceptives. The end result is that no active decision is taken, thus markedly increasing the risk of an unwanted pregnancy.

Gender identity may play an important role in the development of adult sexual preferences. Conformity (or the absence of it) to social norms is a measure of whether there is correlation between our gender identity (perceived femaleness or maleness) and our biological gender (Bell *et al.* 1981). Adolescence is a time for realising the short- and long-term significance of gender identity and sexual preference and of striving to integrate these with all the other aspects of sexuality and self-concept.

Perceived normality of body image strongly influences adolescent sexual development, particularly gender identity and sexual self-concept. Adjusting to a changing body image is especially difficult for adolescents in that this change echoes and compounds other feelings resulting from the multiplicity of simultaneous changes.

Daniel, aged 15, had a family history of calcifications in the brain, mental disability and convulsions. He was admitted to a children's hospital with a history of intermittent colicky abdominal pain which appeared to cause him much distress. The surgeon diagnosed appendicitis and as there was no apparent urgency Daniel was scheduled for surgery the next morning.

Later that day his primary nurse found Daniel curled up in a ball rolling from side to side on his bed. The nurse was very concerned and tried to get him to localise the pain, but when she removed the covers she discovered that Daniel had an old-fashioned alarm clock which he had placed close to his genital area and the vibration of the alarm was the reason for his 'distress'.

How do you feel you would have responded to finding Daniel with the alarm clock? Would you have been embarrassed? angry? disgusted? Reflect on why you would have felt any particular way.

Consider how Daniel and his family's sexual health educational needs should be met in order to help him to make the transition into adulthood.

Am I Heterosexual or Homosexual?

Part of the adolescent's discoveries about sex is the realisation that they are sexually attracted and attractive to people of the opposite sex. Some may feel that they are especially attracted to people of their own sex. Parents may first become aware of this when they find that their pre-adolescent or adolescent child is experimenting sexually with someone of the same sex. Alternatively, their son or daughter may confide in them that they think that they are gay. Whatever the scenario, in order to cope with this period of uncertainty, and possibly guilt and shame, the adolescent needs love and acceptance and to feel that, whatever they finally decide, their parents' feelings for them will remain unchanged.

Psychoanalytic theory puts the 'blame' for the child's homosexuality firmly on the family, in particular the mother. The theory postulates that unresolved Oedipal and Electra complexes (where the child loves and then rejects the opposite-sex parent, choosing instead the same-sex parent as a model) are crucial to this theory. Current evidence suggests that sex roles do not determine sexual orientation (Progebin, 1980). The bottom line for parents is that the origin of heterosexuality or homosexuality is unknown. Care has to be taken, however, when young children are playing with much older siblings or friends of the same sex. There is a risk that inappropriate sex play may take place in which the younger child may be coerced into being a passive participant.

Nevertheless, it is often a stunning blow to parents when they learn that their son or daughter is homosexual. They often feel that they are somehow to blame for how their child has 'turned out' and experience anticipatory grief for the loss of future grandchildren, and in some cases for their son or daughter whom they cannot accept.

To increase their discomfiture even further, homosexuality is very poorly tolerated in a predominantly Christian Western society. Disapproval comes from both a religious and a legal standpoint, whereby homosexual acts have been perceived as either sinful or criminal. Both the religious and the legal prohibitions are possibly as strong as they were in less enlightened times. Furthermore, homophobic prejudice still exists and homosexuality is either construed as some form of deviancy or mental illness and therefore is still not universally acceptable or accepted. The young person who reveals his or her homosexuality has to overcome the kind of institutionalised prejudice which may affect job prospects or finding suitable housing. Moreover, there are the negative stereotypical jokes about 'camp' men and 'butch' women which usually disguise the negative feelings that many heterosexuals have towards gay and lesbian people.

The most important thing, as far as adolescents are concerned, is to come to terms with their sexual identity and gain acceptance by the most important people in their lives, their families. Child health professionals should advise parents experiencing a dilemma over their child's sexuality to remain as loving towards them as usual, including continuing to express affection physically. It also means accepting their child's homosexual friends in the same way that heterosexual friends are accepted and being prepared to listen to their confidences. The relevance of this is that if homosexual adolescents have no adult to confide in they can feel very isolated and depressed, for there may be few if any friends whom they will feel they can trust, especially among their schoolmates who can often be thoughtless and cruel (Petrie, 1990).

Cross-gender Behaviour

The child who persistently chooses play partners, dress preferences and interest patterns stereotypically associated with the opposite sex is said to be exhibiting cross-gender behaviour. The child may be certain of his or her masculinity or femininity but simply has an externally manifested preference for behaving like someone of the opposite sex. Alternatively, the child shows a determination to belong to the opposite sex which persists over time. Ideally, children should be able to transcend gender-role limitations and develop psychological harmony with their inner needs and feelings. This ability to explore a different gender role must follow initial conformity to sex-role differentiation, otherwise this may lead to psychological problems.

CASE STUDY

Simon, aged 16, lives with his mother and two sisters. He has had no male influence on his life since his parents divorced when he was three years old. Simon has an exceptionally close relationship with his mother and sisters.

Simon has developed a liking for silky ladies' underwear which arouses him sexually. Soon he begins to steal items of women's underwear from his family and from neighbours' washing lines. Gradually this progresses to him wearing and becoming very excited by ladies' lingerie. Eventually his mother discovers his secret hoard. Although she expresses her disapproval nonverbally, she does not comment on her discovery. Nevertheless, Simon feels very guilty yet stimulated at the same time.

As time progresses Simon begins to wear female underwear at every opportunity. He also buys very androgynous clothes. Simon is very confused about his sexuality and wonders whether he is homosexual. He is tempted to experiment with his sexuality but he feels that he will jeopardise his relationship with his family and friends.

Why do you think that Simon behaves in this way? It may be helpful to consider Simon's early upbringing and his mother's response to his behaviour.

How may Simon be helped to resolve the difficulties he is encountering with his sexuality?

Promoting Healthy Sexual Relationships from Adolescence into Adulthood

It is often quite difficult for parents to accept that there is a sexual dimension to adolescents' lives as this marks a particular worry that their children are growing up too soon. Inherent in this is the desire to protect their children from premature sexual experience, especially under duress and before the young person feels ready. Nevertheless, parents should teach children that it is quite permissible to refuse unwanted sexual advances. It is also important to teach adolescents to take sexual relationships seriously and to understand the possible consequences of their actions. It is very important to include parents in any programmes devised for sexual health education.

Sexual health covers a plethora of subjects but adults may inadvertently send out negative messages about sexuality in an attempt to impress upon young people that there are risks involved. Consequently, another important message that sex is a part of a mature relationship is overlooked. The sex act is in itself a powerful means of communication which can convey messages of love, trust, tenderness and fulfilment. Conversely, it can also be used as a weapon of power and abuse. As sexual maturity introduces the possibility of a more intimate relationship this should be tempered with teaching about morality, in addition to basic information about:

○ contraception
○ sexually transmitted diseases
○ pregnancy
○ abortion.

Sexual Health for Adolescents who have Physical Disabilities

Adolescence poses a number of psychological challenges for most young people. For the adolescent with a physical disability this can be a particularly testing time. During this time it is usual to become increasingly aware of physical appearance, abilities, limitations and physical problems. This heightened state of self-awareness may lead adolescents with physical disabilities to become distinctly self-critical, resentful, frustrated and may engender feelings of inferiority. They may become angry at their inability to 'hang out' with their peers and bitterly resent dependence on others at a time when they experience the need for independence is heightened. As they achieve sexual maturity, in keeping with other adolescents of the same age, these issues are brought into stark focus. Health care professionals have a significant part to play in helping them to readjust their value systems. They need to be given information about their bodily changes and to be supported in coming to terms with their sexual maturation.

Adolescents with physical disabilities may have very serious concerns about personal relationships and sexual fulfilment. They begin to question their future prospects in relation to career, setting up home with a partner and perhaps most importantly, having a family. The question also arises as to whether any children they do produce will also be disabled.

As has been previously identified, sexual health is not merely about physical relationships, but is inextricably linked with feelings, self-identity, self-esteem and personal relationships. Adolescents who have physical disabilities should have the chance to articulate their feelings, anxieties and exercise personal choice and responsibility. The forum for these discussions should be with a trusted adult such as a parent or a teacher. The school nurse may also be able to assist disabled female adolescents with practicalities such as preparing for and managing menstruation. It is important to remember that whatever constellation of feelings and behaviours adolescents experience, including psychological problems and their attendant problems, the entire family will experience the repercussions.

By definition, adolescence is a period during which young people attempt to define parameters which help them to experience feelings of stability, safety and containment. The adolescent who is disabled is no exception.

CASE STUDY

Ginette is a 14–year–old girl who has spina bifida and hydrocephalus. She has been admitted to hospital on several previous occasions to have her shunt revised but on this occasion she becomes hysterical when she is told that a section of her hair will need to be shaved off.

Why should Ginette suddenly become uncooperative and distressed about having her hair shaved? Could this be related to her age and developing self–image?

How can Ginette's parents and her primary nurse help her to come to terms with what she possibly perceives as a very traumatic situation?

ADOLESCENTS WITH LEARNING DISABILITIES

For an adolescent who has a learning disability the development of the physical and emotional characteristics which herald sexual maturity become problematic not only for his or her parents, but also for society in general. The characteristic attitude of society is to treat people with learning difficulties of whatever age as perpetual children who are therefore asexual. To acknowledge their developing sexuality is to step outside our own 'comfort zones' and to think what many people would regard as the unthinkable. Nevertheless, this difficult area must be addressed, whatever the degree of learning disability that the adolescent has.

Information about normal processes such as menstruation must be given before its occurrence as this can be a frightening experience if the young woman is not psychologically prepared. At another level, sexual health issues can be addressed as a means of protecting the adolescent from people who might take advantage of them sexually.

Some adolescents with learning difficulties will eventually lead independent lives while others will only be able to achieve semi-independence, which makes it even more imperative to explain the basic tenets of reproduction to them.

From the point of view of their developing sexuality, adolescents with learning difficulties need to be made aware of what is or is not socially acceptable behaviour, for example that hugging strangers is inappropriate and that they have the right to say 'no' to anybody's touch or kiss. Issues such as masturbation have to be explained and the adolescent taught the difference between what is acceptable behaviour in public and in private.

FACILITATING SEXUAL HEALTH IN ADOLESCENCE

The definition of the term 'sexual health' in relation to adolescents needs to be clarified if mixed messages to this group are to be avoided. Do we mean encouraging young people to learn to develop and enjoy sexual well-being free from guilt and exploitation? Or is sexual health related to the acceptance of ourselves, irrespective of gender, sexual orientation, culture or physical ability, as long as the individual has the power to make choices, define his or her needs, and arrive at agreements with others about exercising that choice? It would appear that no one definition of sexual health is appropriate for every adolescent, however, most definitions have a common denominator: self-acceptance. Health professionals dealing with adolescents need to be adaptable, open-minded and able to help young people to define their own versions of sexual health. It is very easy to hide behind the 'facts' in sex education, usually as a reactive response to teenage pregnancy or HIV/AIDS. Unfortunately, this purely biological approach can induce guilt, blame and imply a moralising stance by adults which may prove to be counterproductive.

POSSIBLE MODELS FOR ADOLESCENT HEALTH EDUCATION

There are several contemporary approaches that have been advocated in the interests of healthy sexual development. Perhaps the most interesting examples of these include peer-education programmes (Sciacca, 1987; Bernard, 1991; Sloane and Zimmer, 1993) and Freirian praxis (Freire, 1970, 1983; Reed, 1981; Werner and Bower, 1982; Minkler, 1985; Barndt, 1989). Essentially both of these approaches have their theoretical roots in social learning theory with particular emphasis on social learning, imitation and empowerment education. Both constructs represent a hybrid approach to promoting healthy adolescence in the areas of sexual health, drug/substance abuse, behaviour modification, deviancy, smoking, suicide and violence. They represent a synthesis of several major ideas in an attempt to counteract the adultist view of young people's health issues as social problems. These social problems are generally associated with risk-taking, which is part of adolescent culture (Brannen *et al.*, 1994)

Milburn (1995) states that the theoretical underpinnings of early peer education are primarily in school settings and are generally traceable to social learning theory (Bandura, 1986), social inoculation theory (Duryea, 1983) and differential association theory (Sutherland and Cressey, 1974). Much of this work concludes that peer modelling is a basic process in the socialisation of children. Peer education based in social learning may involve:

○ modelling appropriate behaviour
○ teaching social skills
○ conveying factual information
○ peer pressure resistance training (using rehearsal of possible roles and situations).

The appeal of peer sex education for health promotion is that it has always existed on a very informal basis. Young people share information amongst themselves which they have drawn from a variety of sources, including personal experience. Adults often regard this process with mixed feelings as at best it gets them off the hook and the content will not be grossly inaccurate; at worst it raises the spectre of influences resulting in disapproved behaviour being validated by what might be seen as undesirable 'peer pressure' (Milburn, 1995).

Recently, health educators have begun to experiment with harnessing these naturally occurring processes to what they define as positive ends.

Social inoculation theory applied to peer education may be concerned with providing peers with persuasive arguments and facts to counter pressures. Differential association theory is based in criminology and deviance research and asserts that criminal behaviour is learned in small personal groups. This theory is based not just on techniques, but also on their supporting motivations, rationalisations and attitudes (Milburn, 1995).

In the main, the peer education approach is largely concerned with vicarious learning. However, the criticism could be levelled at its approach of being one of social control, particularly if the form and content of such programmes are determined by adults as part of an approved curriculum.

Paolo Freire's social change theory of dialogue and praxis, which underpins his research in the Adolescent Social Action Programme (ASAP) in Mexico, attempts to incorporate a cognitive and empowerment aspect to the process of adolescent health education. According to Freire, the purpose of education is human liberation, which means people are subjects of their own learning, not empty vessels to be filled by a teacher's knowledge. Freire proposes a structured dialogue approach in which everyone participates as co-learners to create a jointly understood reality. Individuals must be involved not only in efforts to identify their problems, but also to engage in critical thinking to analyse the societal context for these problems. The goal of dialogue is the ongoing interaction between reflection and the actions people take to promote personal and community change (praxis). In health education circles there has been a growing interest in the role of Freirian theory in health enhancement by engaging people to collectively move beyond feelings of powerlessness and assume control of their lives (Wallerstein, 1992).

PROTECTION–MOTIVATION THEORY

This is an attitudinal change theory where intention to act is an indicator or predictor of behaviour change. Protection–motivation theory proposes that decisions to act are initiated through a variety of informational sources and mediated through a nonlinear cognitive perceptual process (Rogers *et al.*, 1978), resulting in either an adaptive or maladaptive response.

The emphasis of protection–motivation theory on individual threat in conjunction with coping appraisal processes integrates elements from social learning theory and the health belief model. Individuals showing self-efficacy (belief in the ability to complete a task successfully), and response efficacy are more likely to exhibit self-protective behaviour. It is perhaps important to note that self-efficacy has been shown to be an effective predictor of health behaviours (O'Leary, 1985; Stretcher *et al.*, 1986).

To implement the Freirian model, which integrates threat and coping appraisals, a listening–dialogue–action methodology is used. This three-part process encompasses a participatory orientation to learning rather than passive receipt of information. Nevertheless, listening and dialogue are not linear processes, but are overlapping, cyclical components of learning and change. This is a possible sequence of events:

○ students interview subjects
○ discuss interviews with facilitators
○ select an action project
○ evaluate and revisit their own analysis of the impact of their actions
○ choose alternative actions.

This cyclical process is the embodiment of Freirian praxis and also reflects a cognitive–perceptual process that encourages attitudinal and behavioural change (Wallerstein and Sanchez-Merki, 1994). Stories may be used to portray the consequences of risky behaviour and the rich complexities of problems and solutions. Other triggers in the curriculum are role plays, students' stories about their own lives, songs, videotapes, collages or photographs. Although triggers present open-ended situations, critical thinking does not necessarily occur spontaneously. In order to promote different levels of critical thinking the facilitators may use an inductive questioning guide (Shaffer, 1983). The young people are asked to use the following sequence.

○ Describe the problem.
○ Consider how it affects their personal lives.
○ Develop a critical analysis of the context of the problem.
○ Strategise social actions for its solution.

To move towards an adaptive coping response, facilitators must acknowledge the feelings elicited by the interviews, and help participants to move beyond emotions to a cognitive understanding of the basis for the creation of various problems. Facilitators usually have to give young people a great deal of encouragement to think beyond their peers and families to analysis of societal issues. It is this feature of critical thinking that is the hallmark of the ASAP approach.

Wallerstein's (1989) research into Freirian programmes indicated a central pattern of adolescents' perception of their changing identity. Participatory dialogue encountered on the programme appeared to start a three-stage process of self-identity change. Within each stage the adolescents experienced changes on an emotional, critical thinking and action level (see Table 1).

Table 1   Three-stage model of action orientation

Stage 1	Caring about the problem, each other, and about the ability to implement a course of action
Stage 2	Adolescent institutes action for individual changes and expresses an ability to help others who are close to him or her
Stage 3	Adolescent understands the need for social responsibility and the possibility for larger social actions

From Wallerstein *et al.* (1994).

Griffin (1993) suggests that the two main features surrounding family life and sexuality are biological determinism, which underpins the 'storm and stress' model of adolescence, and social construction. The latter represents adolescence as an age stage characterised by particular and conflicting social and cultural pressures. Once more these views are essentially adultist and reductionist. Because of the risks involved, adults are keen to adopt an interventionist approach in order to exercise either care or control (Milburn, 1995).

If sexual development is to take place in a supportive, nurturing and empowering way, then an approach to education for sexual health needs to be constructed that will cultivate a supportive environment.

The two models explored have clearly identified strengths and weaknesses in their approach, but further research and evaluation of these constructs are necessary. In advocating an approach to promoting the sexual health and development of young people, a synthesis of the more favourable elements of peer education and Freirian praxis would provide a possible basis of a good educational programme.

PRINCIPLES FOR EDUCATIONAL PROGRAMMES FOR ADOLESCENT SEXUAL HEALTH

The promotion of sexual health should involve establishing the needs of young people of different ages in order to discuss relationships and sexuality in an honest and open way. Education toward sexual health should begin in the first years of school with children aged 5–6 years. At this stage children can learn to like their own bodies and also learn to form good peer relationships. With this approach we could develop in a 'more complex and widening spiral' of sexual health education as these children became more mature.

Sex education is important in order for children and young people to become competent and responsible adult members of society. This, as well as the other aspects of their education, is a process that should traverse the age continuum and involves understanding of feelings as well as facts.

Education about sexual health can take place in several milieu, for example a planned series of sessions in the personal and social education (PSE) section of the school curriculum, or in less structured discussions with parents in the home environment. Nevertheless, a great deal of learning about sex is unplanned, taking place in informal settings such as via television and magazines. This may be regarded with some ambivalence since although information acquired in this way may add to young adolescents' knowledge, it can also perplex them greatly. Furthermore, inaccurate conclusions may be drawn when attempts are made to understand the concepts and images portrayed. These young people may not seek clarification from their parents but turn to older siblings and/or friends to answer their questions, even though they are aware that reliable adults such as parents and teachers may very well have the answers to their questions.

It must be borne in mind that media messages about sex and personal relationships may in some circumstances be harmful or misleading by providing an overly romantic or unrealistic picture of relationships between the sexes, while other images may be violent and pornographic. At a time when adolescents are trying to discover their own identities as young women and men, being confronted with negative stereotypes of women as dependent sex objects and men as dominant and 'macho' may have far-reaching implications. These perceived role models can be anxiety-producing in adolescents of both sexes and may also produce feelings of inadequacy.

It is also important to note that the most powerful role models for men and women's behaviour towards each other are the parents. Moreover, although adolescents should have the opportunity to discuss their feelings and opinions on these subjects, it is also important to realise that many parents are uncomfortable, indeed unhappy, about children or adolescents being given (too much) information about sex and sexuality, believing that this may encourage them to experiment earlier and end up with unsatisfactory and unwelcome outcomes. Bury (1984) found that adolescents who were uninformed about sex at home and at school and who relied on information from friends and the media engaged in sexual intercourse at a younger age than their more well-informed peers and were less likely to use contraception. Many teenagers decide, in the absence of trustworthy advice, to learn about sex by experimenting with it. As they are operating without reliable knowledge or understanding of the consequences of their actions, they are not equipped to act responsibly towards their partners and themselves.

Children should be given clear information about their own development as sexual beings and sex if they are to understand and cope with the physical and emotional changes that comprise adolescence. Knowledge is the key to freedom from guilt and anxiety about normal feelings and practical issues such as menstruation and masturbation. Boys need to know that all males experience embarrassing erections from time to time and that this is a perfectly normal occurrence. Good knowledge about healthy development can also increase adolescents' social competence and independence. Those who have been given good quality information are much less likely to succumb to 'behind the bike shed' innuendo, myth and supposition. They are more able to behave in a responsible manner towards other people and themselves and they will be much more able to respect both themselves and others as sexual beings. It can help them to realise that affectionate relationships do not necessarily involve sexual intercourse and that friendship, attraction and affection may be conveyed in a number of other ways. They will understand that sexual intercourse is not obligatory and it is perfectly acceptable to say 'no' if they do not want to engage in sexual activity.

Sexual health education programmes should aim to foster a positive attitude towards sexuality and an acceptance of adolescents' identity as sexual human beings. Becoming sexually mature marks the boundary between childhood and adulthood and opens up options and uncertainties which need consideration. These may be compounded by the unwelcome bodily changes and unwelcome skin eruptions associated with puberty. Adolescents may find it difficult to accept themselves as these changes are giving rise to anxiety about whether they are attractive to members of the opposite sex and whether they will find a boy or girl friend.

It is contended that the adoption of a principled approach would be more likely to facilitate a situation where responsibility for the programme is shared by all the participants and specific learning criteria are arrived at by negotiation and dialogue. The process of empowerment through understanding and reasoned action can facilitate the sensitive journey of our young people from childhood to adulthood in a positive and meaningful manner.

The principles for an effective approach are summarised below.

- There is a sound shared philosophy constructed through dialogue and negotiation.
- The programme is action-orientated and emphasises facilitation of change (praxis).
- Sexual development, behaviour and education is contextualised through reflection and dialogue in order to foster development of reasoned action and self-efficacy.
- The combination of empowerment, information-giving and change models may facilitate responsibility, praxis, a positive climate of shared learning and growth. Individuals may come to feel less isolated and threatened by developmental processes and begin to see their experiences as a natural and more universal experience.

PREVENTING SEXUAL ATTACKS ON ADOLESCENTS

One of the potential risks that children and adolescents may encounter, and therefore need protection from, is sexual harassment or attack of some description. Many young people of both sexes experience unwelcome sexual attention or in some instances verbal or physical attacks. Verbal attacks include remarks about physical development, either about the lack thereof or, in the case of female adolescents, the size of their breasts in particular. The perpetrators would describe their behaviour as teasing! Other unwelcome attention may come from 'flashers' exposing themselves in the park or from obscene telephone calls and/or remarks, inappropriate physical contact on buses or trains, coercion into sexual contact by peers or adults, and ultimately rape.

Adolescents continue to need reminders about 'stranger danger', though familiar adults may also present risks to them. With their growing sexual maturity and greater independence the risks may on balance be increased. Parents need to remind their children that no one has the right to make them embarrassed about their physical development, whether by actions or by making personal remarks. Safety from sexual attack will be one of the considerations behind the arrangements parents make with their teenagers for informing them of their intended destinations and who their companions are, their estimated time of return and the arrangements made for coming home. In spite of care and vigilance, however, some adolescents are still sexually attacked by a member of the family, by an acquaintance or by a stranger.

CONCLUSION

We have acknowledged that adolescence is a turbulent time when young people are bombarded with physical, social, emotional and psychological changes and pressures. However, the resulting inconsistencies in feelings, thinking and behaviour are synchronised at an individual level and clearly affect development of sexuality. This very individuality may create problems for adolescents who compare themselves with others and try to conform to the norms of their peer group and may also create problems for parents and health care professionals who are involved in helping them.

Sexual self-concept continues to form and develop during adolescence and has far-reaching significance. If the sexual self-concept is negative it may prevent or interfere with the formation of all interpersonal relationships. Crucially, if it is positive it will provide a good foundation for the formation of intimate relationships, whether sexual or platonic, throughout life. We have highlighted that it is particularly important to begin education about sexuality from the early years in school. This means teaching children to be comfortable with their bodies and to have a positive regard for their own physical attributes. It is clear that many adults find it difficult to relate to adolescents' sexuality and this may be the result of the reawakening of thoughts and feelings from their past experience. It is also apparent that in the formulation of strategies for helping adolescents to attain and maintain sexual health we are using models based on either retrospective experience or idealised models of how we would like them to behave. We feel that there are models of peer education and negotiation in existence that should be reconsidered for use today, as at the time of their development the timing of their introduction may have been premature.

To give effective health care to adolescents, health professionals must understand the extent to which the development of adolescents' sexuality affects and is affected by virtually every aspect of their overall development.

In the light of the inseparability of sexuality from the whole person, and in consideration of the extensive formative development of the adolescent, the rationale for consistently addressing adolescent sexual health as integral to comprehensive health care becomes apparent.

REFERENCES

Bandura A (1986) *Social Foundation of Thought and Action: A Social-Cognitive Theory.* Englewood Cliffs: Prentice Hall.

Barndt D (1989) *Naming the Moment: Political Analysis for Action.* Toronto: Jesuit Centre for Social Faith and Justice.

Bell AP, Weinberg MS, Hammersmith SK (1981) *Sexual Preference: Its Development Among Men and Women.* Bloomington: Indiana University Press.

Bernard B (1991) The case for peers. *The Peer Facilitator Quarterly* 8, 20–27.

Brannen J, Dodd K, Oakley A, Storey P (1994) *Young People, Health and Family Life.* Buckingham: Open University Press.

Brooks-Gunn J (1988) *Psychological Adaptation to the Early Adolescent Transition: Biological and Social Contributions.* New York: American Psychological Association.

Brown BB (1990) Peer groups and peer cultures. In: Eeldman SS and Elliott GR (eds) *At the Threshold: The Developing Adolescent,* pp. 171–196. Cambridge, MA: Harvard University Press.

Bury J (1984) *Teenage Pregnancy in Britain.* London: The British Birth Control Trust.

Conger J (1991) *Adolescence and Youth; Psychological Development in a Changing World.* New York: Harper Collins.

Demos J, Demos V (1979) Adolescence in historical perspective. *Journal of Marriage and the Family* 31.

Dreyer PH (1982) Sexuality during adolescence. In: Wolman BB (ed.) *Handbook of Developmental Psychology,* pp. 559–601. Englewood Cliffs: Prentice-Hall.

Dunphy DC (1972) Peer group socialisation. In: Hunt FJ (ed.) *Socialisation in Australia*, pp. 200–217. Sydney: Angus and Robertson.

Duryea EJ (1983) Using tenets of inoculation theory to develop and evaluate a preventive alcohol education intervention. *Journal of School Health* **53**, 250–256.

Erikson E (1963) *Childhood and Society*, 2nd edn. New York: Norton.

Erikson E (1968) *Identity: Youth and Crisis*. New York: Norton.

Faust MS (1983) Alternative constructions of adolescent growth. In: Brooks-Gunn J and Petersen AC (eds) *Girls at Puberty: Biological and Psychosocial Perspectives*, pp. 105–126. New York: Plenum Press.

Foster R, Hunsberger M, Anderson J (1993) *Family Centered Nursing Care of Children*. Philadelphia: Harcourt Brace Jovanovich.

Freire P (1970) *Pedagogy of the Oppressed*. New York: Seabury Press.

Freire P (1983) *Education for Critical Consciousness*. New York: Seabury Press/Continuum Press.

Greydanus DE (1982) Adolescent sexuality: an overview and perspectives for the 1980s. *Pediatric Annuals* **117**, 714–726.

Griffin C (1993) *Representations of Youth: The Study of Youth and Adolescence in Britain and America*. Cambridge: Polity Press.

Hyde JS (1979) *Understanding Human Sexuality*. New York: McGraw Hill.

Katchadourian H (1980) Adolescent sexuality. *Pediatric Clinics of North America* **27**, 17–28.

Kohlberg LA (1966) Cognitive–developmental analysis of children's sex-role concepts and attitudes. In: Maccoby EE (ed.) *The Development of Sex Differences*. California: Stanford University Press.

Lamke LK (1982a) Adjustment and sex-role orientation. *Journal of Youth and Adolescence* **1**, 247–259.

Lamke LK (1982b) The impact of sex-role orientation on self esteem in early adolescence. *Child Development* **53**, 1530–1535.

Massad CH (1981) Sex-role identity and adjustment during adolescence. *Child Development* **52**, 1290–1298.

Milburn K (1995) A critical review of peer education with young people with special reference to sexual health. *Health Education Research* **10**(4), 407–420.

Minkler M (1985) Building supportive ties and sense of community among the inner-city elderly: the tenderloin senior outreach project. *Health Education Quarterly* **12**, 303–314.

Odiorne J, Tenerowicz C (1980) Adolescent sexuality. In: Howe J (ed.) *Nursing Care of Adolescents*, pp. 246–280. New York: McGraw-Hill.

O'Leary A (1985) Self-efficacy and health. *Behaviour Research and Therapy.* **23**, 437–451.

Petrie P (1990) *The Adolescent Years: A Guide for Parents*. London: Michael Joseph.

Progebin LC (1980) *Growing Up Free*. New York: McGraw Hill.

Reed D (1981) *Education for Building a People's Movement*. Boston: South End Press.

Roberts D (1987) Adolescence. *Nursing* **24**, 914–919.

Rogers RW, Deckner CW, Mewborn CR (1978) An expectancy-value theory approach to the long term modification of smoking behaviour. *Journal of Clinical Psychology* **34**, 562–566.

Schofield M (1973) *The Sexual Behaviour of Young Adults*. London: Allen Lane.

Sciacca JP (1987) Student-peer health education: a powerful yet inexpensive helping strategy. *The Peer Facilitator Quarterly* **5**, 4–6.

Shaffer DR (1989) *Developmental Psychology*, 2nd edn. California: Brooks/Cole Pacific Grove.

Shaffer R (1983) *Beyond the Dispensary*. Nairobi, Kenya: Amref.

Sloan BC, Zimmer CG (1993) The power of peer health education. *Journal of American College of Health* **41**, 241–245.

Strecher V, De Vellis B, Becker M, Rosenstock I (1986) The role of self-efficacy in achieving health behaviour change. *Health Education Quarterly* **13**, 73–91.

Streigel-Moore RH, Silberstein LR, Rodin J (1986) Towards an understanding of risk factors for bulimia. *American Psychologist* **41**, 246–263.

Sunderland EH, Cressey DR (1974) *Criminology*. Philadelphia: Lippincott.

Wallerstein N (1989) Empowerment Education: Freire's theory applied to health: a case study of alcohol prevention for Indian and Hispanic youth uml., Dissertation Information Service, Michigan, Ann Harbour, USA.

Wallerstein N (1992) Powerlessness, empowerment and health: implications for health promotion programmes. *American Journal of Health Promotion* **6**, 197–205.

Wallerstein N, Sanchez-Merki V (1994) Freirian praxis in health education: research results from an adolescent prevention programme. *Health Education Research* **9**(1) 105–118.

Weitzman L, Eifler D, Hodada E, Ross C (1972) Sex role socialization in picture books for preschool children. *American Journal of Socialization* **7**, 1125–1150.

Werner D, Bower B (1982) *Helping Health Workers Learn*. Palo Alto, CA: The Hesperian Foundation.

FURTHER READING

Conger JJ (1991) *Adolescence and Youth*, 4th edn. London: Harper Collins.
This book reflects the remarkable progress in research on adolescent development that has taken place in recent years and places it in the context of the changing socioeconomic world and the influence of this variable on the process of development. Bibliographic references are detailed and it is of particular value to Diploma and undergraduate students studying the behavioural sciences as well as health care professionals involved in working with developing adolescents.

Shaffer DR (1989) *Developmental Psychology*, 2nd edn. California: Brooks/Cole Pacific Grove.
A comprehensive overview of developmental psychology reflecting the main theories, research and practical advice. Although the book is rigorous and research orientated, there is serious application of theory to practice to illuminate the text and challenge the reader.

Chapter 5

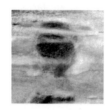

PHYSIOLOGICAL PROBLEMS

ELIZABETH BARTLEY BA PGCE RN RSCN RHV

KEY POINTS

- NORMAL SEXUAL DIFFERENTIATION – OVERVIEW OF PHYSIOLOGY OF SEXUAL DEVELOPMENT, FROM BIPOTENTIAL OF EARLY FETUS TO PUBERTY

- ABNORMALITIES OF SEXUAL DIFFERENTIATION – SEX CHROMOSOME DISORDERS AND AMBIGUOUS GENITALIA, IMPLICATIONS FOR PSYCHOSEXUAL DEVELOPMENT AND SEXUAL IDENTITY

- ORGANIC DYSFUNCTION – IMPLICATIONS FOR SEXUAL FUNCTION

- HORMONAL PROBLEMS – THE EXPERIENCE OF EARLY PUBERTY

- CHILDHOOD CANCER AND DRUG THERAPY – GONADAL DAMAGE AND INFERTILITY

- CHRONIC ILLNESS AND DISABILITY – POOR GROWTH, DELAYED PUBERTY AND ALTERED BODY IMAGE

- LOSS OF CONTROL – SOCIAL/SEXUAL INDEPENDENCE

- IMPLICATIONS FOR PRACTICE

The aim of this chapter is to explore some of the physiological problems that can affect the sexual health and development of pre-adolescents and young people. It is important to acknowledge at the beginning of a chapter that is concerned primarily with physiological problems that sexual identity cannot be equated with a purely biological definition of sex. Sexual identity encompasses many elements including gender, appearance, how we feel about our bodies and how we relate to other people sexually. It is directly influenced by a multitude of factors – family environment and parental behaviour, peer relationships, education, culture – and on a wider scale by the social and political climate in which we live.

Problems of sexual health and development are many and varied; some are relatively common disorders, such as undescended testis or hypospadias, whilst others are rare and

---

therefore less understood, such as pseudohermaphroditism. As health professionals who may be involved in the care of pre-adolescents and young people with sexual health problems, it is important that we appreciate not just the physiology of these disorders, but also the psychological and social implications. This is particularly important when one considers that many of these disorders are likely to have a detrimental effect on sexual identity and function for

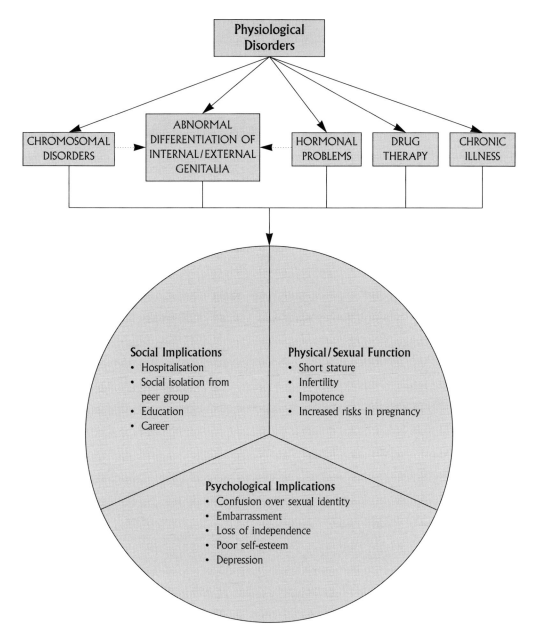

Figure 1 The main causes of physiological disorders that can affect sexual development and sexual function.

the individual concerned. Figure 1 outlines the main causes of physiological disorders that can affect sexual development, sexual function and hence psychological well-being.

Normal Sexual Differentiation

The genetic set of a zygote, the first cell of a new life, is determined at the time of fertilisation (Blair, 1995). The cell division process by which the sex cells are formed is called meiosis (Carola *et al.*, 1992). The gametes, or sex cells, each bring with them only half the number of chromosomes contained in all other cells (in humans there are 46 chromosomes in each cell, and so 23 in the gametes). When the sperm penetrates the ovum and fertilisation takes place, the nuclei of the two gametes fuse together, making the zygote complete with 23 pairs of chromosomes, one of each pair coming from the mother and one from the father.

There are two types of chromosome: sex chromosomes are concerned with sex determination, while autosomes determine other traits and are arranged in 22 matching pairs. The sex chromosome complex of the female is XX, and that of the male is XY. The sex of a zygote depends upon the chromosomal composition of the sperm cell. In the male, half the sperm will carry an X chromosome and the other half a Y chromosome. Therefore if an ovum is fertilised by a sperm with an X chromosome, an XX zygote is produced which will develop into a female. Conversely if an ovum is fertilised by a sperm with a Y chromosome, an XY zygote is produced which will develop into a male (Emery and Müller, 1988). The type of gonads which develop in an individual are determined by the sex chromosome complex.

Gonadal Sex

Before 8 weeks gestation, the gonads of an embryo are undifferentiated (Carola *et al.*, 1992). Regardless of the genetic sex, the embryo and early fetus is bipotential, i.e. it has the potential to develop along male or female lines (Danish, 1992). Bipotential structures that will become either testes or ovaries appear during the 5th week of gestation and consist of cortical (ovarian) and medullary (testicular) tissue (Moshang and Thornton, 1994; Page, 1994). The differentiation into either a testis or an ovary is directed by the genetic information contained within the sex chromosome.

The innate tendency of the embryo and early fetus is to differentiate along female lines. Sexual differentiation begins at 7 weeks and in the absence of a testis-determining factor located on the Y chromosome, and known as the H–Y antigen, the gonads will develop into ovaries. In the presence of the H–Y antigen the gonad will differentiate into a testis.

Testicular Differentiation
Testicular differentiation can be seen by the 7th week of gestation principally with the formation of the seminiferous tubules (Moore, 1988; Danish, 1992; Blair, 1995). The walls of the

seminiferous tubules are composed of Sertoli cells. These secrete a glycoprotein known as mullerian inhibiting factor (MIF) which causes degeneration of the mullerian ducts. In the interstitium of the testis, between the seminiferous cords, Leydig cells appear at around 7½–8 weeks; these produce testosterone which induces masculinisation of the external genitalia (Danish, 1992). As the fetus grows the testes descend, stimulated by MIF initially, and later on by testosterone, so that by the 8th or 9th month they will have reached the scrotum.

Ovarian Differentiation

As with the testes, ovarian differentiation begins at 7 weeks gestation. However, without a Y chromosome gonadal development is slower (Danish 1992; Blair, 1995). During fetal life, the sex cells break up into follicles and form the ovaries. Here germ cells — oogonia — develop into oocytes, so that there are several million oogonia and oocytes by the 5th month of gestation. Most germ cells degenerate *in utero*, leaving approximately 150 000 oocytes in each ovary at birth (Moore, 1988; Moshang and Thornton 1994).

Differentiation of Internal Genital Ducts

Male and female embryos possess two pairs of genital ducts. The stage when both are present is referred to as the indifferent stage; this lasts approximately up to 8 weeks gestation (Carola, *et al.*, 1992) (see Figure 2). These ducts are known as the mesonephric (wolffian) ducts, and paramesonephric (mullerian) ducts. As discussed earlier, the fetal testes produces MIF which causes degeneration of the mullerian ducts. At the same time the Leydig cells secrete testosterone and stimulate the wolffian ducts to differentiate into the epididymis and the vas deferens.

In the female fetus, mullerian ducts differentiate into fallopian tubes, the uterus and upper two-thirds of the vagina. In the absence of testosterone, the wolffian ducts regress and the fetal ovaries do not descend.

External Genitalia

The external genitalia of both sexes are identical for the first 2 months of embryonic life, consisting of a genital tubercle, paired lateral labioscrotal swellings and the urogenital sinus (Muller and Graem, 1993). Masculinisation of the external genitalia is dependent upon the availability of testosterone and its conversion to dihydrotestosterone (DHT) by the enzyme 5-α-reductase. DHT causes fusion of the urogenital sinus and genital tubercle, and development of the scrotum and penis (Moshang and Thornton, 1994; Blair, 1995). DHT binds to specific androgen receptor sites within tissues so that masculinisation can be expressed (see Figure 3).

Development of female external genitalia is related to the absence of androgens, but does not necessitate the presence of an ovary (Blair, 1995). Without androgens growth of the phallus eventually stops, forming the clitoris. The urogenital folds do not fuse but form the labia minora, whilst the remainder of the labioscrotal swellings form the labia majora (Moore, 1988; Blair, 1995).

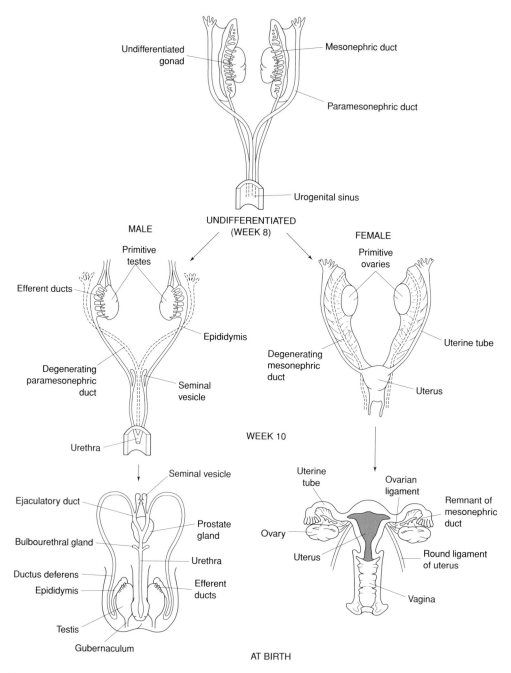

Figure 2 Development of internal reproductive organs. Redrawn from Carola *et al.* (1992).

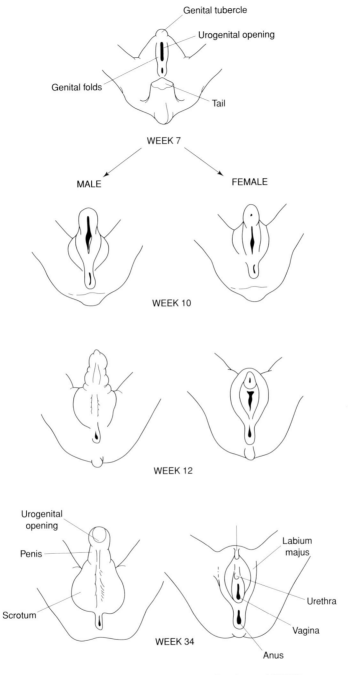

Figure 3 Development of external genitalia. Redrawn from Carola *et al.* (1992).

Secondary Sexual Characteristics

The acquisition of secondary sexual characteristics begins with the onset of puberty, when there are specific endocrinological changes that occur in the hypothalamus and pituitary gland (Berhman *et al.*, 1992).

A gradual pulsatile increase in gonadotrophic releasing hormone (GnRH) from the hypothalamus triggers intermittent serum peaks of lutenising hormone (LH) and follicle stimulating hormone (FSH) at night (Brook and Stanhope, 1989; Wales *et al.*, 1996). Lutenising hormone stimulates testosterone production by Leydig cells in the testes of boys, and FSH combined with high intratesticular concentrations of testosterone stimulates spermatogenesis. In girls FSH stimulates secretion of oestrogen (primarily oestradiol) from the ovary in the first part of the menstrual cycle. Oestrogens are responsible for the development of female secondary sexual characteristics and stimulate the growth of ovarian follicles (Marshall, 1992). Lutenising hormone stimulates ovulation and development of the corpus luteum in the uterus.

Physical Changes

The onset of puberty in boys and girls can occur at any time between the ages of 8 and 18 years (Brook and Stanhope, 1989). On average, puberty for girls commences 2 years earlier than for boys. The major physiological changes that occur are as follows.

Girls   In girls breast budding is usually the first sign of puberty, occurring at approximately 10–11 years. Menstruation is considered to be a late event, and occurs only after maximum growth potential has been achieved. Pubic hair growth commences with or after breast development, but can sometimes precede it (Buckler, 1994).

Boys   Increase in testicular volume is usually the first sign of puberty in boys (Brook and Stanhope, 1989; Buckler, 1994). The pre-pubertal testis is small with a volume of approximately 1–3 ml. In the adult it ranges between 12–25 ml in volume. Enlargement of the testes is accompanied by changes in the texture and colour of the scrotum, followed by an increase in length and width of the penis. The beginning of sperm production usually occurs in the 13th year (Brook and Stanhope, 1989).

Adolescent Growth Spurt

Peak height velocity (PHV) in girls is usually achieved 2 years earlier than in boys and precedes menstruation. In contrast to girls, the PHV of boys follows genital development. The growth spurt at this time is explained by the mediation of growth hormone (GH) by the sex steroids. The decrease in height velocity in the later stages of puberty is due to closure of epiphyseal growth plates, again as a result of sex steroid secretion (Brook and Stanhope, 1989; Buckler, 1994).

Can you remember your own puberty? At what age did it commence and how did you cope with the physical changes?

ABNORMAL SEXUAL DIFFERENTIATION

Abnormalities of the sexual differentiation, or intersex problems, are complex and not readily categorised. A review of the literature reveals that there is no uniformity in the classification of disorders.

A fault in sexual differentiation can develop as a result of erroneous biochemical processes, some of the most common being an absent or extra sex chromosome, an endocrine imbalance, an enzyme deficiency or teratogenic effects of drugs. Whatever the causal factor, interference with the normal fetal process of sexual differentiation can result in a wide range of abnormalities. A full discussion of these is beyond the scope of this chapter and so only the most commonly occurring disorders will be considered here under the following headings:

○ chromosome sex disorders
○ ambiguous genitalia.

Chromosome Sex Disorders

Turner's Syndrome

Turner's syndrome (TS) is a chromosomal disorder in which there is loss of, or loss of part of, an X chromosome. In the classical form of the condition, the chromosome complex is 45 X phenotype (Parkin, 1989; Williams, 1992). The most significant features of this condition in girls are ovarian dysgenesis and short stature.

Ovarian dysgenesis refers to a condition in which ovaries are not fully formed and represented only by 'streaks of tissue' that have no reproductive potential (Huffman *et al.*, 1981). There are no germ cells (oogonia) present in ovarian tissue, and therefore no primordial follicles are formed. Subsequently there is failure of puberty and menstruation, resulting in infertility. It is thought that there is normal embryological development of ovaries in TS up until approximately 16 weeks' gestation (Muller and Graem, 1993), but rapid degeneration thereafter results in no functional ovarian tissue in the majority of TS women (Parkin, 1989).

Some of the other physical features characteristic of the condition have been identified as webbed neck, shield-shaped chest, high arched palate and congenital heart disease, in particular coarctation of the aorta (these are not necessarily present in all cases) (see Figure 4) (Buckler, 1994). Diagnosis in infants is often suggested by small size, lymphoedema of the hands and feet and excess skin at the nape of the neck. Diagnosis is usually confirmed by chromosomal analysis.

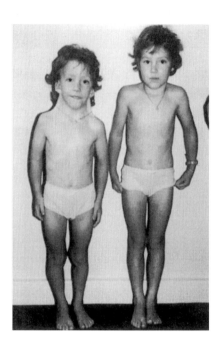

Figure 4 Girl with Turner's syndrome (on the left) with her twin sister at age 5½ years. Reproduced with permission from Buckler (1994).

With regard to short stature in TS, there is a decline in growth velocity throughout early childhood. According to Behrman and co-workers, the rate of growth is normal during the first 3 years of life, although in the lower centiles, but thereafter begins to decelerate (Berhman *et al.*, 1992). Growth hormone is commenced in the early years to maximise growth potential. Sex hormone therapy, either oestrogen or progesterone, is usually given between the ages of 13 and 15 years (Vockrodt and Williams, 1994), but is delayed until an adequate height has been achieved. Although oestrogen therapy will induce puberty, it will also cause cessation of growth (Williams, 1992).

It is claimed that one of the major causes of psychological problems for girls with TS is short stature. Vockrodt and Williams (1994) discuss the need for parents to explain to girls with TS why their bodies do not form functional ovaries, and consequently why their bodies are different (Vockrodt and Williams, 1994). This is particularly important when growth hormone is introduced. Growth hormone therapy involves a long course of treatment, over a period of several years, with an unpredictable outcome in terms of height achieved. For many girls treatment will not just begin and end with hormone replacement therapy. The other clinical manifestations may necessitate further medical and surgical intervention, which inevitably involves periods of hospitalisation, interruption to family life, schooling and relationships with their peer group.

Research into the cognitive characteristics of girls with TS, comparing their cognitive functioning with that of pre-adolescents with non-verbal learning disability, indicates that

CHILDREN AND SEXUALITY: PERSPECTIVES IN HEALTH CARE

there are similarities between the two groups when it comes to memory attention span and visual spatial perception. Williams (1992) argues that inadequate educational and psychological support may affect cognitive development and as a consequence these girls may underachieve academically. She also discusses the tendency of parents to 'juvenilise' their daughters because they appear younger than their chronological age, and suggests that families should be encouraged to expect girls to behave in a way consistent with age, not size.

The other very important issue for girls with TS is infertility. Although female sex hormones are administered at the time of puberty, enabling secondary sexual characteristics to develop, they cannot correct infertility. However, recent advances in assisted reproductive technologies seem to indicate that ovum donation and hormone replacement therapy may provide an option for women with TS who wish to become pregnant (Jones, 1994). One experimental study involving eight women with primary ovarian failure demonstrated that it was possible for some of these women to maintain a pregnancy and give birth to normal, healthy babies (Navot *et al.*, 1986).

Endometrial function was induced through administration of oestrogen and progesterone, followed by surrogate embryo transfers between 16 and 21 days of the induced menstrual cycle. Conception was achieved in two of the eight women. Early gestation was supported by increased doses of oestradiol and progesterone, from which the subjects were eventually weaned. Although in one woman exogenous progesterone was not withdrawn until the 22nd week of gestation, both pregnancies were eventually maintained by placental oestradiol only (Navot *et al.*, 1986).

Klinefelter's Syndrome

In Klinefelter's syndrome, the chromosomal composition is that of a 47 XXY male. Most commonly there is just one extra X chromosome, but there can be variants with up to three or four extra X chromosomes present (Emery and Müller, 1988; Blair, 1995).

As discussed at the beginning of this chapter, sex cell division — meiosis — causes a reduction in the number of sex cells from each parent, to produce a normal 46 chromosomal complement. In Klinefelter's syndrome, the chromosomal aberration results from meiotic non-disjunction of an X chromosome (Berhman *et al.*, 1992). Advanced maternal age has been identified as predisposing to meiotic non-disjunction, but it does not necessarily follow that the mother of boys with Klinefelter's syndrome are older women (Buckler, 1994; Blair, 1995).

The clinical features of Klinefelter's syndrome are tall stature, slim, long legs, hypogonadism (small testes) and infertility (see Figure 5). In many cases there is also gynaecomastia. The diagnosis is not often made until puberty, because the clinical manifestations up until this time can be quite subtle (Hindmarsh and Brook, 1989). At puberty, there is failure of testicular growth, and the phallus is smaller than average. The tall stature results from the presence of additional chromosomal material and a reduced level of sex steroid secretion which fails to close epiphyseal growth plates. Gynaecomastia is caused by elevated levels of the female hormone oestradiol (Berhman *et al.*, 1992; Hindmarsh and Brook, 1989).

Boys with Klinefelter's syndrome are infertile because the testes are small and fail to produce adequate numbers of viable sperm. There is progressive germ cell loss, with seminiferous

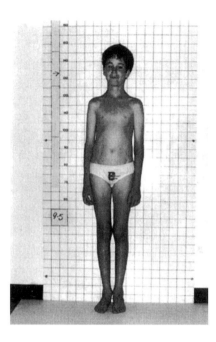

Figure 5 Boy with Klinefelter's syndrome at 9½ years. Reproduced with permission from Buckler (1994).

tubule degeneration throughout infancy and childhood. The testes may produce testosterone but in variable quantities, with differing degrees of masculinisation (Berhman *et al.*, 1992; Muller and Graem, 1993; Blair, 1995). Mental retardation has also been identified as a feature of Klinefelter's syndrome but this can be very mild and limited to learning difficulties at school, which can be appropriately managed with educational support (Buckler, 1994).

Treatment of Klinefelter's syndrome involves inducing secondary sexual development and slowing rate of growth. However, the decision to reduce final height is dependent upon the psychological experience of each individual (Hindmarsh and Brook, 1989; Buckler, 1994). Whilst some boys may have difficulty with their self-image due to tall stature, others may not see it as a problem.

Testosterone is administered, in low doses, to induce puberty. When sex steroids are used to decrease final height they are administered in higher doses, in the form of depot injections. The decrease in final height will be achieved by accelerating epiphyseal fusion. The timing of treatment is vital, so that puberty does not occur at too young an age (Buckler, 1994; Wales *et al.*, 1996).

REFLECTION POINT

Do you think that infertility affects women and men differently?

To what extent do you think the qualities 'feminine' and 'masculine' are associated with reproductive capability?

Ambiguous Genitalia

Probably the first question any parent asks at the birth of their baby is whether it is a boy or a girl. When an infant presents with ambiguous genitalia, parents are likely to be shocked and bewildered. It is a situation that requires sensitive handling. Ambiguous genitalia is the presence of both female and male external genitalia in one individual. In the female it can range from labial fusion to complete virilisation, and in the male it can vary from hypospadia to severe underdevelopment of the sexual organs.

Ambiguous genitalia can be classified into three main groups:

○ female pseudohermaphroditism
○ male pseudohermaphroditism
○ true hermaphroditism.

Female Pseudohermaphroditism

In female pseudohermaphroditism there is a normal genetic female (46 XX) infant with normal ovaries and internal genitalia, but masculinisation of the external genitalia. The masculinisation is caused by androgens, either produced endogenously by the fetus, or transferred placentally from the mother or another exogenous source (Barnes, 1986). The commonest form of this condition is congenital adrenal hyperplasia (CAH), which is an inherited disorder of adrenal steroid hormone biosynthesis (Barnes, 1986; Marshall, 1992).

Congenital adrenal hyperplasia (CAH)   Adrenal sex hormones are produced by the adrenal cortex, and consist mainly of androgens and smaller amounts of oestrogens. Secretion of these hormones is regulated by adrenocorticotrophic hormone (ACTH), from the pituitary gland. Three types of steroid hormones are produced by the adrenal gland:

○ sex hormones
○ mineralocorticoids
○ glucocorticoids.

The biosynthesis of these hormones relies upon specific enzymes, and in CAH there is a deficiency of one of these (Barnes, 1986; Moore, 1988; Savage, 1989). Depending upon which enzyme is deficient, a different form of CAH occurs, but no matter which type of CAH it is, a deficiency in cortisol will result (see Figure 6) (Savage, 1989). This in turn interferes with the negative feedback system to the pituitary, to block the secretion of ACTH. The end result is increased secretion of ACTH, causing adrenal hyperplasia and overproduction of androgens (Barnes, 1986; Moore, 1988; Savage, 1989; Marshall, 1992). Consequently female infants will be masculinised.

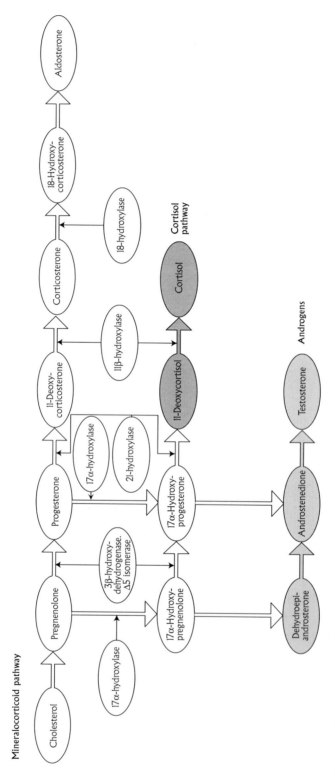

Figure 6 Biosynthesis of adrenal steroid hormones. Cortisol and the androgens are synthesised in the zona reticularis and zona fasciculata of the adrenal gland. 18-Hydroxylase required for the synthesis of aldosterone is present only in the zona glomerulosa. Redrawn from Marshall (1992).

CHILDREN AND SEXUALITY: PERSPECTIVES IN HEALTH CARE

21-Hydroxylase deficiency accounts for more than 95% of cases of CAH in the UK (Marshall, 1992). Presentation can vary from clitoral enlargement to a formed penile structure with a urethral opening at the tip, and complete fusion of the labia majora (Savage, 1989). A very significant problem with 21-hydroxylase deficiency is that a large percentage of these infants are unable to synthesise aldosterone (see Figure 6). An enzymatic block in the aldosterone pathway will result in a decreased production of aldosterone and inability of the kidneys to reabsorb sodium. This constitutes a medical emergency, and neonates may become seriously ill with vomiting and diarrhoea, proceeding to hyponatraemia, hypoglycaemia, hyperkalaemia and Addisonian crisis (Barnes, 1986).

Male Pseudohermaphroditism

In this condition a normal genetic male (46 XY) infant is born with testes but has undermasculinisation of the external genitalia. There can be a large degree of variation in presentation, ranging from complete feminisation of external genitalia in its extreme form, to hypospadias, cryptorchidism or normal male external genitalia. Under-masculinisation is due to interference with production and action of testosterone (Page, 1994). The potential causes of this interference are many and complex, including chromosomal abnormalities, autosomal disorders, enzyme deficiencies and androgen insensitivity (Moshang and Thornton, 1994; Blair, 1995).

The three main causes of the condition are:

○ insufficient production of testosterone
○ inability to convert testosterone to dihydrotestosterone (DHT)
○ androgen insensitivity in target tissue (testicular feminisation syndrome) (Savage, 1989; Page, 1994).

Insufficient testosterone production   Insufficient testosterone production is an autosomal recessive disorder. Five enzymes are required in the adrenal cortex for testosterone synthesis in the Leydig cells of the testes. These enzymes are also necessary in the adrenal steroid synthesis pathway for the production of aldosterone and cortisol (Gamblian *et al.*, 1993; Moshang and Thornton, 1994; Page, 1994). A deficiency in one of these enzymes will interfere with testosterone production.

As with female infants who have 21-hydroxylase deficiency and experience severe salt loss, male infants who have deficiency of 3β-hydroxydehydrogenase will present with the same symptoms of hyponatraemia and hypoglycaemia (see Figure 6). Testosterone production will also be interfered with due to this enzymatic deficiency in the adrenal steroid pathway. Whilst high levels of dehydroepiandrosterone will have mild androgenic effects, it is insufficient to promote adequate masculinisation of the external genitalia (Moshang and Thornton, 1994). The end result is a variation in the degree of ambiguity of genitalia which can range from mild to severe hypospadias, with micropenis. Other enzyme deficiencies are rare. The vas deferens and epididymis are often underdeveloped or absent (Barnes, 1986; Savage, 1989).

Inability to convert testosterone to dihydrotestosterone   In this disorder there is an enzyme deficiency of 5α-reductase, which is responsible for converting testosterone to di-hydrotestosterone (DHT) in target organs. This results in poor masculinisation of external genitalia, but normal development of internal structures, i.e. wolffian structures are present (see Figure 2). Infants present with a small phallus, perineal hypospadias and absent prostate (Savage, 1989; Moshang and Thornton, 1994; Page, 1994). Determination of sex for rearing is difficult and it is recommended that phallic length be used to decide sex assignment, because at puberty these adolescents will masculinise under the influence of testosterone (Page, 1994). Although there is some penile enlargement and descent of testes, external genitalia will remain small (Stock *et al.* 1995). If a pre-adolescent child has been reared as a female, there is also the problem encountered at puberty of a change in psychosexual orientation when mas-culinisation occurs.

Androgen insensitivity   Androgen insensitivity can be partial or complete. It is an X-linked recessive inherited disorder and is due to a deficiency in androgen receptor sites in target tissues.

REFLECTION POINT

What psychosocial readjustment has to be made at puberty by a young woman who is informed that she has the genetic composition of a male?

Complete androgen insensitivity   This is also known as testicular feminisation syndrome. It is a condition where a genetic male (XY) infant presents with normal female genitalia at birth. The vagina is a blind-ended pouch, the uterus is absent and there are testes which can be found intra-abdominally, or in the inguinal canal (Savage, 1989; Moshang and Thornton, 1994).

Due to the feminisation of genitalia, most infants are reared as females, but may present in childhood with abdominal masses or inguinal hernias. Testicular tissue is sometimes dis-covered during a herniotomy (Savage, 1989; Moshang and Thornton, 1994). Otherwise diag-nosis is made in puberty when an adolescent female is investigated for primary amenorrhoea. There is no masculinisation at puberty and affected girls who have not had testes removed before this age will develop normal breasts. This is due to conversion of high levels of testos-terone to oestradiol from defective androgen feedback to the hypothalamic–pituitary axis, resulting in increased secretion of lutenising hormone (Moshang and Thornton, 1994; Page, 1994).

There is little pubic or axillary hair present and psychosexual orientation is female. Oestrogen therapy is recommended at puberty (Savage, 1989). If the condition is diagnosed during infancy, orchidectomy is recommended, prior to 6 months of age, because progressive histological deterioration of the testis begins after this age (Danish, 1992).

Partial androgen insensitivity   With partial androgen insensitivity there is a lesser degree of masculinisation. Infants may present at birth with clitoromegaly and labial fusion and at

---

puberty there is a combination of masculinisation and breast development. Again, it is recommended that a female gender is assigned with plastic surgical reconstruction of genitalia as required (Page, 1994).

True Hermaphroditism

True hermaphroditism, where both ovarian and testicular tissues are present in the same individual, is a rare condition. There are a number of possible combinations of gonadal tissue that can occur.

- An *ovotestis*. This is the commonest gonad. Ovarian and testicular tissue are arranged together in the one gonad but still show clear lines of demarcation (Savage, 1989; Moshang and Thornton, 1994; Blair, 1995).
- An ovotestis can be unilateral with a normal ovary or testis on the opposite side (Blair, 1995).
- There may be an ovary and testis present on opposite sides.

Genetically most infants have a chromosomal complement 46 XX but there can be mosaicisms such as 46 XX/XY (Moshang and Thornton, 1994; Page, 1994; Blair, 1995). Internal and external genital structures are variable; most infants are recognised neonatally due to ambiguous genitalia. The degree of masculinisation is dependent upon the amount of functioning testicular tissue present (Moshang and Thornton, 1994). If a phallus has formed many infants will be reared as male (Page, 1994). Evidence shows that the testicular component of ovotestes is abnormal. In a large number of cases menstruation occurs at puberty, with ovulation, but there remains some uncertainty regarding fertility in these girls (Savage, 1989; Blair, 1995).

Management of Ambiguous Genitalia

At the birth of a child with ambiguous genitalia, it is suggested that parents are informed that the infant's genitalia is unfinished in development, but that a definite gender will be assigned within several days (Danish, 1992; Moshang and Thornton, 1994; Page, 1994). This is, of course, extremely difficult for parents, particularly regarding what they tell family and friends. Parents may require advice and support from health professionals on how best, or when to disclose information.

The aims of clinical management focus upon:

- designating a correct sex of rearing
- correcting any problems early so that the child may develop a normal body image and gender identity
- diagnosing congenital adrenal hyperplasia before the infant has an adrenal crisis (Danish, 1992).

Diagnostic evaluation involves:

(a) *History*
  (i) parents interviewed to find out if there are any relatives with genital abnormalities
  (ii) have any siblings died in infancy?
  (iii) what is the degree of consanguinity?
  (iv) were any drugs taken in pregnancy?
  (v) mother should also be examined for degree of virilisation.
(b) *Physical examination*
  (i) presence or absence of gonads can direct further investigations (Moshang and Thornton, 1994)
  (ii) length and width of phallus should be checked
  (iii) assessment for dehydration should be carried out
  (iv) degree of labial fusion should be assessed, and abnormalities of other organs.
(c) *Investigations*
  (i) buccal smear – chromosomes
  (ii) bloods – to determine karyotype and measure steroid hormone levels
  (iii) pelvic ultrasound – can demonstrate presence of gonads, vagina, cervix (Moshang and Thornton, 1994; Page, 1994)
  (iv) genitogram – radio-opaque die injected into genital orifice to assess internal organs (Barnes, 1986; Danish, 1992).

For most infants with ambiguous genitalia, gender assignment is not a problem (Barnes, 1986; Moshang and Thornton, 1994). Usually sex of rearing is decided when chromosome status and internal organs are known. If bilateral ovaries are present, the infant will be reared as a female, even if well masculinised. This is because these girls are capable of normal female hormone secretion, and are potentially fertile. Genitalia can be corrected by surgical reconstruction.

If bilateral ovaries are absent, the criteria for deciding male sex of rearing is penile size. Consideration needs to be given to decide whether a boy can be expected to achieve normal penile size in adulthood in order to maintain sexual function (Danish, 1992; Moshang and Thornton, 1994). If penile length is very small an infant is best reared as female regardless of chromosomal sex. Infants with androgen insensitivity demonstrate a limited response to testosterone. If these infants are assigned a female gender, surgical reconstruction of genitalia and gonadectomy are recommended before 6 months of age (Page, 1994).

ORGANIC DYSFUNCTION

Hypospadias

Hypospadias is a relatively common congenital abnormality, estimated at 1 in 300 male births (Black and Whitfield, 1991; Stock *et al.*, 1995), and is characterised by an abnormal position of the urethral orifice. This can be located on the ventral side of the penis, in the scrotum or in the perineum. It can be classified into four main types:

○ glandular
○ penile
○ penoscrotal
○ perineal (Moore, 1988).

The majority of cases are either glandular, where the urethra opens in the glans penis, or penile, where the urethra opens on the ventral surface of the penis. Also associated with the condition is a ventral curvature of the penis, known as chordee.

Masculinisation of the external genitalia begins after 8 weeks gestation. Under the influence of androgens the penis lengthens, bringing with it an extension of the urogenital opening. As the penis enlarges, the urogenital folds are pulled ventrally to form the walls of the urethral groove on the ventral side of the penis. This is followed by midline fusion of the genital (urethral) folds, to form a spongy urethra. The end result should be a straight penis with erectile tissue, corpus cavernosa and corpus spongiosum, with a urethra that extends the length of the penis and a meatus opening distally on the glans (Moore, 1988; Sugar *et al.*, 1993).

Hypospadias results from either failure of formation of the urethral groove or incomplete closure of the urethral groove. Factors which are thought to contribute to hypospadias are: inadequate testosterone production, inadequate conversion of testosterone to dihydro-testosterone and a deficiency of androgen receptor sites in tissues (Black and Whitfield, 1991). Chordee is thought to be remnants of fetal tissue — mesenchyme — which should have formed part of the erectile tissue, but instead results in fibrous tissue causing curvature of the penis (Sugar *et al.*, 1993). It is recommended that infants who present with perineal hypospadias and undescended testes undergo chromosomal testing to check for an intersex state (Black and Whitfield, 1991; Sugar *et al.*, 1993).

Functional problems that arise as a result of hypospadias are a poor stream of urine which is often splayed, and difficulty in the voiding of urine whilst standing. Where chordee is present this can result in painful erections and potentially reduce fertility in adulthood (Sugar *et al.*, 1993). Other anomalies associated with hypospadias are undescended testes and inguinal hernias.

The main objectives of surgery are to straighten the penis, open the meatus at the tip of the glans, improve the stream of urine and erections, and the general cosmetic appearance (Sheldon and Duckett, 1987; Stock *et al.*, 1995). Surgical correction of hypospadias is usually performed between 6 and 12 months of age; not only is the anaesthetic risk reduced after 6 months of age (Stock *et al.*, 1995), but it is also recommended that surgery precedes development of gender identity and toilet training (Stock *et al.*, 1995; Sugar *et al.*, 1993; Sheldon and Duckett, 1987). The type of operation performed is determined by the degree of hypospadias. The three commonly used surgical techniques are the Magpi, Mathieu and Ducketts.

The Magpi repair involves meatal advancement and glanulaplasty and is used to connect glanular hypospadias without chordee. This technique is used when the urethra is easily mobilised and has a low incidence of stricture and fistula (Sheldon and Duckett, 1987).

The Mathieu repair is used for distal hypospadias without chordee. Surgery involves the use of a meatus-based flap which is elevated and sutured to the urethral plate. The flap is mobilised with its underlying blood supply intact.

In cases where the meatus is situated towards the centre of the penile shaft, Ducketts repair will be used. This involves separating the inner foreskin from the outer foreskin, and rolling it into a tube which is then rotated and sutured longitudinally to the urethral plate. This extends the length of the urethra, bringing the new meatus to the tip of the glans (Sheldon and Duckett, 1987; Stock *et al.*, 1995). Scrotal and perineal hypospadias require more complex surgery, with the repair being performed in two stages. However, more complex repairs, such as Ducketts, will require some form of urinary diversion, often by means of a suprapubic catheter, and this can involve a stay in hospital for up to 1 week.

Despite improvements in surgical techniques, complications can still occur. It is suggested that complications can be minimised by proper preoperative and intraoperative assessment, so that the appropriate surgical technique is selected. The most common complications post-operatively are urethral fistula or urethral stricture. Two factors identified as major problems are infection and ischaemia (Retik *et al.*, 1988). Prophylactic antibiotics are used to prevent these from occurring.

CASE STUDY

Matthew is 10 years old. He first underwent surgical correction of hypospadias at 9 months of age, but unfortunately due to fistula formation following surgery, he has had three more operations over the past 9 years to rectify the problem. He is about to have his fourth and final operation, but is now frightened of hospital and embarrassed at the prospect of doctors and nurses looking at his penis.

What do you think are the psychological implications for any pre–adolescent who has to undergo repeated genital surgery?

How should Matthew's fear and embarrassment be managed and by whom?

Vaginal Malformations

Vaginal abnormalities are either obstructive or non-obstructive (Blair, 1995). Some of the more common include: imperforate hymen, longitudinal vaginal septa, transverse vaginal septa and vaginal atresia.

The vagina develops from the urogenital opening (see Figure 3), often referred to as the urogenital sinus. Vaginal epithelium in the embryo is formed from ectoderm and endoderm; the muscular wall is formed from mesoderm (embryonic tissues). The vagina remains as a solid epithelial structure until approximately 5 months gestation. At this stage the cells at the inner core begin a process of degeneration and the vagina becomes a lumen. The lumen of the vagina remains separated from the cavity of the urogenital sinus by a membrane, known as the hymen, which usually ruptures during the perinatal period (Huffman *et al.*, 1981; Moore, 1988).

Most obstructive lesions of the vagina do not present until puberty, when girls are investigated for primary amenhorroea. The blockage of menstrual blood can occur with an imperforate hymen or with vaginal septa, which can be complete or incomplete. Presenting symptons are cyclical abdominal pain and vaginal discomfort.

Vaginal atresia occurs due to failure of canalisation of the vagina. The vagina remains as a solid epithelial mass of tissue. An absence of the distal vagina is usually discovered at examination of the newborn. Treatment is normally delayed until puberty, and involves either dilatation or surgical creation of a functional vagina. An opening is formed between the urethra and rectum, followed by insertion of a skin graft (Huffman *et al.*, 1981).

HORMONAL PROBLEMS

Precocious Puberty

Precocious puberty can be defined by the onset of puberty before the age of 8 years in girls, and 9 years in boys. It can be classified into two main types:

○ central precocious puberty
○ pseudo precocious puberty (Wheeler and Styne, 1990; Wales *et al.*, 1996).

Central Precocious Puberty (CPP)

Central precocious puberty results from premature activation of the hypothalamo–pituitary axis, when all the events of normal puberty occur early. It is five times more common in girls than boys (Ludderjackson and Ott, 1990). It can be idiopathic, as occurs mainly in girls, or due to central nervous system tumours, which are more common in boys (Wales *et al.*, 1996). These can be benign, such as hamartomas, or malignant as with gliomas, teratomas and astrocytomas (Brook and Stanhope, 1989; Wheeler and Styne, 1990; Wales *et al.*, 1996). CPP can also follow cranial irradiation (Lee, 1990). It can be characterised by the following:

○ development of secondary sexual characteristics, pubic hair growth
○ growth spurt
○ advanced bone age (Wales *et al.*, 1996).

The major problems for pre-adolescents with CPP are that premature sexual development is out of step with cognitive development (Brook and Stanhope, 1989). Early sexual maturation involves early growth acceleration. Sex steroid secretion stimulates epiphyseal maturation, and bone age progresses rapidly. This leads to premature epiphyseal closure and reduction in the final height achieved (Brook and Stanhope, 1989; Wales *et al.*, 1996). The earlier the onset of puberty, the shorter the final height will be.

Pseudo Precocious Puberty (PPP)

In PPP only some of the events of puberty occur early. Sex steroid secretion stimulates physical changes, but this is not regulated by the pituitary–hypothalamo axis. The most common form of PPP is congenital adrenal hyperplasia, but it can also be due to liver and adrenal tumours, gonadal tumours and follicular cysts in girls. The characteristics of PPP are:

○ excess production of specific hormones, i.e. testosterone, oestrogen, causing hypertrophy of tissues, e.g. clitoral hypertrophy
○ advanced bone age
○ acceleration of growth (Wales *et al.*, 1996).

Management of Precocious Puberty (PP)

Detecting the underlying cause is the first step in the management of precocious puberty. Neurological assessment is required, with CT scan to detect any tumours. Endocrine function should also be assessed, and the timing of the onset of puberty needs to be established (Ludderjackson and Ott, 1990). Bone age can be checked by X-ray.

Because CPP results in a reduction of final height, treatment involves slowing down the progression of puberty. Administration of gonadotrophin releasing hormone agonists as depot injections is used to achieve this. Episodic secretion of gonadotrophin releasing hormone (GnRH) causes pulsatile secretion of gonadotrophin, but a constant infusion of GnRH causes a decrease in pituitary response to GnRH, resulting in decreased gonadotrophin secretion (Wheeler and Styne, 1990). It is also recommended that crypoterone acetate, an oral sex steroid synthesis blocker, is administered for the first 6 weeks of treatment, to prevent progression of puberty (Wales *et al.*, 1996). Any malignancies are treated with surgery, chemotherapy and/or radiotherapy. Psychological support is also a very important part of treatment, both for the adolescent and their family. It has been shown that the self-esteem of pre-adolescents with PP can be adversely affected by their body image. The self-esteem of pre-adolescents with PP has been assessed using a Piers Harris Children's Self Concept Scale, self portraits and structured interviews (Ludderjackson and Ott, 1990).

Results demonstrated that pre-adolescents were confused about their condition. Many of them were anxious, felt insecure and recognised themselves as different from other people. Some even described themselves as 'weird' or as 'a monster of some kind – like on TV' (Ludderjackson and Ott, 1990: 200). Their poor body image and low self-esteem were thought to disadvantage them when it came to forming peer relationships. In some instances, pre-adolescents with PP had been sexually harassed by peers, even to the extent of being touched inappropriately.

It is argued that without adequate knowledge of their condition these pre-adolescents are more likely to feel socially isolated, because inability to discuss their condition increases their sense of being different. Counselling can help pre-adolescents understand their condition, and help them explore ways of developing coping strategies. This in turn leaves less to their imagination and the possible distortion of information (Ludderjackson and Ott, 1990).

The difficulty for parents/carers is having to discuss sexual development with a very young child, who is likely to have a limited understanding of bodily functions. There is also the fear of early sexual activity and its subsequent implications. Psychological support should be made available for the whole family with advice on how to approach sex education.

REFLECTION POINT

How do the media and popular culture influence the concept of 'body image'?

SECONDARY SEXUAL PROBLEMS

Undescended Testis (Cryptorchidism)

Descent of the testes takes place in two stages. First there is the transabdominal descent, where the testis descends to the level of the inguinal canal and remains there for up to 6 months gestation. Secondly there is the descent through the inguinal canal into the scrotum, which occurs at approximately 28 weeks gestation. Full descent is normally achieved by 40 weeks gestation (see Figure 7) (Danish, 1992; Cilento et al., 1993).

Little is known about the cause of testicular descent through the inguinal canal to the scrotum (Moore, 1988; Danish, 1992; Cilento et al., 1993). Descent is thought to be affected by androgens produced by the fetal testes. Undescended testis is associated with decreased levels of lutenising hormone and testosterone in the first few months of gestation (Moore, 1988). Damage to the genitofemoral nerve has also been suggested as a contributory factor to mal descent, since myelomeningocele causes paralysis of the spinal nerves and has been associated with a higher incidence of undescended testis (Wheeler and Styne, 1990; Danish, 1992). The following are abnormalities of sexual differentiation (Danish, 1992):

1. Progressive histological deterioration with changes beginning after age 6 months.
2. Impaired spermatogenesis with a decrease in the number of germ cells after the first year of life (and later reduced fertility potential).
3. Increased (four-fold to ten-fold) risk for cancer in the undescended testis and also in the descended testis in unilateral cryptorchidism.
4. Trauma to the testis that is relatively fixed in position.
5. Torsion.
6. Symptomatic inguinal hernia.
7. Psychological factors relating to altered body image.

The major complications of cryptorchidism are infertility and testicular cancer, and it is for these reasons that surgical treatment is recommended prior to 18 months of age (Danish, 1992; Cilento et al., 1993). Cryptorchidism is bilateral in up to 30% of cases (Berhman et al., 1992), and untreated bilateral cryptorchidism results in infertility. In unilateral cryptorchidism,

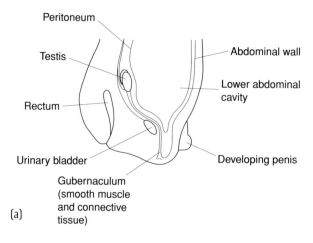

(a)

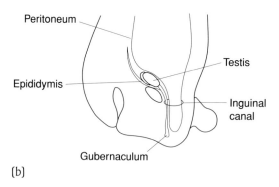

(b)

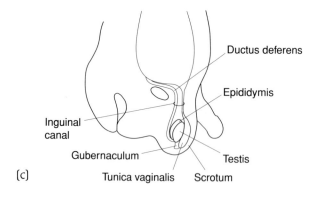

(c)

Figure 7 The testes descend from the abdominal cavity into the scrotum during fetal development: (a) 6 month fetus; (b) 7 month fetus; (c) at birth. Redrawn from Carola *et al.* (1992).

fertility in adult life is dependent upon the age at which surgical intervention takes place. The number of germ cells in an undescended testis is significantly reduced by the end of the second year. Even by the end of the first year there is evidence of atrophy, but a relatively high rate of fertility can be preserved (similar to the adult male population) if surgery is performed between 1 and 2 years of age (Berhman *et al.*, 1992; Cilento *et al.*, 1993). Orchidopexy is not usually undertaken before 6–9 months of age because spontaneous descent of the testis can still occur during this period (Danish, 1992).

Orchidopexy involves relocating the testes in the scrotum. Careful inspection of the testis is made intraoperatively, to assess the degree of atrophy and also to check that the spermatic cord is not twisted. Orchidectomy is recommended if the testis is severely atrophied. Associated anomalies with cryptorchidism include hypospadias and inguinal hernia, inguinal hernia being the most common (Cilento *et al.*, 1993).

There is an increased risk of developing a malignant tumour in later life with cryptorchidism, and orchidopexy does not appear to change the overall risk of being affected by testicular cancer (Berhman *et al.*, 1992). The risk of cancer is linked to the degree of cryptorchidism; boys with intra-abdominal testes are at greatest risk for developing malignancies, in particular the germ cell tumour, seminoma.

Inguinal Hernia

The inguinal canals are pathways by which the testes descend from the abdomen into the scrotum. When the testes descend into the inguinal canals at 28 weeks gestation, they follow the gubernaculum, a ligament which passes through the anterior abdominal wall and attaches to the labioscrotal swellings (see Figure 7) (Moore, 1988).

A diverticulum of peritoneum, the processus vaginalis, attaches itself to the testis, and passes through the abdominal wall along the path formed by the gubernaculum. The portion of the processus vaginalis which is attached to the testis forms the tunica vaginalis. The remainder of the processus vaginalis curls inwards and in so doing obliterates the entrance of the peritoneal cavity in the inguinal canal (Scherer and Grosfeld, 1993). If the peritoneal cavity fails to close it will result in an inguinal hernia, whereby loops of intestine herniate into the scrotum (Moore, 1988).

Inguinal hernias can occur in boys or girls, but are more common in boys, with a predominance of hernias on the right side. One survey reviewing surgical management of hernia repairs over a period of 5 years, found that, out of 348 children undergoing hernia repairs, 245 presented with a right-sided hernia (Harvey *et al.*, 1985).

There is a higher risk of incarceration or strangulation of inguinal hernias during the first years of life and therefore in this age group in particular elective surgery should be performed as soon as possible following diagnosis. However, it is recommended that initially, conservative measures should be used to reduce inguinal hernias when they are incarcerated and not strangulated. This can be achieved by sedation and application of gallows traction, followed by surgery within the next 24 hours (Harvey *et al.*, 1985). This recommendation is based on evidence showing that emergency surgery for inguinal hernias results in more complications. This is due to oedema of the spermatic cord and surrounding tissues, making surgery difficult with possibility of damage to delicate structures (Harvey *et al.*, 1985; Scherer and Grosfeld, 1993).

Herniotomy involves ligation of an empty hernia sac. The sac has to be inspected for contents, such as bowel or gonads. In girls (cases are rare), the gonads must be inspected at the time of surgery, to check for a testis or ovotestis. If any abnormalities are suspected, biopsies should be taken with further evaluation of gender (Harvey *et al.*, 1985). A hydrocele occurs when the processus vaginalis remains open, but is not large enough for herniation of the intestine. Peritoneal fluid leaks through, forming a hydrocele of the testis and spermatic cord (Moore, 1988).

REFLECTION POINT

What are the differences between a 'biological' and a 'sociological' definition of sexuality?

DRUG THERAPY

For many illnesses of childhood and adolescence, drug therapy is an essential component of treatment, particularly for malignancies, autoimmune disorders, haemoglobinopathies and chronic illnesses such as asthma, cystic fibrosis and diabetes. Unfortunately many drugs have deleterious side effects; among the most harmful drugs are the antineoplastics used in the treatment of cancer. The major problem with this group of drugs is that they are not specific to tumour cells but target some normal cells as well (Byrd, 1985), including the cells of the reproductive systems, in both males and females.

Antineoplastics, also known as cytotoxics, are often used in the treatment of malignant disease, in conjunction with radiotherapy and/or surgery (Martindale, 1993). Corticosteroids are also sometimes used, as part of combined therapy. Cytotoxics, radiotherapy and corticosteroids will be discussed here, in relation to their effects upon the endocrine and reproductive systems in pre-adolescents and young people.

Cytotoxics and Radiotherapy

Cytotoxics have low therapeutic indices and frequently cause multisystem toxicity (Folb, 1988). Adverse effects include infertility and hormonal dysfunction (Byrd, 1985). The two main groups of drugs used in the treatment of malignancies are alkylating agents and antimetabolites. Cytotoxic drugs affect all rapidly dividing cells, including those of the bone marrow, gastrointestinal tract and the gonads (Martindale, 1993).

Cytotoxic drugs cause gonadal damage in both sexes, but the severity of damage is dependent upon total dose of drug used and age at which treatment is given (Folb, 1988).

Older women are more susceptible to damage from alkylating agents than pubertal girls, and overall males are more vulnerable than females in the extent of damage sustained by cancer treatment (Leventhal et al., 1996).

Female Reproductive System

Cytotoxic drugs cause loss of primordial follicles in the ovary, with subsequent failure of ovulation and amenorrhoea. Alkylating agents are most likely to cause ovarian failure in post-pubertal females. The pre-pubertal ovary appears to be more resistant to damage (Torano et al., 1996). This is thought to be due to reduced follicular activity prior to puberty, and the larger number of primordial follicles in pre-pubertal girls (Martindale, 1993). Cyclophosphamide, an alkylating agent, has been shown to cause ovarian failure in post-pubertal females. The drug halts follicular maturation and, if therapy is intense, the ova will actually disappear (Byrd, 1985; Torano et al., 1996).

Radiotherapy is often used in combination with cytotoxics for treatment of malignancies. The ovaries of women over 40 years of age appear to be more sensitive to radiation than those of younger women. There is also a correlation between radiation exposure and ovarian dysfunction (Byrd, 1985). Oocytes die within a few hours of exposure to radiation; the proximity of ovaries to radiation treatment fields is a significant risk factor (Torano et al., 1996). Where treatment involves pelvic, abdominal or total body irradiation there is greater likelihood of ovarian failure (Byrd, 1985). Attempts have been made to protect ovaries through shielding, decreasing doses of radiation and oophoropexy (ovarian transposition) (Byrd, 1985; Torano et al., 1996).

Once ovarian failure has occurred, it is suggested that care should be managed by a paediatric endocrinologist, with a view to introducing oestrogen therapy to induce puberty in girls of an appropriate age. Growth hormone may also be considered to increase stature prior to inducement of puberty (Torano et al., 1996).

Pregnancy during treatment for malignancies should be avoided at all costs, since chemotherapy and radiotherapy are potentially teratogenic (Byrd, 1985). In particular they should be avoided in the first trimester of pregnancy; the fetus is at greater risk, at a time of rapid cell division (Folb, 1988; Martindale, 1993). For women who have been treated for malignancy in childhood or adolescence, the rate of birth defects in pregnancy appears to be no more than that of the general population, with the exception of those who received abdominal radiation. For these women, damage to the uterus can result in deformities and premature births (Torano et al., 1996).

CASE STUDY

Anita was 16 years old when she was diagnosed with osteosarcoma. She has had a below knee amputation and has recently been commenced on chemotherapy. She has informed nursing staff that she has missed one last menstrual period and now her next one is overdue. She has a regular boyfriend and had been sexually active a few months prior to treatment, using oral contraceptives. A pregnancy test confirms that she is 10 weeks pregnant.

Doctors have informed her of the teratogenic effects of the drugs she has been receiving, and of her reduced prognosis should she choose to discontinue treatment, in order to maintain the pregnancy. She is advised to have an abortion, but Anita wants to stop her chemotherapy in order to give the baby a chance, arguing that her own outlook is uncertain if she chooses to carry on with treatment. Her parents are distraught and are pleading with her to abort the pregnancy.

What ethical dilemmas does this case present?

Whose wishes should be considered and who has the right of informed consent?

How should nursing staff manage this situation?

Male Reproductive System

In males the germinal epithelium of the testis is particularly susceptible to cytotoxic drugs. Each testis contains seminiferous tubules, which produce thousands of sperm every second in a post-pubertal male. The walls of the seminiferous tubules are lined with germinal tissue which contains spermatogenic and Sertoli cells. The spermatogenic cells develop into mature sperm over a period of 74 days (Carola *et al.*, 1992). Since sperm are continuously produced in adult males, a constant supply of germ cells is necessary for spermatogenesis to take place. It is this high mitotic rate that makes the germinal epithelium so susceptible (Leventhal *et al.*, 1996). As with the ovary, it is the alkylating agents that are the most toxic to the testis. The extent of damage depends on the dose and duration of treatment (Byrd, 1985; Martindale, 1993).

The drug regimen that has been extensively studied is MOPP (mustine, vincristine, procarbazine and prednisone). This causes azoospermia, which can last for more than 5 years (Byrd, 1985; Martindale, 1993; Leventhal *et al.*, 1996). MOPP is generally used in the treatment of Hodgkin's disease. Acute leukaemia is usually treated with antimetabolites (Leventhal *et al.*, 1996), in particular methotrexate. Although less toxic than alkylating agents, it can reduce sperm count significantly in the first few weeks of treatment. However, there is evidence to show that normal testicular function will return (Byrd, 1985).

Leydig and Sertoli cell function are relatively less affected by chemotherapy, and so testosterone concentrations tend to remain normal (Martindale, 1993). Therefore most pre-pubertal males will progress normally through puberty, and post-pubertal males maintain normal male secondary sexual characteristics (Leventhal *et al.*, 1996).

Radiotherapy   Germinal epithelium is sensitive to radiation, but Leydig and Sertoli cells can also be affected, although to a lesser extent. The degree of damage caused to the testis by irradiation is dependent upon the dose administered. Reduced sperm count can be seen

---

within a number of weeks, but late recovery of spermatogenesis can occur over 10 years later (Leventhal *et al.*, 1996).

Management When post-pubertal boys are at risk of post-treatment infertility, sperm banking can be recommended. The intention is that sperm can be stored for future use, up to a maximum of 10 years (Koeppel, 1995). Pre-pubertal boys are too young for sperm banking to be a viable option (Leventhal *et al.*, 1996) and there is also some debate about cryopreserving sperm as an option for post-pubertal males.

Some of the problems encountered with sperm banking are:

○ malignancy itself may reduce the quality of semen; oligospermia may already be present before treatment
○ freezing sperm can reduce sperm motility
○ delaying treatment in order to obtain semen collection is putting the patient at significant risk (Koeppel, 1995; Leventhal *et al.*, 1996).

Several specimens are required, which implies that treatment is delayed up to a maximum of 18 days (Koeppel, 1995). Because there is a potential risk to offspring from semen that is collected once chemotherapy has commenced, it is necessary to collect semen prior to treatment. It is also recommended that patients use reliable contraception from the start of chemotherapy, and up to 6 months after treatment (Meistrich, 1993).

Sperm banking requires written consent and sperm can only be stored for up to a maximum of 10 years. For some young males discussing the practicalities of collecting sperm may prove embarrassing and needs a sensitive approach. Written information should be provided about all aspects of treatment, and counselling from appropriate health personnel should be made available.

It is suggested that health professionals working with cancer patients should discuss issues involving sexuality as soon as possible after diagnosis (Koeppel, 1995). The problem with life-threatening illnesses such as malignancies is that sexual function may not be seen as a priority, particularly if patients are ill at the time of diagnosis. Koeppel (1995: 311) writes:

> *Most patients are unable to think beyond immediate survival at the time of diagnosis; therefore, the health care team must think ahead for patients and offer them a chance at future paternity.*

THE EFFECTS OF ILLNESS ON SEXUAL DEVELOPMENT

Chronic illness, especially in its severe form, will be accompanied by short stature and delayed puberty (Brook and Stanhope, 1989). The effects of chronic systemic illness on psychosocial development in pre-adolescents and young people are well documented. Sparacino (1984) claims that chronic illness has a significant impact on the development of self-concept because society places a great emphasis on physical perfection and beauty.

It is calculated that approximately 5% of children in Western countries have a persistent or recurrent handicapping physical condition, the most common disorders being asthma, eczema and epilepsy (Garralda, 1994). Taylor and Eminson (1994) claim that these pre-adolescents and young people constitute a minority group, and that minority group membership is declared by the 'exhibition of signs or symbols'. They also suggest that the stereotyping of an individual by physical characteristics, especially when they are negative ones, involves a loss of autonomy.

The development of self-image is an integral part of sexual development. The major physiological changes that occur at puberty bring with them a greater preoccupation with body image, as young people attempt to integrate these changes into their self-identity (Sparacino, 1984). A lack of, or delay in, these expected changes can result in a young person feeling extremely isolated from their peer group. If this is coupled with other negative physiological alterations as a result of chronic illness, for example jaundice and dental deformities caused by sickle cell disease, there is a greater likelihood of poor self-esteem (Williams *et al.*, 1985).

The psychosocial aspects of short stature have been explained in several studies. A study of constitutional short stature in 24 pre-adolescents aged 6 to 12 years, using a Piers Harris Self Concept Scale, found that this group had significantly more behavioural problems and less self-esteem than a matched control group with normal height. Negative evaluations appeared to indicate a greater degree of discomfort and vulnerability in social situations (Gordon *et al.*, 1982).

In contrast to this study, Reynolds *et al.* (1995) found a lack of concern about growth in pre-adolescents and young people, but a greater preoccupation with the effects of their illness upon the family (Garralda, 1994). This study looked specifically at short stature and chronic renal failure, comparing the concerns of pre-adolescents and young people with those of their parents. The study of psychological functioning was run alongside a trial of growth hormone treatment. It was suggested that the lack of concern about growth was due to a greater preoccupation made by the demands of illness, and that perhaps short stature can work as a protective factor, because young people will be exempt from peer group pressure if they are considered to look younger than their age. Of course this may also disadvantage them, since this sort of protection is also likely to isolate them from their peer group.

Cardwell Hagenah *et al.* (1984: 31) suggest that isolation from peers during chronic illness hampers normal social growth:

> *Children need experiences with other children to allow validation of their self worth and to give them a sense of belonging. These feelings are important in the development of mental health.*

REFLECTION POINT

How is sexual identity affected by isolation from the peer group during adolescence?

Physical illness is known to be a risk factor in the development of emotional disorders, one of the significant contributory factors being overprotective parenting (Garralda, 1994). Many chronic illnesses involve long periods of hospitalisation, and subsequent absence from school. If educational achievement is affected, there may be a longer period of dependency. There is also the possibility that during acute exacerbations of illness there can be regression to infantile behaviour which encourages others to treat the person like a child. It is also important to acknowledge that illness brings enforced dependency at times, which has little to do with choice (Tong and Sparacino, 1994).

Physical illness not only affects an individual's level of independence, education and future career, but can also have profound implications for intimate sexual relationships. For example, a young person with inflammatory bowel disease, who experiences chronic abdominal pain and diarrhoea, will not only find this stressful to cope with, but may also feel socially compromised. Those with stomas may worry about appearance, odour, and the impact a stoma may have on any type of sexual activity. Chronic illness can also be accompanied by fears that do not affect the peer group, such as the fear of death during sexual arousal, amongst young persons with congenital heart disease (Tong and Sparacino, 1994).

CASE STUDY

Ben is 14 years old and has Crohn's disease. He was diagnosed 2 years ago and up until recently has been managed successfully on oral steroids. However, during the past few months his condition deteriorated dramatically, with increased lethargy, anaemia and significant weight loss. It was decided that he needed a bowel resection and formation of colostomy.

Post–operatively he is depressed. He hates his stoma and refuses to look at it. He has informed his friends at school that he was coming into hospital for more drug treatment only.

How can Ben be helped to come to terms with his changed body image?

What are the social implications for any young person with a stoma?

Sexual activity with some disease states such as congenital heart disease may also involve greater thought and planning, due to the risks associated with certain types of contraception, and with pregnancy. Sex education, accompanied by written information, is essential for the young person with congenital heart disease, because some forms of contraception have inherent risks (Tong and Sparacino, 1994). An intrauterine device is a potential source of infection, putting the young person at greater risk for endocarditis. Contraceptive pills are relatively safe, but oestrogenic types are hazardous for some girls, such as those on anti-coagulation therapy for prosthetic valves or arrhythmias. A progesterone-only pill may reduce the risk of thromboembolic risks, but has a higher failure rate (Tong and Sparacino, 1994).

Similarly there is some debate about the use of oral contraceptives in girls with cystic fibrosis (CF). The progesterone component of these pills is a respiratory stimulant and can increase production and viscosity of mucus, consequently having adverse effects on pulmonary function. Safer options are condoms and barrier methods, but these obviously require compliance and may prove potentially difficult for some young people (Kotloff et al., 1992).

Other important issues that some young people have to cope with are impotence and infertility. Although puberty and sexual maturation can be normal in sickle cell disease, boys may be impotent as a result of priaprism, caused by sickling in blood cells of the penis (Letsky, 1986). In CF, boys are almost always infertile. In more that 95% of CF males, there is absence or atresia of all structures — the epididymis, vas deferens and seminal vesicles (Walters and Hodson, 1989; Kotloff et al., 1992). As a result of this, transport of sperm from the testes to the urethra is impeded.

The majority of girls with CF have near to normal fertility. Girls have normal reproductive tracts, but infertility may occasionally be associated with anovulatory cycles as a result of advanced disease and low body weight. A more common problem is due to altered chemical composition of cervical mucus, whereby the water content is reduced, resulting in a thick mucous plug that blocks the passage of sperm. Increased sodium reabsorption appears to be responsible for this thickening (Kotloff et al., 1992).

When fertility is unaffected by chronic illness, pregnancy is not always a viable option for some young women, owing to increased risks associated with cardiovascular and metabolic alterations that occur in pregnancy. In sickle cell disease many complications can occur in pregnancy, resulting in an increase in fetal loss and maternal morbidity and mortality without appropriate care (Letsky, 1986). Maternal risks are also increased in some cardiopulmonary disorders. Cardiovascular changes that occur in pregnancy include an increased circulating blood volume, by an average of 50%, and a subsequent increase in cardiac output. Alterations in respiratory function include increased resting minute ventilation (Kotloff et al., 1992; Tong and Sparacino, 1994). For young women with congenital heart disease, evaluation of whether pregnancy will be tolerated is dependent upon whether the right side of the heart can cope with the increased blood volume of pregnancy (Tong and Sparacino, 1994). For those who may have undergone surgical correction with prosthetic heart valves, there are further complications to be considered, such as anticoagulation therapy. The risk to the fetus is high, with warfarin causing fetal haemorrhage and wastage (McColgin et al., 1989). It is expected that one third of all pregnancies will be affected by women who took warfarin in early pregnancy, resulting in spontaneous abortion or an abnormal infant.

Other ill effects to the fetus can be caused by reduction of uterine blood flow, owing to a relatively fixed cardiac output, as from a distal valve prosthesis or reduced oxygen transportation caused by cyanosis (McColgin et al., 1989; Tong and Sparacino, 1994). Again, this can result in low birthweight babies, retarded fetal growth and a higher percentage of fetal wastage. Pregnancy therefore needs to be carefully assessed and planned, with counselling beginning before pregnancy. Assessment includes the type of cardiac lesion present, whether or not it has been surgically corrected, cardiac status and risks of heart disease in the fetus (Ramin et al., 1989).

The incidence of congenital heart disease is calculated at 4.05 to 10.20 per 1000 live births, and risk of transmission varies according to the type of defect present (Tong and Sparacino, 1994). Pregnancy in young women with CF also needs careful assessment. Where pre-gravid status is severely compromised by cor pulmonale, hypoxaemia and malnutrition, young women are at high risk for deterioration of their condition and fetal loss, should they become pregnant. In these instances pregnancy should be discouraged (Kotloff *et al.*, 1992). However, for women with mild disease and a good nutritional status, it has been shown that pregnancy is well tolerated. Cohen *et al.* (1980), in a national survey of CF and pregnancy in the USA, found that out of a total of 129 pregnancies, 86 viable infants were born. However, the majority of these women had been diagnosed at a later age than average, with a mean age of diagnosis of 11 years.

As well as considering the impact of chronic physical illness on sexual development, it is also important to acknowledge some of the problems young people with learning difficulties experience on reaching sexual maturity.

When a child becomes ill or has a disability, parents are required to cope with a situation for which they may have had little preparation. They are likely to be thrust into a state of shock and experience many conflicting emotions. Most importantly the desire to protect the child can be overwhelming, when she/he is rendered vulnerable by disease or disability. This includes protection from sexual exploitation.

A study of the control of sexuality in young people with Down syndrome (Shepperdson, 1995) found no consensus amongst parents or carers as to how sex education should be taught. Kreutner (1981) has argued that sexual problems experienced by young people with learning difficulties are only tackled when physical attributes develop, and then the major focus for parents and professionals is the prevention of pregnancy.

Shepperdson's (1995) retrospective study of a 1960s and 1970s cohort of young people with Down syndrome found, amongst parents of the 1960s cohort, a unanimous decision to stop pregnancy. A high proportion of parents and carers were also willing to consider sterilisation as an option. Shepperdson (1995) draws attention to the practical and ethical dilemmas for parents, and the unresolved conflict between their need to protect and the desire for freedom of sexual expression by the young people involved in the study.

Although the study demonstrated that parental attitudes became more permissive over time, few parents encouraged sexual expression amongst their daughters and sons, and generally parents were unwilling to allow their attitudes to be translated into action. With regard to the young person's sexual activity, few had had any sexual experience, mainly because they were hardly ever left unsupervised.

CONCLUSION

The intention of this chapter has been to raise awareness of the effects that physiological problems can have upon developing sexual identity. Regardless of the age at which problems may occur, with many of the disorders described here there is the potential not only for impairment of sexual function but also for psychological damage. 'Sexuality' is not, as society would have us believe, something we acquire at puberty, but is an integral part of our individual identity; it is a complex process which begins at the moment of conception. If we can accept this, then perhaps we are more likely to appreciate the wider-reaching effects of sexual health problems for all pre-adolescents and young people in our care, and not just a select few.

ACKNOWLEDGEMENTS

I would like to acknowledge the support I received when writing this chapter. My thanks go to: Mr DCS Gough, Consultant Paediatric Urologist, Royal Manchester Children's Hospital; Peter Abrahams, formerly Pharmacist with Withington Hospital, South Manchester; Carol Tristan, Staff Nurse, Adolescent Unit, Christie Hospital, Manchester; and to Martin Gahan, who typed the manuscript.

REFERENCES

Barnes ND (1986) Metabolic and endocrine disorders. In: Roberton NRC (ed.) *Textbook of Neonatology.* Edinburgh: Churchill Livingstone.

Berhman RE, Kliegman RM, Nelson WE, Vaughan VC (eds) (1992) Nelson *Textbook of Pediatrics,* 14th edn. Philadelphia: WB Saunders Co.

Black JA, Whitfield MF (1991) Genitourinary emergencies and ambiguous genitalia. In: *Neonatal Emergencies. Early Detection and Management,* 2nd edn. Oxford: Butterworth Heinemann.

Blair JD (1995) In: Reed GB, Claireaux AE, Cockburn F (eds) *The Reproductive Systems in Diseases of the Fetus and Newborn,* 2nd edn, chap. 37. London: Chapman & Hall.

Brook CGD, Stanhope R (1989) Normal puberty: physical characteristics and endocrinology. In: *Clinical Paediatric Endocrinology,* 2nd edn. Oxford: Blackwell Scientific Publications.

Buckler JMH (1994) *Growth Disorders in Children.* London: British Medical Journal.

Byrd R (1985) Late effects of treatment of cancer in children. *Pediatric Clinics of North America* 32(3), 835–850.

Cardwell Hagenah G, Harrigan JF, Campbell MA (1984) Inflammatory bowel disease in children, Symposium of Inflammatory Bowel Disease. *Nursing Clinics of North America* 19(1), 27–39.

Carola R, Harley JP, Noback CR (1992) *Human Anatomy and Physiology,* 2nd edn. New York: McGraw-Hill.

Cilento BG, Majjar SS, Atala A (1993) Cryptorchidism and testicular torsion. *Pediatric Clinics of North America* 40(6), 1133–1149.

Cohen LF, Di Sant' Agenese PA, Friedlander J (1980) Cystic fibrosis and pregnancy. A national survey. *Lancet* 2, 842–844.

Danish RK (1992) Abnormalities of sexual differentiation. In: Fanaroff AA, Martin RJ (eds) *Neonatal and Perinatal Medicine. Diseases of the Fetus and Infant,* 5th edn. St Louis: Mosby.

Emery AEH, Müller RF (1988) *Elements of Medical Genetics,* 7th edn. Edinburgh: Churchill Livingstone.

Folb PI (ed.) (1988) Cytostatic and immunosuppressive drugs. In: *Meyler's Side Effects of Drugs.* 11th edn. Elsevier Science Publications.

Gamblian V, Bivens K, Burton KS, Hoell Kistler C, Kleeman T, Freije MM, Prows C (1993) Assessment and management of endocrine disfunction. In: Kenner C, Brueggemeyer A, Porter Gunderson L (eds) *Comprehensive Neonatal Nursing. A Physiologic Perspective.* Philadelphia: WB Saunders Co.

Garralda ME (1994) Chronic physical illness and emotional disorder in childhood. Where the brain's not involved, there may still be problems (editorial). *British Journal of Psychiatry* **164**, 8–10.

Gordon M, Crouthamel C, Post EM, Richman RA (1982) Psychosocial aspects of constitutional short stature: social competence, behaviour problems, self-esteem, and family functioning. *The Journal of Pediatrics* **101**(3), 477–480.

Harvey MH, Johnstone MJS, Fossard DP (1985) Inguinal herniotomy in children: a five year survey. *British Journal of Surgery* **72**, 485–487.

Hindmarsh PC, Brook CGD (1989) Tall stature. In: Brook CGD (ed.) *Clinical Paediatric Endocrinology,* 2nd edn. Oxford: Blackwell Scientific Publications.

Huffman JW, Dewhurst Sir CJ, Capraro VJ (1981) *The Gynaecology of Childhood and Adolescence,* 2nd edn. Philadelphia: WB Saunders Co.

Jones SL (1994) Assisted reproductive technologies: genetic and nursing implications. *Journal of Obstetric, Gynaecologic and Neonatal Nursing* **23**(6), 492–497.

Koeppel KM (1995) Sperm banking and patients with cancer. Issues concerning patients and healthcare professionals. *Cancer Nursing* **18**(4), 306–312.

Kotloff RM, Fitzsimmons SC, Fiel SB (1992) Fertility and pregnancy in patients with cystic fibrosis. *Clinics in Chest Medicine* **13**(4), 623–635.

Kreutner AK (1981) Sexuality, fertility and the problems of menstruation in mentally retarded adolescents. *Pediatric Clinics of North America* **28**(2), 475–480.

Lee PA (1990) Disorders of puberty. In: Lifshitz F (ed.) *Pediatric Endocrinology. A Clinical Guide,* 2nd edn. New York: Marcel Dekker.

Letsky EA (1986) Sickle cell and thalassaemia. In: Curtis S (ed.) *From Asthma to Thalassaemia. Medical Conditions in Childhood.* British Agencies for Adoption and Fostering.

Leventhal BG, Halperin EG, Torano AE (1996) The testes. In: Schwartz CL, Hobbie WL, Constine LS, Ruccione KS (eds) *Survivors of Childhood Cancer. Assessment and Management.* St Louis: Mosby.

Ludderjackson P, Ott MJ (1990) Perceived self-esteem among children diagnosed with precocious puberty. *Journal of Pediatric Nursing* **5**(3), 190–203.

Marshall WJ (1992) *Illustrated Textbook of Clinical Chemistry,* 2nd edn. London: Gower Medical Publishing.

Martindale W (1993) Antineoplastic agents and immunosuppressants. *Extra Pharmacopoeia,* 30th edn. London: The Pharmaceutical Press.

McColgin SW, Martin JN, Morrison JC (1989) Pregnant women with prosthetic heart valves. *Clinical Obstetrics and Gynaecology* **32**(1), 76–88.

Meistrich ML (1993) Potential genetic risks using semen collected during chemotherapy. *Human Reproduction* **8**(1), 8–10.

Moore KL (1988) *The Developing Human. Clinically Oriented Embryology,* 4th edn. Philadelphia: WB Saunders Co.

Moshang Jr. T, Thornton PS (1994) Endocrine disorders in neonatology. In: Avery GB, Fletcher MA, MacDonald MG (eds) *Pathophysiology and Management of the Newborn,* 4th edn. Philadelphia: JB Lippincott Co.

Muller J, Graem N (1993) The reproductive system. In: *Fetal and Neonatal Pathology,* 2nd edn. London: Springer-Verlag.

Navot D, Laufer N, Kopolovic J, Rabinowitz R, Burkenfeld A, Lewin A, Granat M, Margalioth EJ, Shenker JG (1986) Artificially induced endometrial cycles and establishment of pregnancies in the absence of ovaries. *New England Journal of Medicine* **314**(13), 806–811.

Page J (1994) The newborn with ambiguous genitalia. *Neonatal Network* 13(5), 15–21.

Parkin JM (1989) The short child. In: Brook CGD (ed.) *Clinical Paediatric Endocrinology*, 2nd edn. Oxford: Blackwell Scientific Publications.

Ramin SM, Maberry MC, Gilstrap LC (1989) Congenital heart disease. *Clinical Obstetrics and Gynaecology* 32(1), 41–47.

Retik AB, Keating M, Mandell J (1988) Complications of hypospadias repair. *Urologic Clinics of North America* 15(2), 223.

Reynolds JM, Wood AJ, Eminson DM, Postlethwaite RJ (1995) Short stature and chronic renal failure: what concerns children and parents? *Archives of Disease in Childhood* 73, 36–42.

Savage MO (1989) Clinical aspects of intersex. In: Brook CGD (ed.) *Clinical Paediatric Endocrinology*, 2nd edn. Oxford: Blackwell Scientific Publications.

Scherer LR, Grosfeld JL (1993) Inguinal hernias and umbilical anomalies. *Pediatric Clinics of North America* 40(6), 1121–1131.

Sheldon CA, Duckett JW (1987) Hypospadias. *Pediatric Clinics of North America* 34(5), 1259–1272.

Shepperdson B (1995) The control of sexuality in young people with Down's Syndrome. *Child: Care, Health and Development* 21(5), 333–349.

Sparacino LL (1984) Psychological considerations for the adolescent and young adult with inflammatory bowel disease. *Nursing Clinics of North America* 19(1), 41–49.

Stock JA, Schertz HC, Kaplan GW (1995) Distal hypospadias. *Urologic Clinics of North America*. 22(1), 131–138.

Sugar EC, Firlit CF, Reisman M (1993) Pediatric hypospadias surgery. *Pediatric Nursing* 19(6), 585–588.

Taylor DL, Eminson DM (1994) Psychological aspects of chronic physical illness. In: Rutter M, Taylor E, Herson L (eds) *Child and Adolescent Psychiatry. Modern Approaches*, 3rd edn. Oxford: Blackwell Scientific Publications.

Tong E, Sparacino PSA (1994) Special management issues for adolescents and young adults with congenital heart disease. *Critical Care Nursing Clinics of North America* 6(4), 199–214.

Torano AE, Halperin EG, Leventhal BG (1996) The ovary. In: Schwartz CL, Hobbie WL, Constine LS, Ruccione KS (eds) *Survivors of Childhood Cancer. Assessment and Management*. St Louis: Mosby.

Vockrodt L, Williams JK (1994) A reproductive option for women with Turner's syndrome. *Journal of Pediatric Nursing* 9(5), 321–325.

Wales JKH, Rogol AD, Wit JM (1996) *Colour Atlas of Pediatric Endocrinology and Growth*. London: Mosby-Wolfe.

Walters S, Hodson M (1989) *Fertility, Pregnancy and Contraception in Cystic Fibrosis*. Kent, Bromley Cystic Fibrosis Research Trust.

Wheeler MD, Styne DM (1990) Diagnosis and management of precocious puberty. *Pediatric Clinics of North America* 37(6), 1255–1271.

Williams JK (1992) School-aged children with Turner's syndrome. *Journal of Pediatric Nursing* 7(1), 14–19.

Williams I, Earles AN, Pack B (1985) Psychological considerations in sickle cell disease, Symposium on Sickle Cell Disease. *Nursing Clinics of North America* 18(1), 215–229.

FURTHER READING

Brook CGD (ed.) (1989) *Clinical Paediatric Endocrinology*, 2nd edn. Oxford: Blackwell Scientific Publications.

Ludderjackson P, Ott MJ (1990) Perceived self-esteem among children diagnosed with precocious puberty. *Journal of Pediatric Nursing* 5(3), 190–203.

Moore KL (1988) *The Developing Human. Clinically Oriented Embryology*, 4th edn. Philadelphia: WB Saunders Co.

Page J (1994) The newborn with ambiguous genitalia. *Neonatal Network* 13(5), 15–21.

Reed GB, Claireaux AE, Cockburn F (eds) (1995) *Disease of the Fetus and Newborn*, 2nd edn. London: Chapman & Hall.

Rutter M, Taylor E, Herson L (eds) (1994) *Child and Adolescent Psychiatry. Modern Approaches*, 3rd edn. Oxford: Blackwell Scientific Publications.

Schwartz CL, Hobbie WL, Constine LS, Ruccione KS (eds) (1996) *Survivors of Childhood Cancer. Assessment and Management*. St Louis: Mosby.

Williams JK (1992) School-aged children with Turner's syndrome. *Journal of Pediatric Nursing* 7(1), 14–19.

Chapter 6

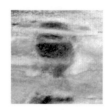

GENDER, SEX AND HEALTH

BRUCE LINDSAY BA RSCN

KEY POINTS

- ○ PROBLEMS IN DEFINING 'SEX' AND 'GENDER'
- ○ THE RELATIONSHIP BETWEEN SEX, GENDER AND HEALTH
- ○ 'FAMILY-CENTRED CARE': ITS INFLUENCE ON APPROACHES TO SEX AND GENDER ISSUES IN CHILD HEALTH
- ○ DEVELOPING A FRAMEWORK FOR CHILD HEALTH CARE

- ○ GENDER ROLES IN THE PROVISION OF CHILD HEALTH CARE
- ○ A PROPOSAL FOR THE CONSIDERATION OF GENDER, SEX AND SEXUALITY IN CHILD CARE NURSING

Existing literature about gender and sex in health care presents us with a complex set of theories, offered from a wide range of perspectives. In support of these theories research studies provide evidence of inequalities in health, in the receipt of health care, and in the outcomes of health care, which appear to arise from differences in sex or gender. Such research evidence is not yet conclusive in terms of the precise nature and effect of these differences, but it does offer sufficient evidence to suggest that all child health professionals should take gender and sex into account when planning and implementing care.

This chapter will consider existing evidence relating to gender, sex and health in children and adolescents, drawing the varied strands of the debate together to produce some suggestions for the incorporation of the evidence into child care nursing practice. In particular it will critically appraise the current most popular approach to child health care, the concept of 'family-centred care', with regard to its impact on and perpetuation of gender bias. The discussion will suggest that despite the growing awareness of the effect of sex and gender on health and health care the philosophy of family-centred care as it is put into practice fails to take these factors into account and, as a result, fails to offer a genuinely contemporary approach to child health care.

WHAT ARE WE TALKING ABOUT?

Mahowald (1996: 22) uses the word 'sex' to refer to '(relatively) permanent biological characteristics and functions that distinguish men and women', the term 'gender' to refer to 'socially induced behaviours' and the phrase 'sex roles' to mean 'socially induced or gender-based behaviours'. Giddens (1993: 162) offers a similar differentiation: 'sex refers to physical differences of the body, gender concerns the *psychological, social and cultural* differences between males and females'.

Archer suggests that 'sex' refers to 'the binary categories of male and female' and 'gender' to 'the "fuzzy" categories of masculine and feminine' (1992: 31). For Taylor and Field (1993: 71–72), sex 'concerns biological or anatomical differences that are universal and unchanging', while gender 'refers to the culturally-specific ways in which men and women behave within any particular society or group that are learnt in the course of childhood and adult socialization'. They go further to pinpoint the differences between the concepts: 'Sex ... refers to the differences between male and female, gender to masculinity and femininity'. This final differentiation will be used here, with the terms male and female being used to refer to sex-related issues and masculine and feminine to gender-related issues.

Within nursing literature the use of terms such as 'gender' or 'sex' is rarely as clear cut as the above definitions suggest it could be. One recent nurses' dictionary views the terms as interchangeable (Duncan, 1989). Roberts (1996) notes that gender and sexuality is a 'complex and contentious issue, and it is wise for those concerned with patient care in this area to read widely around the subject', but adds to the confusion by suggesting that gender can be defined as *either* chromosomal, gonadal, phenotypic or behavioural sex.

None of the three most recent comprehensive children's nursing textbooks published in Britain adequately define 'gender' (Campbell and Glasper, 1995; Carter and Dearmun, 1995; McQuaid *et al.*, 1996). Indeed, the term is given little more than a cursory mention by any of these books and detailed discussion on the possible effects of gender or sexuality on health or health care does not take place.

Sexuality is also a term which is inadequately defined within nursing. Batcup and Thomas (1994) recognise this difficulty with definition, although they fail to resolve it themselves. They also indicate the importance of these concepts to nursing care, stressing in doing so the crucial role an understanding of them must play. Batcup and Thomas also note that there has been a great increase in nursing literature relating to gender and sexuality in recent years. This increase does not, however, appear to have occurred in child care nursing. Undoubtedly there is a body of literature about sexuality and gender in child health care, but it is small, and often fails to consider these subjects in detail, preferring instead to focus on them, and sexuality in particular, when they are seen as 'problems' in specific situations. Does this lack of discussion stem from a view of children as somehow 'neutral' beings, or from a view of child health care as a 'gender-free' or 'sexuality-free' activity?

Historically, child health care has neglected issues of gender, sex and sexuality. But it is also true that historically the client group was much more restricted than it is today. Child health professionals were, until relatively recently, concerned with children no older than 10 or 12 years of age. When one takes into account the slightly later onset of puberty in previous decades, it is easy to see that sexually mature individuals, or even pubescent individuals, would have formed a small minority of a child health professsional's workload. This is not to excuse the lack of consideration, but it does help to explain it. Modern child health professionals are constantly caring for sexually mature young people, both as patients or clients, and also as the parents of younger children: a failure to accept gender, sex and sexuality as important aspects of our care is now even less acceptable.

It is worth remembering that one of the most fundamental divisions in society, and particularly in health care, is what Riska refers to as 'the sexual division of labour in the sphere of reproduction' (1993: 4). This division is inextricably linked with divisions made in terms of gender and has repercussions for all aspects of child health care. Much current thinking about child health care centres on the effect of separation from the mother. The woman's role in reproduction has been an important factor in the place of women in the hierarchies of the health care professions, and the existence of families led by lesbian or gay couples is often condemned because such a setup precludes 'normal' child-bearing. But as Riska notes, this sexual division of labour has only recently been seen as a problem.

THE RELATIONSHIP BETWEEN SEX, GENDER, SEXUALITY AND HEALTH

When does a child become a 'boy'? When does a child become a 'girl'? At the point of conception we are differentiated in terms of sex, in terms of physiological characteristics which do not at that point exist but which will appear as the child develops. As soon as a child's biological sex is known to others, differentiation according to gender can, and does, begin.

On the birth of a child the first piece of information normally given is whether the infant is a girl or a boy. Where more sophisticated pre-natal investigations exist this information may well be given to the inquiring parent during pregnancy. This first assignment of the label 'boy' or 'girl' results from observation of external genitalia: it is based on physiology, and is a decision regarding the child's sex. Once a particular sex has been ascribed to a child then the gendering of that child begins. Birth is 'the moment in which biological characteristics are invoked to assign the new individual to a gender category' (Lloyd and Duveen, 1991: 283). I would suggest that the child's health care needs also become gendered at that moment.

Because the allocation of a biologically defined sex and a socially defined gender occur almost simultaneously in modern Western societies, the task of differentiating the effects that sex and gender have on health care needs and health care provision becomes extremely difficult. In many cases, particularly in practice when such differentiation is unlikely to be given a high priority, it may be impossible to separate the two influences. However, an awareness of the possible effects should always influence the professional's assessment of a child's needs.

But what influences may sex or gender exert? Evidence does suggest that boys and girls, in all age groups, access health services differently. In their review of recent literature Eiser *et al.* (1995) note that teenage girls report more physical symptoms than boys, and more psychological symptoms than boys. They also note that girls are more likely to go to a doctor as a result of their symptoms, regardless of what those symptoms may be, but caution that these differences may be less to do with gender or sex and more to do with variations in self-image (although these variations may in themselves be linked to gender). It also seems that in certain aspects of health care boys and girls are treated differently by health professionals, while outcomes also vary between boys and girls for specific health problems. But to what extent are these differences due to sex or to gender?

REFLECTION POINT

Do you deal differently with children according to whether they are seen as boys or girls?

In many cases sex-related differences are clear, and their existence is acknowledged and accepted by child health professionals. This acceptance perhaps reflects a view of physiology as a discipline which produces hard evidence about our bodies: facts about our metabolism, our bone structure, our reproductive organs. Gender differences are less easily identified, acknowledged or accepted. Gender differences belong to the disciplines of psychology, sociology and other 'soft' disciplines: fields of study which are less accepted by many nurses than the hard sciences and, therefore, which produce research findings which are less easily accepted. Interestingly, Hicks (1996) suggests that research findings are themselves affected by gender stereotypes. Hicks notes that the qualities seen as required by a good researcher are 'archetypally feminine for nursing yet archetypally masculine for research' (p. 1006), a polarisation which she sees as explaining at least partly nurses' own undervaluing of nursing research.

SEX, GENDER AND ILL-HEALTH

Of all the supposed 'facts' quoted in the debate on sex, gender and health, the commonest and perhaps best known is the one which states that women live longer than men. The life expectancy for children born in the UK between 1985 and 1990 is 78.1 years for girls and 72.4 years for boys (Lloyd, 1995). For some, this single statistic is proof that males are less healthy, or less well served by the health care system, than women.

Others counter this assertion by emphasising that women make more use of the health care services during their lives, indicating higher levels of morbidity in women than in men.

For example, in the UK during 1990 males made a total of 67 million visits to general practitioners, while females made 143 million visits (Lloyd, 1995). In the under-16 age group, however, boys are more likely to attend hospital outpatient departments and to be admitted as inpatients (Lloyd, 1995).

These supposed facts are, of course, open to criticism on a number of fronts. With regard to women's supposed longevity in comparison to men, it has been noted that this is predominantly a Western phenomenon, and even here it is a relatively recent occurrence. In many countries today women's life expectancy is markedly lower than men's, due to a number of factors including high levels of mortality during pregnancy and childbirth. Pregnancy and childbirth may also be responsible for the greater use of health services by women rather than men in developed countries, leading to debate about whether this is genuinely a reflection of greater female morbidity, or of differences in biological function. Certainly, the evidence is not yet clear enough to be unequivocal, and it may still be used to support many viewpoints, some of which are more dubious than others.

Sex-related health problems, that is, problems linked directly to physiology, are often easily identifiable. Problems of the reproductive organs, such as hypospadias, torsion of the testis, or ovarian cysts, are readily identifiable examples of this, each affecting only males or only females. However, many more health problems affect boys and girls differently, and these differences cannot so easily be allocated to differences of sex. Pyloric stenosis, for example, affects five times as many boys as girls: this statistic is readily acknowledged as identifying a difference of incidence according to the sex of a child, but it does not prove a variation which is a result of that difference in sex.

SEX AND GENDER AWARENESS IN HEALTH CARE PROVISION

When does a health professional become aware of a child being a boy or a girl? In most cases, just as at the birth of a child, this is one of the first pieces of information which is sought and given. Indeed, when a child is admitted to hospital as an emergency the child's age and sex are often known before the child's name. But when does such information become necessary, and how may an awareness of a child's sex or gender help to improve health care?

Professionals' responses to children do seem in many instances to be based on boy/girl differentiation. Often this differentiation has clinical value, the possible causes of abdominal pain, for example, include some which are specific to boys or to girls and an effective assessment will take such a factor into account. In other cases such differentiation is of more questionable worth, for example when allocating children to 'Mr Men' or 'Little Miss' beds on a ward according to masculine/feminine divisions.

The first of the above examples is one of sex differentiation, the second is one of gender differentiation. Is it therefore true to say that sex differentiation is useful for the professional and beneficial to the child, while gender differentiation is not? Such a statement would be a gross oversimplification: the reality is much more complex.

Effective care, in terms of sex and gender awareness, involves both the conscious aware-ness of sex and gender and an understanding of when their recognition is of relevance and when it is not. It also involves an awareness that we are not simply concerned with the child's sex or gender, but also with those of the carers, family or otherwise. Child health care is so multifaceted that the roles of sex and gender within it cannot be considered solely in terms of the sex or gender of the child.

GENDERING CARE: FAMILY-CENTRED CARE AND GENDER ROLES

Child health care is 'family-centred': contemporary literature continually reinforces this belief, which has developed in recent decades from the work of Bowlby and Robertson, through the research and theorising of numerous health care professionals. Family-centred care is now accepted by health care organisations, by pressure groups and the voluntary sector, and by governments as the ideal framework within which to provide health care for children. The child is seen as 'indivisible from the family unit' and child health professionals, especially child care nurses, have the 'concept of family-centred care as [their] guiding light' (Glasper, 1995: 24).

Family-centred care is far from being a consistent, clearly defined concept, despite its widespread acceptance as a framework for child health care. Definitions do exist. For example, Sidey (1995: 35) suggests that family-centred care occurs 'when carers, and when possible the sick child, are involved as active partners with the health care professionals in management, decision making, treatment and care', while Campbell defines the term as care 'where the needs of all family members are considered during childhood illness' (1995: 26). Smith (1996: 141) identifies the main theme of family-centred care as the focusing of care around the needs of children and their families but acknowledges that the concept is 'a well-used but poorly defined idea'.

REFLECTION POINT

What does 'the family' mean to you? Is your concept the same as those of your friends and colleagues?

It may be assumed that the concept of 'the family' is crucial to any understanding of family-centred care. But the proponents of family-centred care tend to steer clear of defining the family. One commentator actually suggests that a central concept of family-centred care is that 'It accepts the family's own definition of what constitutes "family"' (Campbell, 1995: 28).

For other commentators the family is, amongst other things, an institution which con-tinues to emphasise gender divisions and inequalities to the detriment of women and chil-dren. Burman (1994) notes the traditional image of the nuclear family as a fiction on the one hand but yet still at the centre of social policy (which includes health care policies) in Western societies. These policies then help to reinforce the notion of women as economically dependent on men and children as the property of their parents. Assumptions about the family and its importance, especially those held by the political right, ignore much of the research evidence, ignore the diversity of family structures which can be found in Western societies, and 'legitimise the maintenance of traditional gender and age roles' (Burman, 1994: 67).

Other concepts dear to many child health professionals, and indeed to the philosophy of family-centred care, have also been implicated in what critics see as the perpetuation of gender divisions. Mother–infant bonding, a theory which adds to the evidence for the detrimental effects of maternal deprivation, is described by Bradley (1989) as 'a myth that fully accords with tendencies for men to argue that women are better fitted than themselves to rear small babies, and to see a lack of mother-love as the main cause of children's problems' (p. 159). Burman (1994) offers an excellent discussion of the criticisms of bonding, attachment and maternal deprivation research.

However widely the acceptable definition of the 'family' may be stretched, surely some family setups must be considered unacceptable to child health professionals? Can it really be considered acceptable to support a family in which gender divisions are perpetuated by violence? Are we genuinely ensuring the best interests of a child if we allow that child to be used by a parent for sexual purposes, or to be physically abused because a parent considers the child to have an undesirable sexual orientation?

The answers may well be so obvious as to make the questions ridiculous. Of course we cannot justify violence or abuse on the grounds that it is considered acceptable family behaviour by certain members of a family. It follows therefore that family-centred care cannot get away with an unwillingness to define the family as an acceptable unit within which to promote child health care. Within the context of this chapter, such a definition must encompass issues relating to gender, sex and sexuality.

So powerful is this belief in family-centred care in Western health care systems that no discussion of gender and sex in child health can be adequately carried on without detailed analysis of the concept. But it is important to remember that family-centred care is not a universal imperative: it is not the only framework within which child care can be carried out, it is simply the one which holds sway within Western societies at the present moment. I would suggest that its current pre-eminence is itself one of the major, if not the most important, factors in the continuation of gender bias in child health.

Family-centred care reflects the society within which it has developed. It does not represent a proactive attempt to change society, or to force it to rethink its ideas of child care, child health, or indeed children or childhood. It is a conservative approach to care, based on adults' perceptions of children's needs, not on some universal and unchanging quality of childhood. As such, it falls into the trap identified by Woodhead (1991):

> *Framing professional judgements in terms of 'children's needs' serves to direct attention away from the particular adult value-position from which they are made. Projected on to children themselves, they acquire spurious objectivity.*

In this way, cultural prescriptions for childhood are presented as if they were intrinsic qualities of children's own psychological make-up.

(Woodhead, 1991: 49, my emphasis)

Phillips (1994) also comments on Woodhead's idea, stressing that both children's 'alleged best interests' and their 'alleged needs' are 'social constructions influenced by the fashionable requirements of the age' (p. 71). One of the 'fashionable requirements' of this particular age is for much of society, including much of its health care provision, to be divided along lines of gender and sex.

THE FOUNDATIONS OF FAMILY-CENTRED CARE

It is generally agreed that family-centred care is founded at least in part on the work of two researchers: John Bowlby and James Robertson. Bowlby, working in the 1940s and 1950s, produced influential work on the effects of 'maternal deprivation' on the development of the child. Robertson, who had worked with Bowlby in the early part of his career and who would later work in partnership with his wife Joyce Robertson, studied the effects of separation occasioned by hospitalisation and produced the influential film *A 2-year-old Goes to Hospital.* Gradually, over a number of years, the work of both men came to influence child health care in their native Britain and in many other countries. Open visiting, resident parents, the idea of hospital admission as a 'last resort', indeed the concept of family-centred care itself, all owe a debt to the research and writings of Bowlby and Robertson.

Agreement about the benefits of family-centred care and the other developments noted above appears to be almost universal within Western child health literature. Possibly as a result of this universal agreement the work of Bowlby and Robertson appears also to be accepted uncritically in mainstream child health literature. This uncritical acceptance, taking the work out of its historical context and assuming that it has the same value as a basis for care in the 1990s as it seemingly had in the 1950s, is conceivably one of the worst limitations on the development of truly proactive child health care. More radical child care literature has been more willing to criticise the work of these 'founding fathers' (see, for example, Burman, 1994 and Bradley, 1989). With regard to gender alone this work, and perhaps more importantly the way in which the work has been co-opted into the development of child health care practice, deserves further analysis.

In both Bowlby's and Robertson's research the effects of separating a mother and child receive close consideration. My own experience suggests that their work seems best recollected by child health professionals in terms of their evidence relating to mother–child separation. Bowlby's 'maternal deprivation' and Robertson's filmed evidence of the emotional upset occasioned by the separation of mother and toddler are both accorded almost legendary status by child health students, even if little else of their work can be brought to mind.

But there is much more to the work of Bowlby and Robertson. Bowlby's early work on juvenile delinquency, *Forty-four Juvenile Thieves* (1946), certainly emphasises separation from the mother as a core influence on the development of 'delinquent character', but he also recognises other possible factors, including hostile fathers and traumatic life events, as of importance in the production of 'maladapted children'. Furthermore, Bowlby emphasises that it is *prolonged* separation which creates problems, and defines this as '(*six months or more*) ... during their first five years of life' (Bowlby, 1946: 55).

Bowlby's work was published at a time when British society was undergoing a major upheaval following the end of the Second World War. Men returning from war service found themselves facing unemployment and the Government found itself with a possible social problem to deal with. Research which suggested a link between absent mothers and abnormal child development offered an opportunity for the government to promote the notion of 'a woman's place is in the home', and helped to encourage married women to give up paid employment in favour of full-time motherhood (Burman, 1994). Bowlby's findings thus appeared at an opportune time for the British Government, and also perhaps for Bowlby, for without the problem of male unemployment his work may not have gained the influence it did eventually achieve.

Robertson also considers far more factors than separation from the mother in his work on hospitalisation. The hospital ward to which Laura, the 2-year-old girl who is the subject of Robertson's film, is admitted is an environment devoid of much more than Laura's mother. This ward lacks toys and games, interaction with other children, interaction with adults, and, indeed, it is Laura's father who visits on the fewest occasions. Identifying the effect which separation from the mother has on Laura amongst all these other deviations from normal life is impossible.

Robertson acknowledges this himself (Robertson and Robertson, 1989), and was to follow up his early work with a project which sought to identify the effects of brief separation outside institutions. However, as James and Joyce Robertson became more widely known their work, while gaining influence, became misinterpreted by some. This misinterpretation is acknowledged by Joyce Robertson, who notes that:

> *Some people thought we were implying that mothers and young children had to be together undiluted for twenty-four hours a day for seven days a week until the child went to school.* We have never said this ...
> (Robertson and Robertson, 1989: 200, my emphasis)

Despite the complex interrelationships identified by both Bowlby and Robertson, it was the absence of the mother which was to be seen as the most vital aspect of hospital-based child care in the succeeding decades. During those years open visiting and resident mothers were encouraged by pressure groups (e.g. the National Association for the Welfare of Children in Hospital, now Action for Sick Children), often in the face of strong opposition from health care professionals. The idea of open access to children in hospital broadened out to expand beyond the basic idea of allowing the mother to stay with the child, to encompass the idea of the mother continuing to take on an active role in the care of her child.

In more recent years the idea of parental, rather than maternal, participation in care came to prominence in child health literature, reflecting changes to patterns of employment and child care in the wider society. However, the practical experience of child health professionals still suggests that mothers remain the primary carers for children. The mother is still the most likely parent to accompany a child to an appointment with the GP or outpatient department, and is still the likeliest to remain overnight with the child during an admission. In the community, the sick child is most likely to be cared for by the mother and when both parents work it is the mother who is most likely to take time off to stay at home with the child.

Burman (1994) notes that the newly acquired interest in fathers and fathering within the literature does not simply represent an acknowledgement of equality in child care. Fathers are seen as complementary to mothers, taking over to offer the mother a chance to rest, being encouraged to help with care for their own good as well as for the good of the child, choosing aspects of care which are more fun than others. The father–mother–child relationship remains an unequal one, despite what most people would see as an increasing involvement of the father in recent decades.

Developing a Framework for Health Care Practice

Adopting an 'agendered' or, as Batcup and Thomas call it (1994), a 'gender-blind' approach to health care provision would be as damaging as the inappropriate use of gender differentiation. Children live in social environments which have developed ideas of gender identities and which have sex-based expectations, and while these may not be desirable it is equally undesirable to provide care which does not take account of them. But should care which takes account of gender and sexuality seek to influence how these factors develop in a child's life (a decision which needs to be made, rather than ignored), and if so, is such an approach possible?

In answering the first part of the question, it is useful to remember that neither sexuality or gender are fixed concepts: they are not 'universally true categories' (Batcup and Thomas, 1994: 47) but ones which vary across cultures and across time. Ideas about sexuality and gender, and their application in real life, develop constantly. So if we choose to carry out the health care of children without taking sexuality or gender into account we are not simply allowing the status quo to continue, we are rather allowing change to take place without attempting to exert any influence over that change. We may also be ignoring vital aspects of that child's life to the detriment of care.

REFLECTION POINT

How have ideas about children's sexuality changed over the past 200 years? How might they change in the future? What effect do such ideas have on our expectations of health care for children?

The focus on family-centred care makes the achievement of influence highly improbable. At first, the opposite may seem to hold true: if family-centred care accepts that many different family structures are possible and satisfactory for child-rearing, then surely this acceptance enables the promotion of a wide range of gender roles, without the reinforcement of any which are detrimental to a child's development. But if the predominant family structure is one which promotes gender inequality, then it follows that in most cases family-centred care will do the same.

In the promotion of the family as central to the development of a child, and hence to that child's health and health care, proponents of family-centred care fail to identify clearly the qualities they believe a family needs to achieve its goals effectively in terms of child health care. However, there are some beliefs about the family which do seem to be implicit within family-centred care.

Statements such as – 'It is perfectly correct to emphasise that successful families may exist in a variety of forms beyond that of father, mother and 2 children'; 'It is right and proper that family-centred care should impress on nurses the importance of being open to family structures outside their own experience'; 'It would be unthinkable for child health care to be carried on without informing parents and involving them in care decisions' – are all accepted by, if not crucial to, family-centred care. Yet it would not be difficult to find informed opinion which contradicts all three statements. Many people in Western societies consider any family system which does not centre on a married, heterosexual, pair of biological parents to be abhorrent. They are also likely to consider any philosophy of care which openly promotes such family systems to be equally abhorrent, while other commentators would consider that the health care of a child is best left to professionals who need not inform or confer with parent or child.

Family-centred care therefore accepts ideas about the family and health care which are open to criticism, and which are perhaps increasingly under attack by right-wing political thought. It accepts (although it does not necessarily promote) the notion of gay or lesbian parents, of children with sexually active lives, of child-rearing outside marriage. And yet it steadfastly refuses to identify formally what it considers to be 'ideals' of family construction or function. This omission seems to have been readily accepted within the child health literature. It is as if one was to teach about cardiac rhythm by stating that everyone needs a heart which beats, but any beat will do.

I do not wish to suggest that the identification of these ideals is an easy task. It may not even be an achievable task. But it is one which should be attempted: the debate should be encouraged and used to develop child health care practices. The clarification of ideas about gender and sexuality will be central to this debate.

CHILD HEALTH CARE: PROVISION AND GENDER

The organisation of child health care is not unique in relation to the role of gender within it. Like other aspects of health care, its predominant approach is one in which decisions are made by one group of professionals and carried out by other, subordinate, groups. While the picture is slowly changing the current situation makes it clear to children and parents alike: medical men make the major decisions and women nurses, physiotherapists, care assistants or junior doctors carry them out. This perspective is so entrenched in the minds of the public, and in particular in the minds of children, that even the numerous hospital-based television series which feature male nurses or female doctors seemingly do little to alter it. Even the presence of the word 'nurse' on a man's identification badge cannot prevent greetings of 'hello doc' from parents and children.

Professional child health care promotes a picture which reinforces the traditional gender roles of parental care. The consultant 'father-figure', predominantly absent from the care environment, takes part in direct care only when it becomes too difficult for the, predominantly female, subordinate carers or when major decisions are to be made. The subordinate carers spend far more time with the child, but their roles in caring for the child are often little removed from the activities which the parents would normally carry out. These subordinate carers are not therefore seen as particularly skilled. As child health care shifts back to the community (the home) practical care devolves back to the parents. These parents find their responsibilities for the care of the child seemingly encompassing all of the activities carried out in hospital by the subordinate carers, who become even further de-skilled in the family's eyes.

A Framework for Gender, Sex and Sexuality in Child Care Nursing

If gender, sex and sexuality are to be adequately dealt with in our approaches to child health care, then they must each be given consideration as factors which may affect a child's health state, treatment and outcomes of care. Most nursing models can be said to address these factors as aspects of the patient, but few if any address them as aspects of the carers. Even where a child's gender or sex are considered by nursing models, this tends to be rather cursory, unless the health issue is one such as pregnancy or AIDS/HIV.

It can, of course, be argued that any nursing model which can apply to child health has the scope for gender, sex or sexuality to be considered in detail by any nurse who is undertaking the care of a particular child. But the lack of overt discussion about these aspects tends to give the impression that they lack the importance of other factors such as eating or eliminating. Nurses may also have ethical concerns about raising the subject of sexuality. Few nurses would have problems asking a 16-year-old how many times a month they eat burgers, but asking them how many times a month they have sexual intercourse would be seen as far more invasive a question. Similarly, nurses will happily offer advice about diet following abdominal surgery, but would be far more reluctant to offer a 16-year-old the opportunity to ask questions about returning to their normal pattern of sexual behaviour.

Research into sexuality and sexual behaviour can also be seen as more problematic than research into other aspects of behaviour. Ringheim (1995) suggests that such research raises its own particular ethical issues. Research with children and adolescents also raises its own particular issues (Taylor, 1994). Anyone wishing to undertake research into the sexual behaviour of children and adolescents must therefore confront two sets of difficulties. Such problems are also reflected in health care practice and may explain to some extent the reluctance of health professionals to involve themselves in issues related to sexuality or gender.

Certainly, cultural, religious or ideological beliefs about gender roles or sexual behaviour differ greatly and the 'balancing act' needed to deal with these issues while taking the beliefs into account is one which health care professionals find hard to achieve. However, there is evidence to suggest that many health professionals do not attempt to consider gender or sexuality when dealing with children, considering them to be somehow 'neutral' concepts (Batcup and Thomas, 1994) not warranting consideration. This notion of neutrality may reflect nurses' own social backgrounds, or it may be one which continues to be reinforced by nurses' education programmes. Whatever the reason, the notion of gender and sexuality as neutral concepts increasingly runs counter to the evidence, and results in care ignoring vital aspects of children's lives.

So how can nursing care take adequate and effective account of gender or sexuality? It is clearly not a simple task to develop a framework for this to take place. There are some general areas that can be discussed within the context of a framework, but this must be no more than a general outline of possibilities: more detailed development of such a framework needs to take place outside the confines of this chapter.

FRAMEWORK OUTLINE

Whenever anyone offers a framework for discussion there is always a danger that it will be taken as a prescription for practice. This framework is not intended in such a prescriptive fashion, it is simply a means of discussing how gender, sexuality and sex can be given due consideration in the planning and carrying out of child health care. It is offered because evidence would suggest that despite their importance these three concepts are only rarely given sufficient weight in the provision of child health care. Despite the many nursing models which are used in child health care, issues of gender and sexuality in particular seem to create problems. It should also be remembered that each child is an individual, who will not behave according to neat, over-generalised, academic notions of type.

Within this framework, consideration of sex, gender or sexuality focuses on three processes and six sources of influence. The processes are identification, assessment and integration. The sources are the child, the family, the health care team, diagnosis, treatment, and care (see Figure 1). Each will now be considered in turn.

The processes are aimed at producing a programme of care which adequately considers all aspects of gender and sexuality which may be of influence in the health care of the child. The *identification* stage concentrates on establishing which aspects of gender or sexuality are present in a given situation. The *assessment* stage aims to enable decisions as to the degree of effect each of these influences may have. At this stage irrelevant aspects can be excluded from

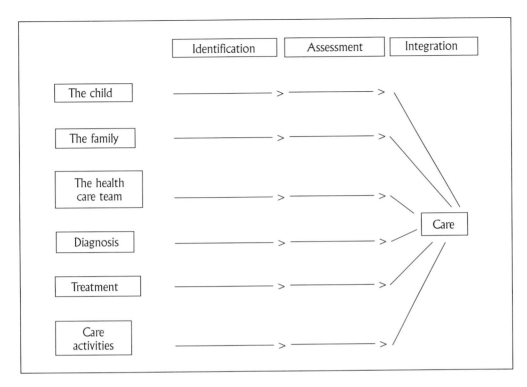

Figure 1 A framework for the consideration of gender, sex and sexuality.

further consideration. The third stage involves the *integration* of relevant aspects of gender and sexuality into the care plan, ensuring that the care encompasses both these factors as well as other more universally accepted ones.

Each process needs to be applied to each of the six sources. It is this stage which departs from most nurses', and most nursing models', ideas of care assessment which persistently focus on the child and family and on the diagnosis. Here I propose that in each individual case we need to consider the relevance of gender and sexuality not only for the child and family, but also for the professionals who will care for them and for the treatment and care strategies which they will employ.

It is worth stressing again that we are interested in *relevant* aspects of gender and sexuality. The framework must be used within the context of the child's health care problem and needs, and not every aspect of gender or sexuality will be relevant. Attempts to consider these factors without recourse to a framework of some kind may, as with other aspects of health care assessment, lead to the neglect of important issues in the child's care (Foster, 1989). A comprehensive consideration of factors such as gender and sexuality is still not easy, even if a framework is used. As I noted earlier, the nurse may have to overcome personal psychological and cultural barriers in order to carry out the process effectively. Even if the child and parents are willing to give out detailed and appropriate information, the nurse may lack the confidence and communication skills needed to ensure such information is forthcoming.

Consideration of treatment and care in this context is perhaps less threatening for the nurse, but still needs skill, knowledge and experience to be effective. Surgical procedures, diagnostic procedures, drugs and other therapies may all affect males and females differently, and not only because of biological differences. For example, the interaction of some anti-epilepsy drugs with oral contraceptive drugs means that this possibility needs to be taken into account when working with adolescent girls, but not with adolescent boys. This is not simply a sex-related difference, but is also related to sexuality.

THE HEALTH CARE TEAM

How can the team effectively consider issues of gender and sexuality in relation to children in their care? Team members may well need to discuss their own attitudes to these issues, their own gender identities, and their own feelings about sexuality and sexual behaviour, in order to develop an awareness of these aspects of the team. This is, of course, threatening to many health professionals. But without this openness the team may well fail to recognise the influence of its own members' gender identities and sexualities on those of individual children in its care. A note of caution must be injected here. It is vital that the team does not identify its own attitudes, identities and behaviours and then go on to understand them as in some way the norm, or, even worse, the ideal. Attempts to identify the team's attitudes, identities and roles will be difficult enough without then attempting to undertake an identification of their relative worth.

Some recent concerns about health care practice have led to a specific consideration of health workers' sex or gender. Problems with mixed-sex wards in mental health institutions have led to the suggestion that staff on such units need to be 'balanced' with regard to gender (Batcup and Thomas, 1994). The same suggestion could be put forward with regard to adolescent units or even for general children's wards, but debate on this point appears to be absent from the literature. However, fears about accusations against nurses of sexual abuse of children have led the Royal College of Nursing to develop policies based on the sex of staff. Recent RCN guidelines include specific advice for male nurses working with children, aimed at minimising the possibility of such accusations being made against them (Royal College of Nursing, 1996).

CONCLUSION

In recent decades many changes have come together to create a climate where issues relating to sex, gender and sexuality must now be of utmost importance in child health care. Child health professionals no longer focus on pre-adolescent individuals. Modern Western society now recognises that adolescents are, for the most part, sexually aware, if not sexually active, people. Modern health care recognises that its role is not simply to treat specific diseases, but to deal with health problems in the context of a person's lifestyle. An ever-increasing body of research suggests that gender and sexuality are aspects of life which influence, and are influenced by, health and health care.

An effective consideration of how sex, gender and sexuality may affect care must be a comprehensive one. We need to be willing and able to look beyond the child, beyond the family, to our approaches to treatment and care and to ourselves as people and as health professionals. We need to clarify our ideas about sexuality and gender, and about the 'family-centredness' of our care. None of this is easy, but all of it is relevant if we truly want to develop care which deals effectively with gender, sex and sexuality.

REFERENCES

Archer J (1992) Childhood gender roles: social context and organisation. In: McGurk H (ed.) *Childhood Social Development: Contemporary Perspectives.* Hove: Lawrence Erlbaum Associates.

Batcup D, Thomas B (1994) Mixing the genders, an ethical dilemma. *Nursing Ethics* 1(1), 44–51.

Bowlby J (1946) *Forty-four Juvenile Thieves: Their Characters and Home-life.* London: Baillière, Tindall and Cox.

Bradley BS (1989) *Visions of Infancy.* Oxford: Polity Press.

Burman E (1994) *Deconstructing Developmental Psychology.* London: Routledge.

Campbell S (1995) Family-centred care. In: Campbell S and Glasper EA (eds) *Whaley and Wong's Children's Nursing.* London: Mosby.

Campbell S, Glasper EA (eds) (1995) *Whaley and Wong's Children's Nursing.* London: Mosby.

Carter B, Dearmun AK (eds) (1995) *Child Health Care Nursing: Concepts, Theory and Practice.* Oxford: Blackwell Science.

Duncan HA (1989) Duncan's Dictionary for Nurses, 2nd edn. New York: Springer-Verlag.

Eiser C, Havermans T, Eiser JR (1995) The emergence during adolescence of gender differences in symptom reporting. *Journal of Adolescence* 18(3), 307.

Foster R (1989) Perspectives on the nursing care of children and adolescents. In: Foster R, Hunsberger M, Anderson J *Family-centered Nursing Care of Children.* Philadelphia: WB Saunders.

Giddens A (1993) *Sociology*, 2nd edn. Cambridge: Polity Press.

Glasper EA (1995) Preserving children's nursing in a climate of genericism. *British Journal of Nursing [British Journal of Children's Nursing* supplement] 4(1), 24–25.

Hicks C (1996) The potential impact of gender stereotypes for nursing research. *Journal of Advanced Nursing* 24: 1006–1013.

Lloyd B, Duveen G (1991) The reconstruction of social knowledge in the transition from sensorimotor to conceptual activity: the gender system. In: Woodhead M, Carr R, Light P (eds) *Becoming a Person.* London: Routledge.

Lloyd T (1995) *Men's Health Review.* 'Working with Men' on behalf of the Royal College of Nursing Men's Health Forum.

Mahowald MB (1996) *Women and Children in Health Care*, paperback edn. Oxford: Oxford University Press.

McQuaid L, Huband S, Parker E (eds) (1996) *Children's Nursing.* Edinburgh: Churchill Livingstone.

Phillips T (1994) Children and power. In Lindsay B (ed.) *The Child and Family: Contemporary Nursing Issues in Child Health and Care.* London: Baillière Tindall.

Ringheim K (1995) Ethical issues in social science research with special reference to sexual behaviour research. *Social Science and Medicine* 40(12), 1691–1697.

Riska E (1993) Introduction. In: Riska E, Wegar K (eds) Gender, Work and Medicine: women and the medical division of labour. London: Sage.

Roberts A (1996) Glands, gender and sexuality. *Nursing Times* 92(7), 38.

Royal College of Nursing (1996) *Protection of nurses working with children and young people* (NPC/2/96). London: Royal College of Nursing.

Siday A (1995) Community nursing perspectives. In: Carter B, Dearwin AK *Child Health Care Nursing: Concepts, Theory and Practice*. Oxford: Blackwell Science.

Smith P (1996) General concepts in child care. In: McQuaid L, Huband S, Parker E (eds) *Children's Nursing*. Edinburgh: Churchill Livingstone.

Taylor J (1994) Research and child care. In: Lindsay B (ed.) *The Child and Family: Contemporary Nursing Issues in Child Health and Care*. London: Baillière Tindall.

Taylor S, Field D (1993) *Sociology of Health and Health Care: An Introduction for Nurses*. Oxford: Blackwell Science.

Woodhead M (1991) Psychology and the cultural construction of 'children's needs'. In: Woodhead M, Light P, Carr R (eds) *Growing up in a Changing Society*. London: Routledge.

FURTHER READING

Burman E (1994) *Deconstructing Developmental Psychology*. London: Routledge.
A detailed critique of many aspects of developmental psychology, including theories which have had a profound influence on child health care.

Lindsay B (ed.) (1994) *The Child and Family: Contemporary Nursing Issues in Child Health and Care*. London: Baillière Tindall.
A reader for nurses and other child health professionals. No single chapter is devoted wholly to gender, sex or sexuality, but chapters 3, 4 and 5 are particularly relevant to a discussion of sex and gender in child care.

Mahowald MB (1996) *Women and Children in Health Care*, paperback edn. Oxford: Oxford University Press.
An up-to-date text which focuses on many issues of gender and sex of relevance to child health care.

Woodhead M, Carr R, Light P (eds) (1991) *Becoming a Person*. London: Routledge.
Another reader, with numerous chapters discussing issues of gender and sex roles in child development which have implications for child health professionals.

Chapter 7

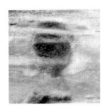

ABUSE, POWER AND SEX

LITA REASON RN RHV MSC

KEY POINTS	
○ DIFFICULTIES WITH STATISTICS	○ EFFECTS OF CHILD SEXUAL ABUSE
○ DIFFICULTIES WITH DEFINITION	
○ THEORIES ABOUT WHY CHILD SEXUAL ABUSE HAPPENS	○ ACCOMMODATION SYNDROME
	○ INTERVENTION
○ FOUR PRECONDITIONS TO CHILD SEXUAL ABUSE	○ SUPPORT FOR PROFESSIONALS
○ POWER OF ABUSER, PROFESSIONALS AND AGENCIES	

The sexual abuse of children has always been a very difficult subject. Society in general has been reluctant to acknowledge that children may be sexually abused in their own homes, by people they know, often by close relatives. Accounts reported in the newspapers of the happenings in Cleveland and the Orkneys have overshadowed advances that were made in the acknowledgement of child sexual abuse. The fact that professionals cannot agree on the incidence of child sexual abuse or on a definition is often used to discredit children and the professionals who try to help them.

This chapter seeks to give some exploration of these difficulties, consider how children get caught up in sexual abuse and why their accounts are often not believed. Some of the populist theories about child sexual abuse are described. Patterns of power and education as a contributory factor are also discussed.

It is not intended to be a definitive text on child sexual abuse, but attempts to encourage understanding of how beliefs and myths around child sexual abuse have arisen, and how practice on how to protect and help children who have been sexually abused is constantly changing as more is learnt about the subject.

EXTENT OF CHILD SEXUAL ABUSE

The sexual abuse of children has always been a controversial and emotive subject. Studies in the subject have been made since the late 1920s (e.g. Hamilton, 1929), but it was the driving force of the women's liberation movement in the 1970s that started to force child sexual abuse onto the public agenda, along with other issues such as domestic violence. Finkelhor (1984) also states that the child protection movement had an effect on this.

Child sexual abuse is a difficult subject to think about and most of us would prefer to believe it does not really occur. This is, of course, much more helpful to the abuser than to children.

Alongside the slow recognition of child sexual abuse as a social problem came a call for statistics so that the true extent of the problem could be recognised. Research has been undertaken to try and estimate how often the sexual abuse of children occurs. This has presented many difficulties. The two most common methods used have been either incidence or prevalence studies.

Incidence studies are usually undertaken by identifying the number of cases that have come to the attention of professionals or the child protection agencies. There is a general acknowledgement, however, that for numerous reasons many cases are never brought to the attention of professionals, and, therefore, these studies do not reflect the true extent of the problem.

The reasons children do not talk of their abuse are many and varied but include the fact that many children find it very difficult to talk about their abuse, many are frightened of their abusers and what may happen if they do tell, and many think nobody would believe them anyway.

DISCUSSION POINT

Why do you think children find it difficult to tell that they are being sexually abused?

Peters *et al.* (1986) made a comparison of incidence and prevalence studies and came to the conclusion that incidence studies underestimated the problem. Prevalence studies attempt to measure the prevalence of child sexual abuse through victim or offender self-reports. Prevalence studies are usually retrospective and involve asking adults about their childhood experiences. These again have proved very difficult, with no general agreement being reached on the extent of the problem; there have been some widely differing results.

There are various explanations for those differing results. One reason for the variation is that there is no real agreement on what is actually meant by child sexual abuse. In his early studies, Landis (1956) specified no definition at all; other researchers (e.g. Russel, 1983) restricted their research to activities ranging from fondling to oral/vaginal intercourse, i.e. contact abuse; other researchers include suggestions or an invitation to partake in sexual behaviour; and others such as Di Vasto *et al.* (1984) include such activities as obscene telephone calls.

Another explanation for the wide variation of results is the different samples of the population that have been used. Some have been based on college student samples, others on inpatient samples, outpatient samples or patients in general practice.

In 1985 Baker and Duncan carried out research in the UK to attempt to estimate the national prevalence of the problem. They used a definition which included contact and non-contact abuse. They reported a prevalence rate of 12% among women, but concluded, however, that their reported rate is almost certainly an underestimate.

Many writers, including Finkelhor (1986) and Kelly *et al.* (1991), have argued that the way sexual abuse is defined has an effect on prevalence estimates with narrower, restricted definitions producing lower rates. Finkelhor (1986), Vizard (1989) and others have also described how the number and phrasing of questions designed to find out the details of sexual abuse can also affect the estimate of the prevalence of child sexual abuse.

Public attention was drawn to the subject of child sexual abuse by the publicity attracted by the events in Cleveland in 1987. The Report of the Inquiry into Child Abuse in Cleveland (Department of Health and Social Security, 1988) noted that there were no reliable incidence or prevalence estimates available in this country and made a recommendation that attention be given to measuring the extent of the problem. It was felt that reliable information was needed to enable prevention, diagnosis and support services to be planned. Many people working with children who have been sexually abused echoed this. As part of a programme of research on child protection, and in response to public, professional and political concern, the Department of Health commissioned a feasibility study for a national survey of the prevalence of child sexual abuse. The findings of the feasibility study were published in 1995 and the conclusion was that it would be possible to carry out a national survey of the prevalence of child sexual abuse (Ghate and Spencer, 1995).

DEFINITION OF CHILD SEXUAL ABUSE

Alongside the difficulties associated with the problems of recognising the true extent of child sexual abuse comes the problem of definition. What do we really mean by child sexual abuse? There is no universally accepted definition. The most commonly used definition is that written by Schecter and Roberge (1976: 60) 'Sexual abuse is defined as the involvement of dependent, developmentally immature children in sexual activities that they do not fully comprehend and to which they are unable to give informed consent or that violate the social taboos of family roles'.

This definition starts to concentrate the mind on what is meant by child sexual abuse, but it does not tackle the problem of contact or non-contact. It also raises issues about family roles and a child's ability to consent to sexual contact. In reality children do not have a choice of consent. Not only do they lack the knowledge and experience of adult sexuality, but they are existing in a world where they must rely on adults to feed, clothe and shelter them;

children are taught to obey adults, and adults have power over children, no matter how powerless the adult may perceive themselves or be perceived in the wider strata of society.

La Fontaine (1990) wrote the following:

> The sexual abuse of children refers primarily to the activities of adults who use children for their sexual gratification … Sexual abuse refers to bodily contact of all sorts: fondling, genital stimulation, oral and/or anal intercourse. Some people may extend the meaning to include suggestive behaviour, sexual innuendo or exhibitionism (flashing).

This is a more detailed definition and starts to describe some of the behaviours that perpetrators might be involved in.

In their writing Driver and Droisen (1989)

> take child sexual abuse to be any sexual behaviour directed at a person under 16 without that person's consent. Sexual behaviour may involve touching parts of the child or requesting the child to touch oneself, itself or others, ogling the child in a sexual manner, taking pornographic photographs or requiring the child to look at parts of the body, sexual acts or other material in a way which is arousing to oneself; and verbal suggestions or comments to the child which are intended to threaten the child sexually or otherwise to provide sexual gratification for oneself. It must be defined by every circumstance in which it occurs: in families representative of all classes, races and social strata; in state run and private institutions; on the street; in classrooms; in pornography and films.

This is a very broad picture of sexual abuse.

Driver (Driver and Droisen, 1989) goes on to say in her notes, however, that exhibitionism is among the types of assault that is trivialised. She goes on to quote an article in *The Independent* in 1987, in which a child psychiatrist said that the much quoted figure that one in 10 children are sexually abused should be subject to scrutiny. Half of these cases of abuse involved 'flashers' and did not involve physical contact.

This is interesting as it appears professionals have a perception of a 'ranking' of sexual activity and the damage it does to children. In her interviews with professionals working in the field of child sexual abuse, Davenport (1988) found that penetration was considered the most abusive of all acts. The law would reinforce this. However, this may not always reflect the effect the act has had on the child, and does not mean that perceived 'lesser' acts of abuse should be trivialised and not taken seriously.

I recall a few years ago a young girl I know very well, who was then 12 years old, returning home from school extremely frightened and distraught. A man had stood at the window of a house she passed dressed only in a towel; on seeing her he removed the towel and exhibited himself to her. She ran all the way home, scared that the man was chasing her. She was extremely upset, and could not understand why the man had done it. A complaint by her parents to the police revealed this had happened on other occasions to other schoolgirls. Advice given by the police was not to proceed any further with the complaint, as if the case should go to court, the inference would be that the girls had in some way led this man on. Fortunately, this particular girl had family support and, although upset and withdrawn for a time, she does not appear to suffer from any long-term effects. She was able to take another route home from school, although it was much longer, but was protected from further abuse. Does the fact that she appears to suffer no long-term effects from the incident make it less abusive? She did not appear to have many rights in this case – she was the one who had to take a much longer route home or be escorted home.

This young girl was protected by her family. Society believes this is where children should be protected, but we also know a lot of child sexual abuse takes place within the family. What, then, if her family experience had been different? What would have happened to her then? What if the 'flasher' had been her father? An adult woman may have dealt with the situation differently but that is not the point, as we are discussing the effects on a child.

REFLECTION POINT

Does the fact that a child receives support and is cared for make the actual act of abuse any less abusive?

David Mann (1995) writes about ' "Sexual abuse" as any sexual behaviour from the parent which the child felt transgressed acceptable parental activities'. Although this definition only discusses sexual abuse within the family it is, at least, child-centred.

This also brings further discussion around the whole problem of definition of child sexual abuse. Whilst clear, narrower definitions may help professionals when working with child sexual abuse, how helpful will this really be to children? In fact, it could be argued that a narrower definition may be of much more use to some professionals and to some perpetrators than to the children we are seeking to protect. However, the converse of this is the fact that because at present there is no conclusive study of how often child sexual abuse occurs, the lack of agreement between the various definitions used is often quoted in arguments to minimise the number of children who are sexually abused, and to trivialise its effects.

This is, of course, not a new phenomenon. Psychoanalytical theory, especially the work of Freud, has had over the years a major impact on professional and public perception of child sexual abuse. Freud initially accepted the reality of sexual abuse encountered by some of his female patients, but later went on to deny them, and expressed a view that the experiences were most often fantasies that expressed a child's oedipal conflicts and did not really happen (Rushe, 1984). This is regarded by Conte and Burliner (1981) as having contributed to the dismissal of women's experiences of abuse to the realms of fantasy. Although this ideology perhaps has less influence than it used to, the emergence of so-called 'false memory syndrome' has come along to further complicate the issue.

The belief around 'false memory syndrome' is based on the idea that it is impossible for people to suppress memories of parts of their childhood and then recall them with any degree of accuracy. People who talk about 'false memory syndrome' argue that the memories are brought about by such things as inappropriate counselling, self-help literature or groups for survivors.

Perhaps another of the reasons people find it so difficult to believe in child sexual abuse is that only in a minority of cases is there any forensic proof or medical evidence. This means that we have to rely on the word of a child or sometimes an adult who has intervened on behalf of the child. There appears to be an unproved theory that children lie and adults speak the truth. If the abuser denies the abuse, very often the child is not believed, especially in a legal setting.

DISCUSSION POINT

Why do you think there is a mistaken belief that children lie and adults tell the truth?

A study in America by Jones and McGraw (1987) found that false allegations are rare. This study found a rate of false allegations of 1.5% but also found all the children had been previously sexually abused. However, despite all the difficulties with definition and statistics, we do know that a significant number of children are sexually abused, they are damaged by the experience, particularly emotionally, and often the damage is long term.

The Report of the Inquiry into Child Abuse in Cleveland (Department of Health and Social Security, 1988) says:

> We have learned during the Inquiry that sexual abuse occurs in children of all ages, including the very young, to boys as well as girls, in all classes of society and frequently within the privacy of the family.

EFFECTS OF CHILD SEXUAL ABUSE

One of my first experiences of working with survivors of child sexual abuse was as a generic health visitor based in a busy health centre. There were a number of people who frequently visited the doctors with anxiety, stress and depression. We tried to identify what we could offer to help these people. I decided, with another professional, to offer some group work to try and help them identify some of the sources of their stress and anxiety, and consider ways of helping them deal with this, having first consulted with them and been told by them this would be helpful.

During the course of the groups some people started to ask tentatively if things that had happened to them as children could be having an effect on them now. Six women and two men went on to disclose serious sexual abuse as children, and were offered further help and therapy. This group was not about sexual abuse, but these survivors, who were mainly middle-aged, were able to talk for the first time about their childhood abuse and its effects.

The effects of child sexual abuse have been written about extensively by professionals, researchers and survivors. Many writers have shown links between child sexual abuse and low self-esteem, inability to trust others, depression, the confusion of sex with affection which may be displayed by indiscriminate sexual activity, and difficulties in sexual relationships (Forward and Buck, 1981; Boon, 1986). Nelson (1987) noticed an increasing link between sexual abuse and eating disorders. It is being increasingly noticed that a high number of female psychiatric patients have been the victims of incest.

Children may be sexually abused by:

1. close family members, e.g. parents, grandparents, aunts, uncles, siblings, step, adoptive or foster parents
2. people well known to the family, e.g. neighbours, close family friends, parents of school friends
3. people who are in a position of trust or care, e.g. teachers, doctors, nurses, psychiatrists, psychologists, residential social workers
4. people who run organisations or clubs for children, e.g. cubs, brownies, Sunday schools, sports teams
5. strangers, e.g. in the street or the park.

There has been debate about which may have the most harmful effect emotionally to the child. It would appear that many factors may influence this. Finkelhor (1979) and Russel (1986) felt that abuse by a close relative, especially if they were in a caring role, may have the most harmful effects. However, it would seem that no direct correlation between the closeness of the relationship and the effect on the child has really been established. In my experience the effect and quality of other non-abusing relationships has had an effect on the outcome.

Furniss (1991) described how the work of himself and others allowed a 'very careful and very preliminary conclusion' that psychological damage in sexual abuse may be related to the following factors:

1. the age at onset of abuse
2. the duration of the abuse
3. the degree of violence or threat of violence
4. the age difference between abuser and abused child
5. how closely abuser and child are related
6. the absence of protective parent figures
7. the degree of secrecy.

Secrecy is essential to child sexual abusers. This means that quite often the family setting offers the abuser the safest choice, and minimises the chances of being discovered. The abuser can control and manipulate the child, either by coercion or threats. Bentovim *et al.* (1988) found that in many cases of child abuse within the family the abuse started soon after birth, and continued throughout childhood and further. This can result in some women having their father's child, continuing to live within the family, and the abuse being perpetrated in the next generation. This may be one of the reasons some women refuse to give the name of the father of their child to midwives and health visitors, something that I have come across on frequent occasions.

The need for secrecy may be a reason why children with special needs are at particular risk of sexual abuse. McCormack (1991) wrote that the rates of abuse in handicapped people are higher than in the general population. The sexual abuse of children with special needs is gradually being recognised as a major problem and again may happen at home, school, residential home or any other setting. This is a particularly difficult fact for professionals to accept, but it is essential that they do. Children with impaired hearing appear to be particularly vulnerable and Kennedy (1989) found that up to 50% of such children had been abused at home, during transport to school, or at school. If you consider the care children with special needs may require, especially with intimate tasks such as bathing and toiletting, some understanding of their vulnerability can start to be gained. In addition, a parent's relationship with a child with disabilities may be different and become distorted. There seems to be an increasing recognition of the sexual abuse of older sons by their mothers. Even if the child with special needs recognises and is upset by his/her abuse, he/she may not have the means to tell us. It is essential that ways of communicating with these children are found, and that they are protected.

WHY DOES CHILD SEXUAL ABUSE HAPPEN?

Various theories and models have been put forward to try and explain the phenomenon of child sexual abuse. The problem of child sexual abuse has been put into different theoretical perspectives and different remedies are suggested for it.

System Model and Dysfunctional Family

Child sexual abuse as a symptom of a dysfunctional family is one way that child sexual abuse has been viewed. This particularly concentrates the attention on sexual abuse perpetrated by parents and other family members. It takes the view that incest is a product of family pathology and that, except on the rarest of occasions, all family members contribute in some way to the pathology that breeds incest (de Young, 1982).

The theory of family dysfunction developed during the 1940s and there is a large volume of literature that uses this theory to explain familial child sexual abuse and its treatment. In nearly all family systems models the families are described as patriarchal and authoritarian. Fathers are often described as using force to exert control over their wives, and often also over their children. Mothers are often described as being emotionally absent or withdrawn. This leaves the children vulnerable to a powerful man, although he may not be seen as powerful outside the family.

Furniss (1991) also describes a theory of family function of child sexual abuse. He talks about child sexual abuse as 'conflict avoider' and 'conflict regulator'. Furniss describes emotional and sexual difficulties being controlled by the development of inappropriate sexual and emotional bonds with the children. He argues that some families use this to avoid conflict, e.g. if marital or sexual estrangement threatens to break up the family, and the family members cannot cope with this or do not recognise its reality, incest may arise between father and daughter, removing one source of stress and keeping the family held together in a veil of secrecy. The second type of family pattern Furniss describes is 'conflict regulation'. These families are frequently disorganised and violent, with weakened unclear generational boundaries and confused roles. It is argued that for these families the terror of abandonment is great and this leads them to stay together, whatever the cost.

Child Sexual Abuse as Syndrome of Addiction

Furniss (1991) describes this as being complementary to child sexual abuse as a syndrome of secrecy for the child, the abuser and the family. Furniss describes high levels of sexual arousal which lead to the need for frequent gratification and a cycle of addiction. The sexual abuse often serves to relieve tension and the child is not seen as a person but as a tool for arousal. Furniss (1991) describes the egosyntonic aspect of sexual abuse and the 'kick' the abuser gets from it (p. 33).

Paedophiles

Paedophiles are described as being sexually fixated towards children. They are increasingly organised and may be in touch with others, exchanging information and publications. Driver and Droisen (1989) describe how over recent years paedophiles have grouped together and fought for their interests as a 'politically oppressed minority'. They claim that sexual involvement with adults enriches children's lives.

Sociological

Sociologists examine the aspect of power in relationships. In society men are seen as more powerful than women; both are more powerful than children. The misuse of power of adults over children to fulfil their own needs, whilst denying the needs of children, is seen as being a contributory factor in child sexual abuse.

Feminism

Feminists argue that child sexual abuse is an expression of male dominance over women and children. Somers-Flanagan and Walters (1987) discuss child sexual abuse as being seen as an extension of male attitudes to women in a patriarchal society, in which women are regarded as the sexual property of men. To help explain why the men account for a much higher proportion of abusers feminists have looked at the process of male socialisation and sexuality.

Holloway (1984) describes *'the male sexual drive discourse'* and discusses the idea *'that men's sexuality is directly produced by a biological drive, the function of which is to ensure the reproduction of the species'*. This idea of male sexuality is one that is often used by abusers themselves to free them of responsibility for their actions. The idea that masculine sexuality is pre-determined means it is possible to circumvent questioning the processes through which male sexuality is constructed, and avoid discussing the issues which cause problems for many men. There are various accounts of the processes which construct masculine sexuality, ranging from the accounts about 'male sexual drive' to the writings of radical feminists who see masculine psychology as an organisation of forces to oppress women.

MacLeod and Saraga (1988) described how from an early age men are taught that masculinity is characterised by domination, and that sexual domination is equated with personal success. Some writers such as Eichenbaum and Orbach (1982) have discussed the negative impact of gender-differentiated child care. Seidler (1985) wrote:

> *Masculine sexual identity is established through feeling superior to women we are close to and through establishing our sense of identity in a masculine competitive world. It is as if we only know how to feel good ourselves if we put others down.*

Many feminists view the process of male socialisation and sexuality within a society that sees male sexuality as being aggressive, active and uncontrollable, whilst female sexuality is seen as being receptive and passive. Many feminists argue that in particular the family dysfunction theory allows the blame for child sexual abuse to be spread between all the family members and takes the responsibility from the abuser. They also criticise that within the family dysfunction theory there is no questioning of traditional family roles, and the belief that families are functional when men's needs are met (McLeod and Saraga, 1988).

THE EDUCATION SYSTEM

It may also be helpful to consider the roles of schools and education at this stage. Schools are institutions where children are supposed to be cared for and protected. However, a lot of research has shown that the education system can institutionalise sexism, that male pupils harass female pupils.

Equal opportunity policies that have developed in schools have concentrated on allowing particular groups of pupils to study subjects to which they have been previously denied access. Driver and Davidson (1991) query *'an equal opportunities analysis which ignores the brutality and violence underlying the relative subtlety of educational discrimination'*. They suggest that incidents in school are often *'neutralised as bullying'*, and no consideration is given to the underlying power relationships between social groups which children are acting out. They go on to argue that the surface structure of this model involves child on child violence, but that the deeper structure would be adults using their own children to manipulate the children of the subordinated social group and ensure that subordination continues from generation to generation. They argue that *we cannot stop sexual or racial oppression in society without stopping parents from using their children to perpetrate it within schools*. Many schools now have strong anti-bullying policies, but it would seem that school policies must also start to tackle the more complex issues of structuralised powers.

However, on a more personal note, for some sexually abused children school can be a place where they feel safe from the abuse that may be happening at home. Some sexually abused children distance themselves from the abuse at home by engrossing themselves in their work and perform very well at school. Others become disruptive and uncontrollable and their work deteriorates. Teachers and school nurses may be the 'trusted' professional to whom the child chooses to talk about their abuse, and it is important that professionals are familiar with their local procedures and guidelines so they know what to do if this should happen. These guidelines have been developed to avoid inappropriate handling of disclosures and it is important they are followed.

Four Preconditions to Child Sexual Abuse

One of the problems with all the theories and models about child sexual abuse is that no one theory accounts for the diverse events that practitioners see and know happen to children.

The family system model has been developed mainly from work with father–daughter sexual abuse. Theories about offenders have been developed by professionals working with men who have molested many children, often outside the family. However, we know that some children are abused by other family members, e.g. grandfathers or older brothers. We know that some women sexually abuse children. The suggestion has been made that women sexually abuse children more frequently than is supposed. Finkelhor (1984) explored this and did not find, at that time, a particularly significant amount of sexual abuse by women within or outside the family. However, knowledge on this subject is increasing and there is an awareness that the problem may be greater than once thought.

I have known three young people, a boy and two girls, who have been sexually abused by women. Their anger towards women in general mirrored the anger that children usually have towards men, when they have been sexually abused by a man. It is interesting to note, however, that none of them voiced the same amount of anger towards their fathers, for not protecting them, as children who have been sexually abused by men often voice about the failure of their mothers to protect them. It is not helpful to ignore the facts that some women do abuse children, *if we do not accept it, then we lose important links as to why child sexual abuse occurs* (MacLeod and Saraga, 1988). More literature about female child sexual abuse is slowly being published.

We also know that boys are sexually abused, and that sometimes older children sexually abuse young children. Hobbs and Wynne (1987) found that 25% of the children in Leeds diagnosed as being sexually abused were abused by teenagers. Many teenage abusers report sexual abuse as children, but not all of them.

The theories and models described also tend to ignore sociological factors. In 1984 Finkelhor developed a model that brought together knowledge about victims, offenders and families, which incorporates explanation at both psychological and sociological level and could be applied to many different types of child sexual abuse from father–daughter incest to compulsive and fixated molesting outside the family. The model is called the Four Preconditions Model of Sexual Abuse:

I. A potential offender needed to have some motivation to abuse a child sexually.
II. The potential offender had to overcome internal inhibitions against acting on the motivation.
III. The potential offender had to overcome external impediments to committing sexual abuse.
IV. The potential offender or some other factor had to undermine or overcome a child's possible resistance to the sexual abuse.

This model allows us to consider some of the information we do have about child sexual abuse.

Precondition I

Precondition I considers why a person may be motivated to have sexual contact with a child. This would include sexual gratification and the fulfilment of emotional needs for power and to degrade.

Precondition II

Precondition II considers how offenders overcome their inhibitions. Research seems to suggest that large numbers of men may be sexually aroused to children but do not act on this arousal because they are inhibited from doing this. Finkelhor says that we presume most members of society have such inhibition, but if some do not, then this also needs to be explained.

There are various ways, based both in individual behaviour and social/cultural beliefs, that offenders may overcome their internal inhibitions. Factors which assist this process include: a distorted understanding by the abuser about children's ability to consent to sex with adults; a distorted reframing of the abuse as love; a belief by the abuser that it is unlikely they will be caught; sexual imagery of children created externally through pornography or other images of children, and internally by fantasy. Readers might like to consider here the messages that using very young girls as models may give, and that males are usually socialised into seeking a female partner who is younger and smaller than them.

DISCUSSION POINT

As some abusers use pornography to overcome their inhibitions, do you think the increase and availability of pornography via videos and the Internet may lead to an increase in child sexual abuse?

Finkelhor (1984) would also cite such issues as weak criminal sanctions against offenders and the ideology of patriarchal prerogatives for men as being disinhibitors. Alcohol is also known to assist in the process of erosion of inhibitions and the experience of people who work in sexual abuse also suggests that alcohol may be used by the perpetrator to diminish the awareness of others who could protect the child.

Precondition III

Preconditions I and II attempt to account for the behaviour of offenders. An offender who is motivated to abuse and has overcome his inhibitions may not do so, or not with a particular child, why not? Precondition III looks at external inhibitors.

Outside the child and the offender, Finkelhor (1984) cites as being the most important the supervision a child receives from other persons. Family members, neighbours and the child's own friends can exert a restraint on a potential offender. The presence of others does not at first sight seem a particularly safe sort of deterrent, but it is frequently noted in the literature about child sexual abuse how important the influence of third parties is in creating a vulnerability to abusers. Henderson (1972, in Finkelhor, 1984) found that children who live in isolated settings, have fewer friends and fewer social contacts are at greater risk of abuse.

One external inhibitor is quite simply the opportunity for abuser and child to be alone. Many abusers spend a lot of time and energy creating situations in which they can be alone with the child they are going to abuse. Finkelhor (1984) expresses the opinion that mothers, in particular, appear to be crucial in protecting children from sexual abuse. Feminists have, quite rightly, disputed the fact that mothers are to blame for abuse, and it is important that responsibility is put where it belongs — on the abuser. It is important that the recurring theme that women are to blame, whatever goes wrong in a family, is disputed. Mothers' and women's roles in child sexual abuse are complex and vary from complete ignorance to what was going on to denial or collusion, while in a small number of cases the mother herself is the perpetrator. In my experience mothers often do not know that their child is being sexually abused. They nearly always believe they should have known, and often believe that everybody else believed they knew, and they did nothing to stop it. It is important to recognise this as mothers need a lot of help and support themselves, if they are to be able to protect and help their child/children.

Studies have shown that there is a correlation between educational inferiority in women in a partnership and sexual abuse of the children, and that girls whose mothers are powerless may fall more easily into the victim role. Some of this may arise from the educational system, and some from women in a family structure having to depend on men economically, but it does seem an area that requires further research to ensure we do not miss vital information that may prevent some child sexual abuse. Russel (1986) found that the daughters of more powerful women were less likely to be abused. It would seem, then, that greater equality between the sexes would enhance the well-being and protection of many children.

DISCUSSION POINT

What do you think may be the reasons why the daughters of more powerful women seem to be less likely to be abused?

Many child sexual abusers may gain access to families by starting a relationship with the mother of the child; this would include a sexual relationship. This means that mothers believe they are visiting because of the relationship with themselves and would not consider that an additional motive may be to gain access to the child and abuse them. People who work with perpetrators have found that many are having a sexual relationship with an adult as well as abusing children. A lot of the information we have about child sexual abuse has been learnt from perpetrators when they have been caught. This can lead to a tendency to consider perpetrators as being 'the experts' on child sexual abuse. This is a concept I find particularly difficult as it seems to still leave the perpetrator in a position of power. Driver (Driver and Droisen, 1989) comments further on this.

Precondition IV

Finkelhor (1984) expresses the opinion that some children have the capacity to avoid abuse. He says that this must not be seen in a narrow way, but some children will avoid abuse without knowing it, when an abuser decides not to approach that particular child but goes onto another one. People who work with abusers tell me that abusers say they can pick out the more vulnerable child almost by instinct. This does not mean the child is to blame in any way, but may give further information about the complexities of child sexual abuse. It may be, of course, something abusers have learnt to say. It is important to recognise that whatever the child does, or however the child behaves, they are in no way responsible. Responsibility lies with the adult.

Force may sometimes be used, and the combination of child sexual abuse and physical abuse and sometimes murder should never be forgotten.

However, force may not be used. The abuser may be a trusted figure to the child or a family member. The child complies because he/she knows them. The abuser spends time playing with the child. It is common in sexual abuse that non-sexual contact games are used by perpetrators to get the child used to being touched, before going on to abuse them. Threats may be used toward the child's mother, siblings or others, e.g. 'if you tell anyone your mother will go to prison', etc., and by whatever means the abuser overcomes the child's resistance. If a perpetrator knows a child has been abused previously, they may interpret this as a signal for future opportunities to abuse.

The four preconditions help us to understand some of the factors around child sexual abuse, although much more research needs to be done to help us gain further understanding.

POWER OF THE ABUSER

In my experience as a practitioner I have always been aware of the power of the abuser and the extremes to which they go to set up the conditions which enable them to abuse children. Power, or abuse of power, seems to me to be a very big factor in child abuse, including child sexual abuse. Adults hold power over children, and this remains one of the most unequal relationships in our society. Children are still often seen as the 'possessions' of adults, and are expected to obey and please adults. Abusers are seen as very powerful people by the children they abuse. They seem to retain this power even if the abuse has been disclosed and stopped. Children I know who have been abused often report feeling frightened they will come face to face with the abuser on the way to school. They take different routes to school to avoid them. Even if the abuser is in prison there is still a feeling that they exert power, and children worry about what will happen when they are released. If the abuser is removed from home and bailed to another address they may make contact on the telephone, or by letter or walk near the house. Restrictions placed on them to stop them doing this do not always seem to be followed and children and young people often say they do not feel protected by the law or the services.

Unfortunately, the problem of power and its abuse does not only affect abusers and children, but may be apparent in relationships between the child, parents and professionals, as well as between the different professionals involved and the agencies from which the professionals are drawn. This may mean that systems used to try and protect children are less effective than they could be as professionals and agencies vie with each other for power (Reason, 1994). Professionals need constantly to ask themselves whose needs they are really serving. The guidance in documents such as *Working Together* (1991) on joint investigation in child sexual abuse between the police and social services has led to the development of joint protocols, interviewing techniques and training, resulting in a very strong collaborative relationship between the police and some social workers. This can have the unintended effect of excluding the other agencies (Evans and Miller, 1992; Reason, 1994).

However, it is members of the other agencies, e.g. health and education, who have contact with the vast majority of children in this country. It is important that members of all professions involved with children are aware of their role in protecting children, and that a common perspective between all organisations is developed and maintained (Reason, 1994).

Children may be abused by professionals. Readers will now be aware of many of the cases coming to public attention of child sexual abuse in hospitals, schools, children's homes, etc. Some abusers actually go into jobs that give them access to children, often vulnerable children. Again, issues of sexual gratification, power and betrayal of trust must be considered. In the past it seems these perpetrators may have sometimes been protected by other professionals not telling, or by the agencies for whom they work, but they are being increasingly threatened by exposure. Many organisations have now recognised this problem and have specific procedures about what to do if it is suspected a professional is abusing a child. It is essential all health service personnel are aware of, and familiar with, their organisation's procedures and feel empowered to act on them.

Child sexual abusers take time to set up very intricate situations which enable them to be alone with and go on and abuse the child. They may move in with families, be caring and loving towards the mother, and have a sexual relationship with her whilst planning to abuse one or more of the children. I have heard accounts of abusers taking the child in the car alone to the shops on the pretext of helping them choose a mother's day present and then abusing them when alone, or going with them to the garden shed to mend a much loved toy and then abusing them.

One young woman who had been sexually abused from being a young girl said to me:

> If you met my father [her abuser] you'd like him. Everybody likes him. He wears a suit and tie to work, has his own business, carries a briefcase, and works for lots of charities. After I told about what he had done to me lots of his friends wrote to me saying they didn't believe it.

Some theorists claim that child sexual abusers are powerless outside the home, and so seek dominance within. This man appears to be dominant and powerful wherever he is.

Some of the many feelings children are left with include a betrayal of trust, very often having been abused by the very people who should have been caring for them. This often leads to difficulty in forming trusting relationships. Children who have been sexually abused often feel guilty; they believe the abuse was their fault and that they should have stopped it. Some children have asked me if they have something tattooed on their foreheads which told the abuser to abuse them. Anger and rage are often expressed in self-hate, self-mutilation, aggressive antisocial behaviour, depression, drug and alcohol abuse, and rejection of the non-abusing parent who 'did not stop the abuse'.

The psychological effects of child sexual abuse are damaging to both the child and their families. Children can be further harmed by the response of the family and by the professional system. Disbelief or denial by people in responsible positions, e.g. mother, father, may further harm the child.

Retraction is common. An unsympathetic response by families, and sometimes by professionals, tells children they had better say they had made it up; this encourages disbelief of the disclosure. Jones and McGraw (1987) found that false allegations are rare, but the myth persists that children lie and people much prefer to believe this rather than that children are sexually abused.

ACCOMMODATION SYNDROME

Summit (1993) described the accommodation syndrome, which describes how a child caught up in sexual abuse may react in a certain way. The five components are listed below.

1. *Secrecy.* The child is told not to talk. In later years victims have explained that they believed nobody would believe them, or they believed nobody would be able to protect them. Some who did try and talk were punished or there was a pretence that nothing had happened.
2. *Helplessness.* The child is unable to stop the abuse and after initial resistance may protect themselves by 'switching off', pretending to be asleep and distancing themselves from what is going on. This can be wrongly interpreted as compliance by the abuser and society.
3. *Entrapment and accommodation.* Trapped in a position of helplessness and secrecy the child holds him- or herself responsible for what is happening. The abuser, by telling the child such things as 'if you tell anyone the family will break up' or 'it's a good job I have you or I'd have to turn to your little sister' puts the child in the position of having the power to destroy the family or keep it together, and having to protect other children. This is a reversal of parent and child roles. The child has accommodated to the situation. If he/she does this effectively they will cover up the reality to protect the family, but allow themselves space to survive. They do this in various ways, sometimes by doing well at school or in some cases developing different personalities to cope with their complex feelings.
4. *Delayed, conflicted and unconvincing disclosure.* Much child sexual abuse is ongoing and most of it is never disclosed, especially outside the family. Sometimes family conflict triggers disclosure after many years of abuse; this often means the child is asking for help when he/she is least likely to get it. Sometimes the disclosure is viewed as a way of the child getting back at the abuser's attempt to achieve reasonable control and discipline. Disclosure can be a slow process, and the child or young person often conceals more than they reveal. This makes criminal investigation difficult.
5. *Retraction.* Summit (1993) says that whatever a child says about child sexual abuse, he/she is likely to reverse it. Guilt and the obligation to preserve the family, often coupled with a hostile response from the family and outsiders, lead the child to say they made up the story. Adult expectation that children lie is confirmed. Children learn not to complain and adults not to listen.

The accommodation syndrome describes the most typical reaction of children to child sexual abuse and disclosure (it is most clearly seen when the abuser is a trusted carer). A knowledge of these reactions can help adults challenge some of the myths about child sexual abuse and help them act as advocates for children.

Even when disclosures are believed, the disruptions to the child may still be devastating.

REFLECTION POINT

How do you think you would react if you were suddenly informed your partner was sexually abusing your child?

INTERVENTION

The aims of intervention should be to bring about an end to the abuse in the least harmful manner to the child. There is a belief by some professionals that the consequences of intervention may be worse than the abuse itself. However, retrospective studies show that people who were repeatedly abused as children and did not disclose suffered adversity. However, others who have had reasonable outcomes in adult life have been able to disclose and be believed, supported and protected (Glaser and Frosh, 1988).

Duration of sexual abuse appears to have a significant effect on the severity of long-term outcome, so a priority must be to stop it. Intervention techniques are constantly being evaluated. Despite the knowledge that intervention is difficult and can cause problems in itself, professionals have responsibility to intervene if the abuse is to be stopped and the child protected.

It is important that professionals should be aware of their local procedures. These should be based on a good working relationship between all the local agencies, which will enable them to intervene on behalf of the child.

DISCUSSION POINT

What would you do if you suspected a child was being sexually abused?

Listening to the disclosure of child sexual abuse and working with children who have been sexually abused can be painful and distressing. It is essential that professionals have a chance to express their own feelings and reactions and receive support in this difficult area of work.

REFLECTION POINT

How might you feel if a child disclosed to you they were being sexually abused?

How would you support a colleague who was in that situation?

CONCLUSION

Knowledge about the effects of child sexual abuse is increasing all the time. It is important that children are protected and that abuse is stopped. It is important that practitioners who work to protect and help children who are being sexually abused constantly update and evaluate procedures and practice, and that intervention is done with sensitivity and does not further harm the child.

The needs and welfare of the child must be the paramount consideration, not the needs of practitioners or the agencies for which they work. All health professionals have a responsibility to assist in the protection of children. To enable them to do this effectively, they need to have received some training on the subject, have been given a chance to reflect on their feelings about it, and be aware of their local procedures.

REFERENCES

Baker A, Duncan SP (1985) Child sexual abuse: a study of prevalence in Great Britain. *Child Abuse and Neglect* 9(4), 456–467.

Bentovim A, Elton A, Hildebrand J, Tranter M, Vizard E (1988) *Child Sexual Abuse within the Family: Assessment and Treatment.* London: Wright.

Boon C (1986) Betrayal of trust: father–daughter incest. In: Schlesinger B (ed.) *Sexual Abuse of Children in the 1980s*, pp. 80–82. Toronto: University of Toronto Press.

Conte J, Berliner L (1981) The impact of sexual abuse on children: clinical findings. In: Walter L (ed.) *Handbook on Sexual Abuse of Children: Assessment and Treatment Issues.* New York: Springer-Verlag.

Davenport C (1988) The Traumatising Effects of Child and Sexual Abuse. Public and Professional Opinion, University of Leicester. In: Hobbs CJ, Hanks HGI, Wynne JM (eds) (1993) *Child Abuse and Neglect.* London: Churchill Livingstone.

Department of Health and Social Security (1988) *Report of the Inquiry into Child Abuse in Cleveland* (Cleveland Report). London: HMSO.

de Young M (1982) *The Sexual Victimisation of Children.* Jefferson WC. McFarland.

Di Vasto PV, Kaufman A, Rosner L *et al.* (1984) The prevalence of sexually stressful events among females in the general population. *Archives of Sexual Behaviour* 13(1), 59–67.

Driver E, Droisen A (1989) *Child Sexual Abuse: Feminist Perspectives.* Basingstoke, London: Macmillan Education Limited.

Eichenbaum L, Orbach S (1982) *Outside In – Inside Out.* Harmondsworth: Penguin.

Evans M, Miller C (1992) *Partnership in Child Protection: The Strategic Management Response.* London: Office for Public Management, National Institute for Social Work.

Finkelhor D (1979) *Sexually Victimised Children.* New York: Free Press.

Finkelhor D (1984) *Child Sexual Abuse: New Theory and Research.* New York: Free Press.

Finkelhor D (1986) *Source Book on Child Sexual Abuse.* London: Sage.

Forward S, Buck C (1981) *Betrayal of Innocence: Incest and its Devastation.* Harmondsworth: Penguin.

Furniss T (1991) *The Multi-Professional Handbook of Child Sexual Abuse.* London: Routledge.

Ghate D, Spencer L (1995) *The Prevalance of Child Sexual Abuse in Britain.* London: HMSO.

Glaser D, Frosh S (1988) *Child Sexual Abuse.* Basingstoke, London: Macmillan Education Limited.

Hamilton G V (1929) *A Research in Marriage.* New York: Albert and Charles Bon.

Henderson J (1972) Incest: a synthesis of data. In: Finkelhor D (ed.) (1984) *Child Sexual Abuse.* New York: Free Press.

Hobbs CJ, Wynne JM (1987) Child sexual abuse – an increasing role of diagnosis. *Lancet* III, 793–796.

Holloway W (1984) Gender difference and the production of subjectivity. In: Hennqries J, Holloway W, Unwin C, Venn C and Walkerdine V (eds) *Changing the Subject.* London: Methuen.

Jones DPU, McGraw JM (1987) Reliable and fictitious accounts of sexual abuse of children. *Journal of Interpersonal Violence* 2, 25–45.

Kelly L, Regan L, Burton S (1991) *An Exploratory Study of the Prevalence of Sexual Abuse in a Sample of 16–21 year olds.* Child Abuse Studies Unit, University of North London.

Kennedy M (1989) The silent nightmare. *Soundbarrier,* March 1989.

La Fontaine J (1990) *Child Sexual Abuse.* Cambridge: Polity.

Landis JT (1956) Experience of 500 children with adult sexual difficulties. *Psychiatric Quarterly* 30, 91–109.

MacLeod M, Saraga E (1988) Challenging the orthodoxy: towards a feminist theory and practice. *Feminist Review: Family Secrets. Child Sexual Abuse* 28, 16–55.

Mann D (1995) Transference and counter transference issues with sexually abused clients. *Psychodynamic Counselling* 1, 4.

McCormack B (1991) Sexual abuse and learning difficulties. *British Medical Journal* 303, 143–144.

Nelson S (1987) *Incest: Fact and Myth.* Edinburgh: Stamullion.

Peters SD, Wyatt GE, Finkelhor D (1986) *Prevalence in a Source Book on Child Sexual Abuse.* London: Sage.

Reason L (1994) *Partnership in Practice.* MSc Dissertation, University of Hull.

Rushe F (1984) *The Best Kept Secret: Sexual Abuse of Children.* New York: McGraw-Hill.

Russel D (1983) The incidence and prevalence of intrafamilial and extrafamilial sexual abuse of female children. *Child Abuse and Neglect* 7, 133–146.

Russel D (1986) *The Secret Trauma: Incest in the Lives of Girls and Women.* New York: Basic Books.

Schecter M, Roberge L (1976) Child sexual abuse. In: Helter R, Kempe L (eds) *Child Abuse and Neglect: The Family and the Community.* Cambridge, MA: Ballinger.

Seidler V (1985) Fear and intimacy. In: Metcalfe A, Humphries M (eds) *The Sexuality of Man.* London: Pluto Press.

Somers-Flanagan R, Walters H (1987) The incest offender, power and victimization: scales on the same dragon. *Journal of Family Violence* 2, 153–175.

Summit R (1993) The child sexual abuse accommodation syndrome. *Child Abuse and Neglect* 7, 177–193.

Vizard E (1989) Incidence and prevalence of child sexual abuse. In: Ouston J (ed.) *The Consequences of Child Sexual Abuse,* Association for Child Psychiatry, Occasional Paper no. 3.

Working Together (1991) Under the Children Act 1989. London: HMSO.

FURTHER READING

Campbell B (1988) *Unofficial Secrets: Child Sexual Abuse – the Cleveland Case.* London: Virago.
An alternative analysis of the 'Cleveland Case'.

Driver E, Droisen A (1989) *Child Sexual Abuse: Feminist Perspectives.* Basingstoke, London: Macmillan Education Ltd.

A thought-provoking analysis of child sexual abuse.

Finkelhor D (1984) *Child Sexual Abuse: New Theory and Research.* New York: The Free Press.

An excellent resource book.

Saradjian J (1996) *Women Who Sexually Abuse Children: From Research to Clinical Practice.* Chichester: Wiley.

Information book on recognition, prevention and treatment when women are perpetrators of child sexual abuse.

Chapter 8

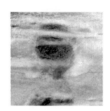

PROMOTING YOUNG PEOPLE'S SEXUAL HEALTH

GRAINNE GRAHAM BA MA MSC

KEY POINTS

- MODELS OF SEXUAL HEALTH PROMOTION
- EDUCATIONAL FRAMEWORK
- LEGAL FRAMEWORK
- CHILDREN'S RIGHTS AND PARENTS' RESPONSIBILITIES
- THE WAY FORWARD – EDUCATION AND SERVICE PROVISION
- MORAL ISSUES
- YOUNG PEOPLE WITH DISABILITIES
- INTERNATIONAL APPROACHES

This chapter considers the promotion of young people's sexual health. It argues that young people have a right to sexual health promotion through appropriate and accessible education and service provision. The difficulties of doing this within the current educational and legal context are discussed, despite the existence of some enabling legislation. The differing perspectives on young people's sexual health promotion are explored: the views of the 'moral majority', who disagree with the whole concept of sexual health promotion, are considered alongside those of the 'liberal educators', who consider sexual health promotion essential for the healthy physical and emotional development of young people. Successful national and international approaches are considered; these include both educational strategies and models of service provision. The possible ways forward for the sexual health promotion of young people in Britain is then considered. These include peer education, outreach and detached work and the provision of specialist young people's health services. Finally, the notion of young people's rights and parental responsibilities is discussed and the need is identified for

---

co-operation between parents, schools and service providers, to ensure that young people's needs are met and their rights are not violated.

In this chapter the term young people refers to anyone under the age of 18 years, children refers to young people up to the age of approximately 13 years, and adolescents to young people aged over 13.

SEX EDUCATION AND SEXUAL HEALTH PROMOTION

Sexual health promotion can be seen as comprising several different elements. Just as health promotion has been described as an all-encompassing term for a range of activities (Downie *et al.*, 1990), so sexual health promotion can be thus described. In Downie's model, health promotion comprises of three overlapping areas: health education, health protection and ill-health prevention. Health education refers to educative / teaching activities, which generally increase knowledge, examine attitudes and develop skills. Health protection relates to policies and legislation, etc., which protect and improve people's health at a structural rather than an individual level. The final element, ill-health prevention, refers to a range of services and treatments which provide primary, secondary or tertiary prevention of ill health. Within this framework sexual health promotion can be seen as comprising sex education, sexual health protection and sexual ill-health prevention. Bloxham (1995) describes a model for sexual health promotion with young people which contains similar elements to Downie's areas of health promotion. Her model also comprises three areas: education, services and information and support. She argues that the start of good sexual health promotion for young people is basic personal and social education, progressing to 'young person friendly' community health services.

One criticism of this type of model is that it has a tendency to be narrowly individualistic. The area becomes problem focused, and the problem is seen in terms of the young people and their behaviour, for instance underage pregnancies. Within this framework some of the real issues may not be addressed. It could be argued that the problem of sexual health and young people is not simply one of sexually active young people putting themselves at risk, but of deprivation. It is surely no coincidence that young people from low income and socially deprived backgrounds with low academic achievement are much more likely to become teenage parents than someone from a more affluent background (Babb, 1993; Smith, 1993).

REFLECTION POINT

It is possible that this link is caused by the lack of social and economic opportunities open for these young people. With few education achievements and little hope of a job, early pregnancy may seem an attractive option for some young women, giving them a purpose and a sense of worth that they may not get elsewhere. Seen in this context the 'problem' becomes not the young person's behaviour but their social and economic circumstances.

This is not to say that the health promotion models described above have nothing offer. Quite the opposite – it is a fact that children and young people are growing and developing sexually and so the model of education, protection and prevention has much to offer any consideration of young people and sexual health promotion. However, when using this model it is important to acknowledge the influence of structural factors and to be aware of the wider context of young people's lives.

Sex Education

Sex education can be interpreted in the same way as wider health education. That is, as being concerned with knowledge, attitudes and skills. The National Curriculum Council, in its guidance to schools on health education, describes sex education as:

○ *providing knowledge of the processes of reproduction and the nature of sexuality and relationships*

○ *encouraging the acquisition of skills and attitudes which allow pupils to manage their relationships in a healthy and responsible way.*
(National Curriculum Council, 1990)

Similarly, Massey (1995) describes good sex education as fostering knowledge and skills. Sex education can therefore be seen as including any activity which aims to educate people about sexual health matters. It aims:

○ to increase knowledge about the biological facts of human sexuality and relationships
○ to allow people to clarify their own attitudes and examine the attitudes of others towards sexuality and relationships
○ to help people acquire the skills necessary to make healthy sexual decisions.

As Massey says:

Sex education is not simply about the absorption of mechanical facts; it embraces issues of ethics, morality, faith and values.
(Massey, 1995)

The definition of sex education is, however, a matter of current and ongoing debate and that debate will be explored within this chapter.

Sexual Health Protection

Sexual health protection refers to structural measures which are undertaken by the government, local authorities, health authorities and charities, etc., which aim to provide protection

for people's sexual health needs. This could include legislation which makes sexual health services available, in particular to priority or vulnerable groups, for instance young people,
people with disabilities and people from minority ethnic groups. It also includes legislation
which enables the provision of sex education. It is generally aimed at whole populations
rather than individuals. In the recent past there have been several high profile educative and
legal measures relating to sexual health protection and young people, all of which have
aroused considerable controversy. The issues involved in these cases and the implications of
them for the sexual health promotion of young people will be explored in this chapter.

Sexual Ill-health Prevention

This refers to a range of services and treatments which will either prevent an individual from
experiencing sexual ill-health, or will provide treatment for sexual ill-health. For the general
population this would include family planning services, genitourinary medicine services and
infertility treatment. However, as with the other aspects of sexual health promotion and
young people, there is considerable divergence of opinion over the question of provision of
sexual health services to young people. Issues relate to whether services should be available
to young people at all and, where services are provided, how accessible and appropriate are
they.

REFLECTION POINT

When considering these issues we should reflect upon whose best interests should be
considered paramount – the child's, their parents', or individuals and groups with
strongly held views and philosophies?

EDUCATIONAL AND LEGAL PERSPECTIVES

The Educational Background

It is only since the Education Act of 1986 that schools and local education authorities have
had any obligations placed on them with regard to sex education. The 1986 Act said schools
and governing bodies had to state whether they were going to provide sex education and, if
they were, they had to promote moral values (Harris, 1996). With the advent of the National
Curriculum health education, including sex education, was classed as a non-statutory subject,
which schools were recommended, but not obliged, to cover. In 1990 The National
Curriculum Council produced a guidance document for health education (National
Curriculum Council, 1990). It recommended nine health education areas, which included sex
education and family life education. The guidance was comprehensive in detailing issues

schools should address at both primary and secondary ages. It was also helpful in that sex education was not viewed in an isolated, biological framework, but in a wide context of relationships and friendships. However, the lack of statutory provision in the 1986 Act meant many schools either ignored sex education, or covered it incompletely. The emphasis on moral values also clearly illustrated that the Department for Education was coming from a traditionalist and moralistic standpoint.

The 1993 Education Act

Under the 1993 Education Act (Department for Education, 1993) sex education became a compulsory subject for secondary schools. Primary schools, however, had no obligation to provide sex education. A policy on sex education was a requirement for all schools providing sex education. A circular was also issued, which gave guidance on how schools should interpret the Act (Department for Education, 1994). This circular contained several important elements:

○ The decision over the content and approach of sex education in a school should be determined by the governing body, whose role and responsibilities in this respect were laid out.

○ The rights of parents were emphasised. In particular their right to withdraw their children from sex education, other than that taught as part of the national curriculum, without question. Parents should also be informed, consulted and involved in the development of the sex education policy and programme.

○ The importance of 'a moral framework for sex education', which was not 'value free', was also emphasised (Department for Education, 1994: 6). Pupils should be encouraged to appreciate the value of a stable family life including marriage, the importance of self-restraint, dignity, etc. Whilst teachers were encouraged to acknowledge that many pupils do not come from backgrounds which reflect these values and experiences, they were advised to help pupils from all circumstances to 'raise their sights' (Department for Education, 1993: 6).

○ The pace of sex education should be not be determined by 'the pace of the most precocious pupils'.

○ There was no guidance on how much sex education should be provided or what the content should be, other than that it had to include HIV/AIDS education and that it should include broad ethical and emotional considerations of sexual attitudes.

○ It was inappropriate to deal in the classroom with particularly explicit issues raised by individual pupils. Instead, the concerns of that child should be discussed with the child's parents.

○ It was inappropriate for teachers to give contraceptive advice to pupils under the age of 16, without parental knowledge and consent. If individual pupils approached teachers for contraceptive advice, the pupils should be directed to their parents and/or relevant health service professionals. If teachers felt that pupils were placing themselves at moral or physical risk, or were likely to break the law, then the head teacher should be informed. The head teacher should inform the pupils' parents and arrange for the pupils to be counselled.

Whilst the Education Act (Department for Education, 1993) and the Sex Education in Schools Guidelines (Department for Education, 1994) rightly place importance on parental consultation and involvement, they can be criticised on a number of counts.

○ It has been argued that instead of facilitating good quality sex education, the guidelines, especially the right of withdrawal, has encouraged schools to do as little sex education as possible (Thomson, 1996a). If children are withdrawn the school has to provide alternative educational provision for the child. As many schools are stretched to find enough teachers to cover existing classes, finding alternative provision for an extra child, or several children, every time sex education is taught is likely to cause problems for many schools. As a consequence they may opt for one lesson a year to minimise the disruption, making a good quality, planned programme of sex education impossible.
○ The guidelines interpret 'moral' in a limited way and do not acknowledge as valid the experience of a large number of young people, whose family backgrounds do not reflect the mythical stable family which is held up as the ideal.
○ The emphasis on the rights of parents could be seen to contradict the Children Act's emphasis on the rights of the child being paramount.
○ Although recent studies have shown evidence for the effectiveness of possibly controversial approaches to sex education in schools, for instance school-linked contraceptive provision, the guidelines do not address this issue and give no guidance on how schools, and others involved in school-based sex education, should respond to such new directions.
○ The guidelines fail to give practical guidance or support to those involved in sex education. A study of school nurses and sex education (Few *et al.*, 1996) has shown that whilst a majority of school nurses involved in the survey were involved in sex education, many felt isolated and unsupported in this role. Many school nurses and teachers in this survey also reported fears of a backlash from parents, governors and senior teachers if they attempted to raise the profile of sex education in school.
○ In general the tone and content of the guidelines fail to support those involved in the challenging and difficult area of sex education. It does not acknowledge the good work which is already taking place in some schools and it tries to threaten teachers with talk of parents taking teachers to court. In short, it peddles a narrowly conservative and morally prejudiced view.

The Legal Background

The Gillick Ruling
The DHSS Guidance of 1980 to Health Authorities on family planning services to young people noted that the question of giving contraceptive advice and treatment to young

persons under the age of 16 was a 'sensitive area' (Department of Health and Social Security, 1980). It emphasised that doctors who were asked for such advice should encourage the young persons to involve their parents. However, it also acknowledged that confidential advice and treatment could be given in exceptional circumstances.

In 1982 Mrs Gillick took her area health authority to court in an attempt to overrule this guidance. She believed that a doctor or health professional should not be able to give contraceptive advice or treatment to young people under 16, in any circumstance, without their parents' consent. Mrs Gillick initially lost her case, then won it in the Court of Appeal, then lost it again in the House of Lords in 1985. This final and definitive House of Lords ruling stated that a doctor, or health professional, could give contraceptive advice and treatment to a young person under 16 if they were acting in the best interests of the child, i.e. to prevent an unwanted pregnancy. The health professional should, however, be sure that the young person was mature enough to understand what they were doing, otherwise they would not be able to give valid consent. Bridgeman (1996) convincingly argues that this principle could be extended from health professional to others, for example school teachers. The Gillick ruling therefore established the principle that a young person could give valid consent to any medical treatment, even if they were under 16, providing they were judged to be of sufficient maturity to understand what was proposed and the implications of the treatment.

In practice many schools, and health professionals, do not interpret the ruling in this way. Possibly because the case achieved some notoriety in the press, there is an awareness of the existence of the Gillick ruling. However, there is confusion as to what it actually states. There appears to be the knowledge among some that the case had been won by Mrs Gillick, but no awareness of the fact that this was overturned. In consequence many health professionals and teachers wrongly believe that contraceptive advice and treatment cannot be given to a young person under 16.

It is possible that some health professionals are happy to misinterpret the Gillick ruling because they personally feel that young people should not be having sex and that the provision of advice and treatment might encourage, rather than discourage them in this. It would appear that this view is held by the Department for Education, as their Guidelines on Sex Education (1994) do not explain the reasoning behind the Gillick judgement, and state that the legal position of teachers giving contraceptive advice to under 16-year-olds has not been tested in the courts. It is likely that this failure to reflect the approach of the Gillick ruling has caused some of the misunderstanding among teachers. As Bridgeman (1996) argues, this is most likely a deliberate use of uncertainty which reflects the particular moral stance of those devising the guidelines.

It is concerning that some health professionals appear uncertain as to how the ruling affects their professional practice. Press interest in school nurses providing sex education lessons in schools has undoubtedly done nothing to reassure health professionals involved in either general sex education or specific contraceptive advice. The notorious chocolate bar incident concerned a sex education session in a primary school, undertaken by a school nurse. The children asked some rather explicit questions, including one about oral sex. The school nurse answered the questions openly and honestly. However, one of the parents, on hearing the content of the session, took exception and reported the matter to the tabloid press, who made great play of the degenerated nature of sex education being taught in schools and the destruction of childhood innocence. There were calls for the school nurse to be sacked or disciplined. Much of the media failed to report that it was a planned programme of sex education which had been approved by both the governors and the parents, in line with the Department for Education Guidelines. Nor was it generally reported that the teaching staff, the governors, the majority of parents in the school and the health authority which employed the adviser, all stated that they supported the school health adviser and were happy with both the sex education programme and her input into it (Hancock, 1995). Although the school nurse was backed by her employers and the school, it is likely that the alarmist press reporting has discouraged many other health professionals in similar positions from undertaking such work.

Clause 28

It has been argued that lesbian and gay sexuality are either not considered in sex education, or are considered less favourably than heterosexuality. This is no doubt a reflection of wider societal attitudes which perceive homosexuality to be unacceptable. Given this, and the extreme conservative nature of the government over the last decade, it is no surprise that much legislation that relates to sexual health has been either heterosexist or outrightly homophobic. The Department for Education Guidelines (Department for Education, 1993), which effectively skirt the issue of homosexuality within sex education, can be seen as heterosexist, whilst Clause 28 of the Local Government Act (Department of the Environment, 1988a), is undoubtedly homophobic. Clause 28 states that:

> 2A(1) a local authority shall not —
>
> (a) intentionally promote homosexuality or publish material with the intention of promoting homosexuality;
>
> (b) promote the teaching in any maintained school of the acceptability of homosexuality as a pretended family relationship.
> (Department of the Environment, 1988a)

This clause has been interpreted by many, including teachers and health professionals, as effectively prohibiting discussion on homosexuality within local authority establishments. It has doubtless deterred many teachers and health professionals from addressing the subject in sex education (Bibbings, 1996). There is possibly a fear among health professionals that the law could be interpreted as applying, not just to local authorities, but also to health authorities. Given that it is a Local Government Act, this is also extremely unlikely. In fact all such concerns, both by health professionals and teachers, are unnecessary because it is incorrect to interpret the clause as preventing the provision of education or services. The clause goes on to state:

(2) Nothing in sub section 1 shall be taken to prohibit the doing of anything for the purpose of preventing the spread of disease.

Issues around homosexuality, and indeed the provision of contraceptive services, can therefore be addressed in relation to the prevention of HIV and other sexually transmitted diseases. In addition, the circular issued with the Local Government Act stated that the clause did not affect school governors or teachers and did not prevent objective discussion of homosexuality in the classroom, or counselling of individual pupils as to their sexuality (Department of the Environment, 1988b).

It seems that, as with the Gillick ruling, teachers and health professionals are misinformed; this may have caused undue circumspection in the provision of sexual health information and education. Harris (1996) argues that the Department for Education Guidelines could enable teachers to include discussions of homosexuality more easily, because parents will have been informed of the content and can withdraw their children from lessons where homosexuality will be included. In reality, however, the one thing most schools are concerned about is parents exercising their right of withdrawal, because the school then has to provide alternative educational activities for those pupils whilst they are withdrawn. It is quite likely that it is the threat of withdrawal, more than the fear of Clause 28, which causes schools to be cautious in addressing issues around homosexuality. For health professionals there is little to fear from the legislation as regards education, advice or treatment.

REFLECTION POINTS

○ Given the education and legal backgrounds should health professionals feel wary teaching about and responding to sexual health issues with children and young people?

○ In what ways can teachers and health professionals teach positively about lesbian and gay issues within the current frameworks?

CASE STUDY

Helen is a school nurse who works in one secondary school and five primary schools. She is often asked to input sex education sessions for some, though not all, of the primary schools. The secondary school has its own sex education programme, delivered by the teachers, to which she does not contribute. There is a nearby youth club, which many of the young people from the local schools attend in the evening. Tom, who is a youth worker from the club, asks Helen to do a session for a group of 12–year–olds who have been asking questions about sexual matters in the club. Helen agrees and arranges to go to the club one evening. When she arrives, Tom says he's busy as one of the workers is off ill and asks Helen to do the session without a worker being present. Helen is a little reluctant, but agrees and has a question and answer session with a mixed–sex group of about 12 young people.

The discussion is wide ranging and includes oral sex, prostitution, homosexuality and contraception. Helen is surprised at the level of questions, as she is used to working with a slightly younger group in a classroom situation, with a teacher present, where the questions are less explicit. However, she felt the session went well and was useful to the young people. Two days later Sheila, the youth leader who manages the youth club, whom Helen has never met before, comes to see Helen and says a parent has complained about the sex education session in the youth club. The parent did not know the session was taking place and felt that the content was 'disgusting' and is worried that it might encourage the children to become sexually active. Sheila says she was not informed that the session was taking place and she understands the parent's concerns and is considering making a formal complaint to Helen's manager on the parent's behalf.

○ Is there any course of action that Helen can take to prevent the youth leader making a formal complaint?
○ Should Helen discuss the issue with her manager?
○ Should Helen offer to meet with the parent to discuss his or her concerns?
○ What could Helen have done to avoid the situation?

You might like to consider the following issues:

○ She could have refused to do the session because she is not experienced with the age group or the situation.
○ She could have met with Tom before the session to agree the content.
○ She could have checked that both the youth leader and the parents knew about and agreed to the session.
○ She could have refused to carry out the session without a youth worker present.

PERSPECTIVES ON SEXUAL HEALTH PROMOTION AND YOUNG PEOPLE

The whole area of sexual health promotion among young people is strongly debated. There would appear to be two main camps in the argument. There are those who are sceptical about the whole concept of promoting young people's sexual health, and those who see it as a crucially important part of promoting the health of young people.

The Moral Majority

The first group regard promoting young people's sexual health as little more than promoting promiscuity. Although there are doubtless many people who have concerns about the possible adverse effects of sexual health promotion for young people, the majority probably have mild, understandable concerns. However, there are some with extreme views and, as is often the case, the most vociferous are also the most vocal. The views of this group are best exemplified by the Family Education Trust, an organisation which aims to promote the family and respect for the family. They produce books, pamphlets and articles, some aimed at exposing what they see as the evils of sex education, homosexuality, etc., and some aimed at promoting respect for family values in young people. For them the purpose of sex education should be to instil in young people due respect for family values. They see most of the current provision of sex education as value-free and possibly to blame for the rise of the permissive society (Whelan, 1995).

Sex education, they argue, should be about teaching young people to 'say no' to pre-marital sex. Given this premise they see no need to be concerned with the provision of sexual health services for young people. Quite simply young people should not be having sex before marriage, and therefore there should be no need to provide sexual health services for them. They argue that abstinence-based programmes, which are popular in the USA, and tell young people to say no to sex, are the only sex education necessary. Homosexuality appears to be singled out for particular criticism by many of the moral majority. The Family Education Trust advertises for sale a book which purports to be a guide to the gay rights movement. The book's premise is that the gay rights movement is made up of paedophiles, who realised that their demands for access to children were unacceptable and so adopted the language of civil rights to make the cause respectable (Family Education Trust, 1995). This view is offensive, homophobic and entirely without foundation.

In Britain the origins of groups such as the Family Education Trust can be seen quite clearly in the rise of the 'moral majority' and 'pro life' movement in the USA, with whom they have natural affinities. Generally conservative and right wing, both in the USA and in Britain, the moral majority in the USA has spearheaded calls for abstinence-based sex education. This 'new sex education movement', as it has been called (Family Planning Today, 1994), requires young people to take a pledge of sexual abstinence until marriage and emphasises the negative aspects of early sexual activity. In some of its more absurd forms it even allows for young people to 'reclaim their virginity'. Thus young people who have already been sexually active before marriage can reclaim their virginity if they refrain from any more sexual activity for several years.

In Britain the views of the moral majority are similar to their American counterparts. They perceive themselves to be on a crusade to save young people from moral degeneration. The malefactors in their view are not so much the media, which is happy to give them space and time to put their 'controversial' viewpoint forward, or the individualistic values of the Western, free-market, capitalist society. They perceive the real enemy to be the depraved sex educators who, by 'educating' rather than moralising, are somehow encouraging young people to be sexually promiscuous. They feel that the best sex education is either no sex education, or sex education which unequivocally says 'no' and very little else. In particular the Family Education Trust appears to feel that there is an international conspiracy, orchestrated by the 'sex education lobby' and the population control movement, which is using value-free instruction in sexual activity for the purpose of social engineering (Riches, 1994). They state categorically, though with rather dubious evidence, that sex education, other than abstinence-based programmes, increases the likelihood of young people becoming sexually active (Whelan, 1995). International evidence which shows that sex education does not lead to sexual activity and in some cases can actually delay the onset of sexual activity is dismissed as being anti-family. For example, research by the Guttmacher Institute in 1985 is seen as having a:

> ... not-very-hidden agenda to discredit the American way of life.
>
> (Whelan, 1995)

Similar over-the-top suggestions are made about publications produced by one of these suspect organisations, that is, the Health Education Authority (HEA), a government agency charged with promoting health at a national level. Whelan refers to the controversial banning of two of the HEA's publications by the Minister of Health. According to Whelan these books were banned because they were of a 'lewd and coarse nature'. However, he fails to mention that one of the publications, *Your Pocket Guide to Sex* (Fisher, 1994), was subsequently published by Penguin and was deemed to be so inoffensive that it is still sold quite openly in many bookshops. The other publication, *Teaching about HIV/AIDS* (Health Education Authority, 1988), was banned solely because it contained a list of gay and lesbian agencies and organisations. Despite the initial ban, it was subsequently published and information on gay and lesbian agencies was included. Whilst it is certainly true that the effectiveness of sex education needs to be more rigorously researched and evaluated (Oakley *et al.*, 1995), much of the criticism of the moral majority seems to be based more on entrenched and blinkered presupposition, rather than any concern for what is most effective.

It would seem that the right wing, conservative values which have been dominant in society during the last 17 years of Conservative governments have created the right atmosphere for the moral majority view to expand and to influence government policy. It is certainly true that Ministers in the Departments of Health and Education have had avowedly conservative attitudes towards sexual matters and this has been evident in legislation, for example the Department for Education's Guidelines on Sex Education (1994). There are also high ranking people in other related government bodies who have extreme moral majority views. For example Dr Nick Tate, the Chief Executive of the Schools' Curriculum and Assessment Authority (SCAA), a government body responsible for overseeing curriculum issues for schools. At a conference in January 1996 he castigated society's lack of a clear moral framework and its subsequent 'moral relativism' (Thomson, 1996b). He said that personal and social education and the promotion of self-esteem in schools was partly to blame for this. Too much emphasis was placed on self-esteem and not enough on traditional moral values, he argued. This view no doubt caused amazement to many involved in schools' health education, who perceive self-esteem raising as essential to give young people the skills to make their own choices, rather than be pressurised into possibly unhealthy choices.

For Tate, society's moral ills were also to be blamed on sociology, post-modernism, and society's:

... desire to respect the views of others ... in particular in relation to those who in the past have been discriminated against, or excluded, or who in other ways have been outsiders.

(Thomson, 1996b)

He appears to be saying that by respecting the views of gays, lesbians, ethnic minorities, etc., society has allowed itself to become morally degenerated, a view which appears to contradict equal opportunities and is offensive to many people from all sexualities and cultures.

The 'Liberal Educators'

On the other side of the debate on sexual health and young people are what might be called the liberal educators. They are represented by such organisations as the Family Planning Association, Barnardos, The National Children's Bureau, the Health Education Authority, Brooke Advisory Centres and the Sex Education Forum, which is an umbrella group of many health, education and religious groups. All of these organisations are well known and they generally have reputations which are nationally respected, except by those whose views place them firmly in the moral majority camp.

These 'liberal educators' argue that sexual health promotion, and in particular sex education, is of prime importance to young people. It is necessary to equip young people with the knowledge and skills to make healthy and responsible sexual decisions, which protect both themselves and others. They argue that avoiding sexual health promotion does not protect young people's innocence, it merely serves to prolong their ignorance. In a world where sexual images and innuendoes are all around, young people are being educated, and often mis-educated, about sexual matters from an early age. Gender stereotypes are also enforced on young people, practically from the moment they are born. For these reasons balanced sex education is imperative to allow young people to make sense of the confusing mixed messages they are receiving. Nor do they think that the provision of sexual health services to young people encourages sexual activity. They argue that some young people are having sex anyway, and the provision of appropriate services is therefore essential to minimise the harm such young people can cause to themselves and others. They argue that the current sexual health promotion provision for young people is insufficient and they point to the alarmingly high British teenage pregnancy rate as testimony to this. It is the highest rate in Europe and one of the highest in the developed world, second only to the USA (Babb, 1993).

Sexual health promotion is therefore seen as important to help young people avoid teenage pregnancy, the effects of which can be disastrous. Fifty one per cent of under 16s who are pregnant have abortions (Babb, 1993; Office of Population Censuses and Surveys, 1994), with the resultant physical and psychological problems that abortion can bring in both the short and long term. For those who go ahead with the pregnancy the problems may be different, but are often just as deleterious, both for the individual and the state. For a solution they look to Western countries, for example The Netherlands, which have a higher than average age at first intercourse and the lowest pregnancy and abortion rates (Babb, 1993). These factors are widely attributed to the fact that these countries have an open climate about sexuality, provide comprehensive sex education programmes in schools and have adequate sexual health services for young people (Denman *et al.*, 1994).

The argument that abstinence-based programmes are the only way to reduce teenage pregnancy is discounted. As Doreen Massey says:

> It is ironic that we should look to the country with the highest pregnancy rate in the Western world for the way forward.
>
> *(Family Planning Today, 1994)*

In fact when Whelan, writing for the Family Education Trust, cites Oakley *et al.*'s study as evidence of the lack of effect of sex education programmes, he fails to mention that the only programme shown by that study to have an adverse reaction and actually increase sexual activity was an abstinence programme (Oakley *et al.*, 1995). Instead the liberal educators think that, far from encouraging young people to have sex, promoting young people's sexual health, if it is done well, can discourage early sexual experimentation and increase safer sexual behaviour. They point to the very research that the Family Education Trust disputes (Baldo *et al.*, 1995) as evidence of this.

They argue that honest, open and well-planned sex education is necessary from an early age (Hayes, 1995). Education that answers children's questions honestly and provides them with information on how their bodies work is necessary to ensure that they grow up aware and understanding, not frightened and confused. The content of sex education for liberal educators is precisely that advocated by the government in the National Curriculum Council's Guidelines on health education (National Curriculum Council, 1990). That is, sex education which is age appropriate to the pupils and is developmental.

- Primary school pupils would therefore be taught about growth and development. They would also be prepared for the physical and emotional changes which are going to take place at puberty.
- Secondary school pupils should be taught in more depth on reproduction, sexual attitudes and behaviours, sexually transmitted diseases, parenting skills and family planning.
- Education which explores relationships, decision making, moral attitudes and values, and sexuality should be ongoing from primary all the way through to secondary school.

This education should not be condemning and disparaging of the situations of young people who do not come from stable two-parent families, as the Sex Education Guidelines 5/94 (Department for Education, 1994) suggest. It should be giving them the space to develop their own attitudes and skills to make their own decisions (Ray, 1995).

Sex education, however, is seen as only one part of the equation. Sexual health services which are appropriate and accessible to young people also need to be provided. There is an awareness of the fact that the average age of onset of sexual activity has dropped quite dramatically over the last few decades, from 21 for those aged 55–59 to 17 for those aged 16–19. Many young people under 16 are sexually active: 19% of women and 28% of men currently aged 16–19 claim to have had sexual intercourse before they were 16, compared with less than 1% of women and 6% of men currently aged 55–59. The liberal educators do not condone early sexual activity, but they accept it as a fact. They see it not as a failing of sex education, but as a reflection of society and in many instances of young people's own families. Although sex education, by alerting young people to the realities and consequences of sexual activity, can prevent some young people from becoming sexually active, it is recognised that many young people will become sexually active, if not before 16 then probably before marriage. For those young people the provision of advice and treatment is necessary to prevent harm and ill-health to themselves and those around them. They see the moral majority as burying their heads in the sand and ignoring the fact of adolescent sexual activity, something which they refuse to do. Instead they are aware of the need to prevent not just unwanted pregnancies, but the spread of disease, including HIV.

The contrasting views of the moral majority and the liberal educators are obviously at extremes of a spectrum. There are doubtless many people, including health professionals, who see a need for sexual health promotion for young people, but share some of the concerns of the moral majority. However, the basic difference between those who advocate sexual health promotion and those who oppose it does exist.

In general, research evidence would appear to favour the views of the liberal educators rather than those of the moral majority. Baldo's paper (Baldo *et al.*, 1995) provides evidence that sex education does not have a detrimental effect in terms of earlier or increased sexual activity among young people. Although the paper is contested by the moral majority, on the grounds of lack of academic rigour, Oakley's study of sex education programmes (Oakley *et al.*, 1995) found no evidence for earlier or increased sexual activity, except with the abstinence-based programme. In addition, a recent report on effectiveness has concluded that the most effective approach to school sex education is a skills-based one which is linked with access to contraception (Effective Health Care, 1997). This is just the sort of approach that the moral majority most deplore.

DISCUSSION POINTS

Can education which promotes only the 'just say no' approach really be called education, or is it merely propaganda?

How widespread is the moral majority view among:

○ the government and political parties

○ parents

○ health professionals

○ teachers?

Can liberal educators be accused of not taking legitimate moral concerns seriously enough?

Can the rise in teenage sexual activity and pregnancy be seen as a consequence of, rather than a reason for, liberal sex education?

Is there any possibility of a middle ground between the two views?

How far are the perspectives rooted in political, rather than moral concerns?

REFLECTION POINTS

As health professionals we should ask ourselves:

○ where do our views lie?

And what effect on our views and practice do the following have:

○ our professional experience and judgement?

○ the values, morals and ethics instilled on us in our childhood, both at home and school?

○ consideration of the rights and needs of children and young people?

YOUNG PEOPLE WITH DISABILITIES

One area of sexual health promotion that has received more attention recently is the needs of children and young people with disabilities, particularly learning difficulties. It is an area that has been neglected, possibly through ignorance and prejudice. Many people, and this can include parents, often think of people with a disability as asexual. The more profound the disability, the more likely it is that people will think they have few or no sexual needs and therefore no sexual health promotion needs. If the young person's sexuality is recognised it is usually seen as a problem, often of inappropriate behaviour. In reality young people with a disability grow and develop physically, just as people without a disability do, and they also experience emotional changes, although they may express them in different ways. Therefore they, too, need opportunities to gain information and to explore their attitudes and feelings about sexual matters. In fact their disability may create a greater need for education and support for several reasons:

○ *If they have a learning difficulty they may be less able to understand what is happening to them or why and so more time is needed to explain and allow them to come to terms with their emotions.*

○ *They will probably experience more limited access to sources of information about sexual matters, because of their particular disability and because their parents and teachers may be unsure about what or how to discuss the issues with them.*

○ *They may need support in dealing with the effects of social attitudes, which may deny their sexual identity.*

○ *They are more at risk of sexual abuse and sexual health promotion can help protect them from this. In particular, sex education can make young people with learning difficulties more aware of what is OK and what is not OK, both in themselves and others and of the fact that they have the right to say no to things that they feel unsure about.*

(Craft and Stewart, 1993).

Once it has been accepted that young people with disabilities are sexual beings the reality that they may become sexually active must be recognised. For this reason they must have the opportunity not just to wide-ranging sex education, but to sexual health services. The rights of people with disabilities to accessible contraceptive services should be acknowledged, similarly their desire to have a family must be considered. For people with profound learning difficulties the issues are more complex, in particular the ethics of preventing young women with severe difficulties from becoming pregnant by compulsorily administering injectable contraceptives. Many institutions do practice this because they are all too aware that young people with learning difficulties are sexually active, without any real conception of what pregnancy will mean or how to cope with it. The implications of the Children Act may be of importance to these issues (Department of Health, 1992a). For the first time children with disabilities are recognised as having the same rights to services as other children in need. It could therefore be argued that under the Children Act young people with disabilities have the right to sexual health promotion services which meet their need, not what statutory authorities consider to be their need.

In relation to sex education there are now many resources available which address the needs of children and young people with learning difficulties (Health Education Authority, 1995). However, there have been criticisms that there are insufficient materials which acknowledge the diversity of young people with learning difficulties. In particular there is a need for resources which are appropriate for young people with severe learning difficulties and for those who are also female, black, lesbian or gay, and therefore likely to be affected by double discrimination (Landman, 1994).

As far as services are concerned there is still a long way to go. With few services aimed at young people in general, the service needs of young people with disabilities are seldom accepted as even existing.

REFLECTION POINTS

Providers of services need to examine:

○ whether the service they currently offer is appropriate and accessible to young people with learning disabilities

○ whether specialist services, or some sort of specialist provision is necessary, this could be through schools, or social service departments involved in providing care to these young people.

Health professionals need to examine:

○ their attitude to disabilities

○ their attitude to the sexuality of young people with learning difficulties.

CASE STUDY

Eileen and John are a young couple aged 16 and 18 with learning difficulties. Eileen lives in supported accommodation and John lives with his parents. They met at a day centre 18 months ago and have been having a relationship for just over a year. Eileen and John would like to have a sexual relationship and possibly get married. Eileen's family are happy about the relationship becoming sexual and feel with the right support and help they could marry. However, John's parents are deeply opposed to the idea of a sexual relationship or marriage. They have told John that if he starts a sexual relationship with Eileen they will stop him seeing her and will stop him attending the day centre. As a health professional supporting John, you are concerned that John and Eileen have had little, if any, sex education and might embark on a sexual relationship anyway.

You might like to consider the following possible ways of responding to the situation:

○ *Leave the situation because you have no right to interfere between parent and child*
○ *Discuss the situation with John's parents in the hope of changing their minds*
○ *Give John contraceptive education, even though it is against his parents' wishes*
○ *Give John contraceptive education only if his parents agree*
○ *Speak to Eileen's health or social worker about the possibility of her receiving contraceptive education.*

International Models of Sexual Health Promotion

As already stated there is a lack of good research evidence on the effectiveness of sex education (Oakley *et al.*, 1995). This is also true for wider sexual health promotion programmes for young people. The evidence that does exist tends to come from the USA, where there have been several pregnancy prevention programmes which have been designed and implemented with a specific evaluation element (Frost and Forrest, 1995). These programmes have several limitations. One is that they are concerned with preventing pregnancy, rather than promoting sexual health in its general sense. Although it can be clearly argued that preventing teenage pregnancy, in itself, promotes sexual health, it is possible that such programmes may have a narrow focus which ignores wider considerations of sexual health, for example sexuality.

Another limitation is that often they only measure levels of sexual activity and use of contraception. Although some measure attitudes towards the above, they tend not to measure whether young people feel any more empowered in relation to sexual health as a result of the programme, surely as important a measure of the effectiveness of sexual health promotion as levels of sexual activity and teenage pregnancy. Despite these problems, the programmes do yield useful information.

School-based Programmes

Early school-based interventions in the USA in the 1960s and 70s were based on knowledge and values clarification. Most of these programmes were rather poorly evaluated. The results, although mixed, generally increased knowledge but had little effect on behaviour. Subsequent programmes were therefore developed which were based on specific theoretical approaches that had been demonstrated as effective in other health areas and were more rigorously evaluated. These programmes are not value-free as the earlier programmes were, but neither are they moralistic as abstinence programmes are. Instead, they emphasise the benefits for young people of delaying sexual intercourse and the importance of using effective contraception when they do have sex (Kirby and DiClemente, 1994).

'Reducing the Risk' is one such programme (Kirby *et al.*, 1991). It is based on social learning theory, social inoculation theory and cognitive behaviour theory. It consists of 15 sessions presented to adolescents by specially trained teachers. The programme uses role play and rehearsal to encourage young people to resist the pressure to become involved in risky behaviour. It also includes parental involvement, and the young people have to ask their parents what their views are on the issues. It is not of itself a full sexuality programme, but can be part of a wider sexuality programme. The results of the programme showed that although it had little impact on young people who were already sexually active, it had a big impact on those who were not sexually active at the start of the programme. It significantly reduced the likelihood that they would become sexually active in the 18 months following the programme.

If and when they did become sexually active, it significantly increased their use of contraceptives (Kirby *et al.*, 1991; Frost and Forrest, 1995).

'Postponing Sexual Involvement' is another similar programme. However, it has a hospital-based outreach component and instead of using specially trained teachers it uses slightly older peer educators, aged 16–18 years, to deliver parts of the programme to young adolescents, i.e. aged 13–14 years. The programme is also focused on young people from low income families. The hospital outreach component is delivered by nurses and counsellors from a young persons' service at the local hospital and it looks at human sexuality, including information on contraception. The peer education element considers skills building and, although delivered by older school pupils, is supervised by the same nurses and counsellors. The results of the programme were similar those of the 'Reducing the Risk' programme. Young people not already sexually active were more likely to postpone sexual activity than those not involved in the programme. Young people in the programme who did become sexually active were also more likely to use contraception than those not involved in the programme (Howard and McCabe, 1992).

In Britain a similar programme, which is also based on social learning theories, has shown promising results. In common with Postponing Sexual Involvement, on which it is based, it used teachers and medical staff to deliver lessons and supervise peer educators. In total 25–30 one-hour lessons were delivered and the content included puberty and reproduction, contraception and negotiating relationships. Methods used included role play and group work. The programme was evaluated over 3 years and showed changes in attitudes, increase in knowledge and lower levels of sexual activity in the intervention group when compared with the control group (Mellanby *et al.*, 1995).

School- and Community-based Programmes

The School/Community Program for Sexual Risk Reduction Among Teens is a programme that uses community education to reduce sexual risk taking (Vincent *et al.*, 1987). It was initiated in 1982 in Denmark, South Carolina, and involved a community outreach and training programme for 'Adult Leaders' to enable them to give sexual risk reduction messages to young people. The adult leaders included teachers, religious leaders, parents and professionals involved in community-based work. The programme involved educational programmes in schools, churches and community agencies. The main messages were chastity, family unity and 'wise sexual choices'. The programme was evaluated in 1987 and found to be highly successful in reducing teenage pregnancy rates (Vincent *et al.*, 1987).

A re-analysis of the programme some years later (Koo *et al.*, 1994) found that the programme had been successful. However, when certain programme and non-programme elements were reduced or discontinued in 1987–88, the pregnancy rate had risen considerably. These elements were a reduction in the number of school teachers receiving training and the discontinuation of a school nurse contraceptive counselling service. The school nurse service was not part of the programme, but was complementary to it. It comprised a school nurse inputting into the school-based programme and the establishment of a clinic based on the school site. The school nurse and a family planning nurse provided counselling and contraceptive supplies to the school students from the school-based clinic. This service was ceased in 1988 because of legislation that was passed to stop contraceptive provision by school-based clinics. The discontinuation of the service and the reduced numbers of teachers being trained coincided with an increase in teenage pregnancy rates. The conclusion that has been drawn from this evidence is that the success of the initial programme was due to the overall, community-wide commitment and effort, which included the school nurse contraceptive service (Koo *et al.*, 1994). Taking away one important element of that community-wide programme therefore reduced the effectiveness of the whole programme.

The provision of school-linked contraceptive services has been a recent development of sexual health programmes for young people in the USA. By 1993 more than 400 school-based health clinics, providing a wide range of services, including sexual health ones, had been opened in schools throughout the USA. Owing to their recent development there has as yet been little evaluation on their impact. The few studies which have been published show mixed results (Kirby and DiClemente, 1994). Increasingly, schools in the USA, including those which do not have clinics, are also supplying condoms to young people, particularly in response to the threat of AIDS. In Britain school-based health services are also starting to be established. In Lancaster and Morecambe drop-in health advice services have been established in some of their secondary schools. School nurses usually run the clinics, providing advice and services on general health issues, including sexual health (Bloxham, 1995). In Few's survey of school nurses (Few *et al.*, 1996), 52% of the school nurses questioned said they provided on-site drop-in clinic services in schools, including sexual health advice and education to pupils. Unfortunately most were not reviewed or monitored and sometimes teachers responsible for sex education in the same school were unaware of the service. Although there has not been a lot of research published on this approach, the evidence that is available is encouraging, so much so that the most recent survey on effectiveness in sex education has concluded that school-linked contraceptive services show most evidence of effectiveness in sex education (Effective Health Care, 1997). It is likely, therefore, that accessible contraceptive service provision, linked to school and community-wide education, may be the most successful approach to sexual health promotion for young people.

Abstinence-based Programmes

As mentioned previously, abstinence programmes are popular in the USA. They have developed out of a dissatisfaction with other sex education and sexual health programmes which were felt to be value-free. They emphasise the message that young people should abstain from sexual activity until marriage, for example the 'Pet your dog, not your date' programme. They use fear-based messages to deter young people from having sex and usually omit any information, discussion or provision of contraceptives. If contraception is included it is usually to highlight its limitations. Some of the most widely used abstinence programmes have been involved in litigation, on the grounds that they violate the law on separation of church and state (Sex Education Matters, 1995). Where sexual orientation is included in these programmes, it is usually to outline homosexuality in a negative way. These programmes have been evaluated and they have demonstrated a short-term impact on attitudes towards pre-marital sex. However, where long-term impact has been measured, the effect greatly decreased over time. Only a few studies have looked at effect on behaviour and these have shown that the abstinence programmes did not delay intercourse or reduce frequency of intercourse (Kirby *et al.*, 1994). As shown earlier, one abstinence programme actually showed an adverse impact. The 'success express' programme aimed to prevent pre-marital sexual activity. It consisted of school-based lessons which focused on information about reproduction, the implications of sexual activity and developing decision-making skills. The programme had a high drop-out rate in both intervention and control groups. None of the desired changes in attitude occurred in the intervention group and more young men in the intervention group than in the control group claimed to have initiated sexual intercourse before the end of the programme (Oakley *et al.*, 1995). Nevertheless it is an approach which appears to be increasing in popularity in Britain and some newspapers have been calling for this approach to sexual health to be adopted in Britain (Sex Education Matters, 1995).

| REFLECTION POINT |

In the current moral climate in Britain is it likely that school- and community-based programmes will be adopted, or are abstinence-based programmes more likely to be adopted?

YOUNG PEOPLE'S RIGHTS

The Children Act

The Children Act was passed in 1989 and took effect from 1991 (HMSO, 1989). It is primarily aimed at the responsibilities of Social Service Departments (SSDs) in regard to individual children deemed to be in 'need'. However, it has general implications for sexual health promotion and a range of other issues related to young people in general, through the *ethos* and the *implications* of the Act. At the heart of the Act is the need to act in the best interests of children and as such it is based on the premise of parental responsibility, rather than 'parental rights'. The Act has been described as a charter for children, whose overriding purpose is to promote and protect children's welfare (Department of Health, 1993a).

The Act states that children have the right to be kept informed about what is happening to them. They also have the right to participate in any decisions that are made about their future. A key element of the Act is that support should be given to families of children in need. A child in need is defined as anyone:

○ who is unlikely to achieve or maintain a reasonable standard of health or development without the provision of services by a local authority

○ whose health or development will be impaired without the provision of such services

○ who is disabled.

Although it is local authority services which are stipulated, the implications for the provision of sexual health-related services are clear. Without the provision of sex education and sexual health services many adolescents are at risk of teenage pregnancy, or acquiring sexually transmitted diseases. As a consequence of these their health and development would be impaired and they would be at risk of not attaining or maintaining a reasonable standard of health or development in the future. The Children Act puts a duty on SSDs to provide the necessary service for children in need. Although it might be inappropriate to expect a social service department to provide sexual health services for young people, it could certainly be argued that under the Act such services should be available to young people. The Act also stipulates that health authorities have a duty to co-operate with SSDs in helping them to exercise their functions if so requested. SSDs could therefore request health authorities to provide appropriate services to meet the sexual health needs of young people. This highlights one of the main issues to emerge from the Children Act — the need for interagency co-operation in planning services. The Act placed responsibilities on SSDs, health and local education authorities to co-operate together to consider overall development needs, including physical, social, intellectual, emotional and behavioural ones. The need for health practitioners to work together with local authorities, for instance in identifying needs, was also recognised.

The Children Act is important for sexual health promotion because it means children's wishes, feelings and best interests should be taken into account in any decisions which affect their health and development. As a result the desire for education and services in relation to sexual health which young people have repeatedly expressed (Walsall Health Promotion Unit, 1992; West *et al.*, 1995) should not be arbitrarily ignored, although in practice it frequently is.

The UN Convention on the Rights of the Child

The Convention on the Rights of the Child was adopted by the United Nations in November 1990. It is a document that seeks to enshrine in international law the rights of young people under 18 years old all over the world. By 1995, 176 of the world's 191 countries had ratified the convention. It contains 54 articles pertaining to young people's rights and responsibilities. In the Convention the notion of young people's rights as expressed in the Children Act is seen in a much broader context and developed much further. As a consequence, the implications for sexual health promotion and young people are more obvious and much greater.

In general the articles relate to the following areas:

○ Survival rights — *this refers to their most basic needs and includes access to health care*

○ Development rights — *to enable children to develop to their fullest potential*

○ Protection rights — *to guard them against all forms of abuse and exploitation*

○ Participation rights — *to enable children to have free expression and take an active role in decisions which affect them.*

[*United Nations Children's Fund, 1995*]

These general principles have clear bearings on the rights of young people to sexual health promotion. In particular, development and participation rights can be seen as ensuring that children and young people have the right to information, education and services that will enable them to grow and develop healthily and make healthy decisions on sexual matters. Of the 54 articles there are several which have specific bearing on sexual health promotion:

Article 3   This states that the best interests of the child should be the primary consideration of any decisions, actions or legislation which affect the child.

Article 12   This states that a child who is capable of forming his or her own views has the right to express those views and they should be given due weight in any decisions affecting the child.

Article 17   This recognises a child's right of access to appropriate information, especially that which promotes her/his social, spiritual, moral, physical or mental health and well-being.

Article 23   This states that children with disabilities have the right to a full and decent life. Signatory states should promote the exchange of appropriate information in relation to disabled children and preventative health care.

Article 24   This states the right of the child to health and health services. In particular, signatory states should:

> ... *develop preventive health care, guidance for parents, and family planning education and services.*
>
> [*United Nations Children's Fund, 1995*]

Therefore by acknowledging the rights of young people to involvement in decisions affecting their health and to information, education and services which promote and protect their health, the convention can be interpreted as an endorsement of sexual health promotion for children and young people. It should be possible to use the convention to argue for the provision of sex education and sexual health services.

The Health of the Nation

Many health professionals are interested in the notion of sexual health promotion as a direct result of the Government's health strategy, 'The Health of the Nation' (Department of Health, 1992b). In this strategy sexual health and HIV/AIDS were identified as key areas and a specific target was set in relation to young people and sexual health. The target was:

○ to reduce the number of conceptions in under 16-year-olds by at least 50% by the year 2000.

In addition, a target to reduce the incidence of gonorrhoea among people aged 15–64 years by at least 20% by 1995 has had implications for reducing sexually transmitted diseases, including HIV/AIDS, among young people from age 15 upwards. As well as the specific targets, the general objectives of the sexual health and HIV/AIDS key area relate to young people. They include:

○ *generally reducing the incidence of HIV and other sexually transmitted diseases*

○ *reducing unwanted pregnancies*

○ *the provision of effective family planning services for those people who want them.*

(Department of Health, 1992b).

The Health of the Nation Key Area Handbook on HIV/AIDS and Sexual Health (Department of Health, 1993b), acknowledges the value of a combined approach to sexual health promotion and young people. This would involve both sex education and service provision. The Netherlands are cited in the handbook as a good example of such an approach. The handbook also contains specific guidance on the following areas:

Improving contraceptive services for young people The handbook identifies the need for services that attract young people and give them the confidence to seek help and advice. It states that young people should be free to attend to the service of their choice, where they feel most comfortable, be that their local GP or a specialist young person's service. The establishment of young persons' advice centres is recommended on the grounds that young people do not identify with 'family planning services'. The need for services to be accessible to young men is highlighted. It recommends that all staff in GP practices should endeavour to be non-judgemental and welcoming to young people seeking sexual health advice.

Education for young people The importance of sex education in promoting 'sexual well-being' and reducing unwanted pregnancy is recognised. The implementation of sex education which is planned, ongoing and based on developing interpersonal and negotiating skills, rather than merely providing information, is recommended.

Developing a local strategy for the sexual health education of young people   The need for intersectoral collaboration and the development of local alliances, to ensure effective provision of sex education and family planning services, is stressed.

The Health of the Nation's guidance can be seen as based very much on the needs, and rights, of young people and as such fits very well with The Children Act and The Convention on the Rights of the Child. All of these can be interpreted as justifying sexual health promotion, in terms of young people's rights to information, education and services. It is ironic that a little more than a year later the Education Act (Department for Education, 1993) and the Guidelines on Sex Education in Schools (Department for Education, 1994) emphasised parents' rights and schools' responsibilities, but said little of the young people's rights to education and service provision. It would seem that there was a conflict between the agendas of different government departments. Indeed, it may be arguable that some of the principles in the Education Act and the Guidelines run counter, not just to the Health of the Nation, but also to the Children Act and the Convention on the Rights of the Child.

REFLECTION POINTS

To what extent does the 1993 Education Act contravene the Convention on the Rights of the Child, the Health of the Nation and the Children Act?

How far can the Children Act be used to justify sexual health promotion and young people?

What implications does the conflict between the Health of the Nation and the 1993 Education Act have for sexual health promotion and young people?

CASE STUDY

Lowstock is a co–educational secondary school, which has recently reviewed its sex education programme and has instituted a planned programme of six lessons per year for years 9–11. Year 9's sex education sessions are due to start in the spring term and letters have been sent out to parents before the Christmas break informing them of the programme and their right to withdrawal. The parents of Susan, a 14–year–old pupil, contact the school to say they wish her to be withdrawn from all the sessions. Susan, however, does not agree to her parents' decision and goes to see her form teacher to complain. She argues that she has the right to the same education as her classmates and intends to go to the sessions despite what her parents say.

Is the school more likely to abide by Susan's wishes or those of her parents?

If the school prevents Susan attending the sessions, how can her rights be protected?

Can the situation be satisfactorily resolved without recourse to legal action?

The Way Forward

It is clear from the evidence above that the way forward for young people's sexual health promotion is a complementary approach of both education and service provision. This section will examine the future directions of both these approaches and the implications they have for good practice in young people's sexual health promotion.

Peer Education

At present peer education is an extremely popular approach to health and sex education. It is used extensively in North America and Canada and appears to be growing in popularity in Britain. It is based on the premise that peer influence has a large impact on young people's behaviour and so the best way to affect young people's behaviour is to utilise peer influence. This is done through the use of young people themselves who become involved in the education of their peers. They present positive role models, advocating healthy behaviour, whose views and actions the recipients will hopefully emulate (Milburn, 1995).

In peer education programmes a group of young people are recruited to become peer educators. The grounds for recruitment vary, but usually include some measure of street credibility, reliability and empathy for the projects aims. These young people are then trained by adults to deliver health education messages to another group of young people. The approach would certainly appear able to afford results. Both the Postponing Sexual Involvement Programme in the States (Howard and McCabe, 1992) and the programme reported by Mellanby *et al.* (1995) in Britain showed successful results for sex education with the use of peer education. It is also being used for sex education in informal youth groups (Hamilton, 1992).

However, although there is some evidence for the success of peer sex education, it is advisable to sound a cautionary note:

○ Peer education programmes take many very different forms. There is no one set peer education approach to follow; instead, programmes have a variety of different aims, objectives and methodologies (Milburn, 1995). There is no consensus even on what the term 'peer' means. Does it refer to someone of the same age, or a few years older, or younger? Are different social and cultural backgrounds taken into account?
○ There are ethical issues over whether the peer educators and the recipients are being educated, or manipulated by adults into 'acceptable behaviour'.
○ There is another ethical issue of whether older peer educators, who may themselves be sexually active, are necessarily good role models for young people who are not sexually

active. Parents in particular may be concerned that some peer educators may, either purposefully or inadvertently, be giving messages about sexual activity that they are unhappy with.

○ As with sex education in general, there is a lack of good evaluation into the effectiveness or otherwise of peer sex education (Milburn, 1995).

These criticisms do not undermine peer education as a whole. The examples of successful peer education projects show a very definite potential for benefit. It is important, however, that peer sex education programmes:

○ are clear about their aims and objectives
○ ensure that the peer educators are adequately trained, supported and supervised
○ wherever possible rigorously evaluate their effectiveness.

Outreach and Detached Approaches

Outreach and detached approaches are ways of making information and services accessible to young people. They do not expect young people to access existing services themselves. Instead, workers from the services go out to where young people are, either in schools, youth clubs or on the streets, and either promote or provide services. Outreach work has been described as going to where young people are and making them aware of existing services and encouraging them to use those services. Detached work has been described as actually taking services out to where young people are (Driscoll, 1993). However, there appears to be no agreed distinction between the two approaches and in practice the terms are often used synonymously. It is also true that one approach often overlaps with the other. For example, detached work may also involve a certain amount of awareness raising about other existing services.

Outreach approaches are often incorporated into sex education programmes in schools and youth clubs. Sometimes this is done explicitly, i.e. a health professional, often a nurse or a doctor, will go to the school or youth club to talk about the service they offer in the local GP surgery or family planning clinic. The intention of this approach is to encourage young people to use the service by increasing awareness of the services offered and by putting young people at ease and allaying any concerns they may have relating to the service, for instance about confidentiality. Outreach approaches may also be done less explicitly. In this case a nurse or doctor may input into a programme of sex education, not to talk explicitly about the service they offer, but about other related matters, for instance puberty or contraception. They might also 'drop into' a school or youth club for an informal chat to young people. Both of these approaches provide opportunities whereby services can be mentioned, either by the health professional or the young people, but in an informal manner. The principle of both types of outreach work is that by meeting people from the service, the young people will feel more comfortable and confident in going to the service for advice and treatment.

An example of an outreach approach is the Portslade Village Centre (Burke, 1995). A successful peer health education programme had already been run in the centre and young people from the programme were invited to facilitate a meeting of sexual health service providers. The young people told the service providers, who included the Health Authority, Hospital Trust, school nurse and health visitor, the type of service they wanted. They described a flexible, drop-in service. It was agreed, therefore, that a practice nurse from the local GP practice should be integrated into the local youth centre to offer a friendly face, specific health advice and a gateway to the local GP service. The result was that one-to-one sessions with the nurse in the youth centre, usually with young women who were concerned with avoiding pregnancy, were followed up by visits to the GP practice. The workers felt that these young women would not have visited the surgery if the practice nurse had not visited the youth centre, because contacting such service was not within their experience or expectations.

Another project, AIDS Action North Humberside, is described as an outreach project (Jarvis, 1992). However, it would appear to fit better into the model described for detached projects. It was started in Hull in 1987 and involves 'outreach workers', working directly with young people on the streets, giving them information about HIV prevention, etc. in an informal way, directed very much by the young people on the street. The outreach workers were young people who were specially trained to give HIV/AIDS education and to engage with the young people on the streets in an informal and relaxed manner.

In Norwich a detached sexual health project was set up through the appointment of a community development worker with a specific brief for detached HIV/AIDS prevention with 16- to 25-year-olds (Driscoll, 1993). She initiated a project called 'Under the Stars', which entailed training volunteer young people in sexual health. The volunteers were trained over a residential weekend and then they undertook detached work with young people in the city. They engaged young people on the streets in discussion about safer sex and generally provided information, support and advice on safer sex and HIV, including the provision of condoms. The project was evaluated favourably, with on average 20–27 young people being contacted per night.

Detached work is therefore much more about starting where young people are, finding out what their sexual health needs are and meeting them, as far as possible, on the streets.

Services

Many young people are unaware of the existence of sexual health services (Francome and Walsh, 1995). Other research has shown that whilst there is some knowledge among young people that 'family planning' services exist, in general they do not use these services (West et al., 1995). It is not that young people do not want sexual health services, but quite the opposite. Young people feel there are insufficient sexual health services for them, because mainstream services are not suitable for them (Walsall Health Promotion Unit, 1992; West et al., 1995). There appears to be a problem of appropriateness – young people simply do not feel that traditional family planning services are suitable for their needs. The main problems have been identified (Tameside & Glossop Health Authority, 1992; Mawer, 1995; West *et al.*, 1995; Health Education Authority, 1996).

○ *Confidentiality*   Young people fear that their parents will be informed if they go to their GP for contraceptive help and advice. Similarly if they attend a GUM clinic they fear their GP will have to be told, who may in turn tell their parents.

○ *Accessibility*   Many young people do not want to attend a local service for fear of being recognised. To attend a service away from home may be difficult because of time and travel costs. Many family planning clinics are offered at times when their absence may be noted. By attending a family planning clinic young people feel that they are 'labelled' as being sexually active, and are unhappy with this.

○ *Appropriateness*   The very term 'family planning' is something which young people do not identify with. Often they are not planning a family, but planning to prevent a family.

○ *Embarrassment*   Young people often feel embarrassed if they do access services. The attitude of staff, particularly receptionists, often makes this worse and has been identified by young people as a particular barrier to them using sexual health services.

As well as identifying problems with the current service provision, young people have also been forthcoming in identifying what they do want from sexual health services. The following is a summary of what young people say they would like in terms of sexual health services (Tameside & Glossop Health Authority, 1992; Mawer, 1995; West *et al.*, 1995; Health Education Authority, 1996).

○ *Confidential services*   Young people need to be assured that any service will provide confidentiality.

○ *Dedicated services for young people*   Specialist young person's health or advice services are preferred. These should not be advertised as just sexual health services, because that would label attendees as being sexually active and might prevent some young people from attending for fear of parental disapproval. Instead, general health services for young people should be provided which include sexual health services.

○ *Convenient location*   Services should be conveniently situated, either locally, in a town centre, or easily accessible from home and school.

○ *Information*   Information on what services are available and where and when, should be easily available to young people. This information should be available at school.

○ *Timing*   Clinics should be open early evening, for example 3.30–8 pm, to allow young people to attend on their way home from school. They should be open on at least Fridays, Saturdays and Mondays, because the weekend is when most young people will be at risk.

○ *Friendly, understanding and welcoming staff*   In one survey female staff were preferred to male staff, even by young men.

Specialised young people's services such as described above have been established for some time in the USA. For example, the Door project in New York, which was set up in 1970, was

---

an innovative young person's centre, offering a wide range of health-related services in an informal, young person-centred manner (Finn, 1986). In Britain, Brooke Advisory Centres have been providing sexual health services to young people for many years. However, specialist services are now becoming increasingly popular with statutory services, usually local health authorities. A recent compendium of family planning provision for young people listed 65 specialist young person's services in Britain. It is probable that the support and encouragement for such clinics in the Health of the Nation has helped their expansion in recent years.

Although some of the services are solely sexual health ones, many are described as general health services, although the primary focus is often sexual health. The Woodehouse Park Clinic in Manchester is an example of a specialist young person's clinic with an emphasis on sexual health (Williams *et al.*, 1994). It was opened in 1988 in a multipurpose community health centre. The aim of the clinic is to reduce the teenage pregnancy rate in the area, however, advice on all health topics is offered. All staff involved in the clinic participated in training prior to the opening of the clinic. Weekly advice sessions are offered to young people between 3.30 and 5.30 pm. The clinic is staffed by school nurses, a midwife, a family planning doctor and a parentcraft tutor. Attendance at the clinic has grown dramatically since 1988. Average attendance in 1993 was 39 per session, of whom 24 were existing clients. Young men aged under 16, who are usually difficult to attract to such sessions, have also attended the sessions. Outcome data on levels of teenage pregnancy in the small geographical area where the clinic is situated is difficult to extract from the wider figures. However, the high level of attendance at the clinic is felt to be an indication that the service is meeting the needs of the young people.

Bodywise is another sexual health service for young people (Brown and Savage, 1993). However, it is based in youth and community, rather than health service settings. It was set up in Kettering in 1990. It is a joint venture between the Health Authority and the local youth services. Clinics have been set up in local youth or community centres and operate a drop-in, rather than appointment basis. The clinic staff are also involved in outreach work. They visit local youth clubs and groups and with outreach/detached youth workers they meet young people on the streets. The aim of this is to make young people feel more comfortable about attending one of the clinics. A specially designed double decker bus also visits the rural areas to undertake outreach work. In addition to the clinics the project operates a weekly drop-in service at two local colleges of further and higher education. Once again outcomes are difficult to evaluate, partly because of the informal nature of the service, and good attendances at the clinics are taken as a measure of success.

Base 51 in Nottingham is a different model of young person's service (Read, 1993). Rather than operating through existing health and community venues it is a specific young person's drop-in health centre, housed in a converted factory in the centre of Nottingham. It was opened in 1993, and although the primary concern behind the project was sexual health, it offers a wide range of health services including sexual health ones. There was already an existing teenage sexual health clinic in the city, but that was felt to attract largely middle class young people, who had the confidence and skills to access services. Base 51 was therefore designed to complement the existing service and meet the needs of disadvantaged young people, including those who are homeless. It is based very much on the Door project in New York and it is open both during the day and evening. It has washing facilities and can refer young people onto a range of agencies for overnight accommodation. It also has crèche facilities for young parents. In addition to these services other activities are offered, for example drama, dance and aerobics. The design of the centre is intended to appeal to young people's taste. It is colourful, welcoming and friendly — it does not look like a clinic.

The services described above are all specialist young person's services, in line with what young people have asked for. There is, however, an argument that rather than creating new services for young people, we should be making existing services more accessible to young people (Burke, 1995). It is certainly true that specialist services may be letting existing providers off the hook and it may be more beneficial for young people to get used to using mainstream services, because when they reach 18 or 24, they will have no choice but to use those services. However, at the moment existing services are clearly not meeting the needs of young people and it may take a long time to change the attitudes of staff in health centres and society at large. An alternative should be the provision of contraceptive advice in schools, provided in partnership with sex education programmes, such as suggested by the Effective Health Care Report (Effective Health Care, 1997). However, given the prevalent social, media and political attitudes, which are often sympathetic to the moral majority views, it is likely that such an approach would encounter severe opposition. Until the necessary changes in social attitudes take place, if they ever do, specialist services will have to be the way forward for young people's sexual health services.

REFLECTION POINTS

Can mainstream sexual health services ever meet the needs of young people?

Who is in the best position to educate young people about sex — professionals or other young people?

Are we placing an unfair responsibility on young people when we ask them to be peer educators?

Can we be sure that outreach and detached services are appropriate, or are we giving young people something they have not asked for and therefore may not want?

CHILDREN'S RIGHTS/PARENTS' RESPONSIBILITIES

The issues at the heart of sexual health promotion for young people are really those of children's rights and parents' responsibilities. Children and young people have the right to sex education and sexual health services for several very important reasons:

○ All people, whether children or adults, are sexual beings. We are not born sexless, with our sexuality suddenly appearing at puberty. Instead we are born with sexual attributes, which grow and develop throughout life. This sexual growth brings with it understanding and needs which are constantly developing and changing and which are different from person to person. The very fact that all people have these sexual attributes, and experience these growths and developments, gives them sexual rights. These include the right to information and support to enable them to develop in a sexually healthy manner.

○ Young people are not growing up in a sexual vacuum. Sex education and sexual images are all around children and young people, from the earliest of ages. They are on the television and the radio, in the papers, in advertising and in the playground. This information arouses children's curiosity and interest and it often gives conflicting messages, causing confusion and anxiety. If young people are to be truly sexually healthy they need accurate and honest answers to their questions. Many adults worry that when a child asks a question about sex an answer is required which will have to go into great detail about sexual acts. This is seldom true, since most children are satisfied with a very simple, basic answer. If we do not answer questions truthfully and give appropriate information, the confusion and misunderstanding will continue. As a result of this ignorance young people may put themselves at risk.

○ Many young people are at risk of sexual abuse. A recent NSPCC survey revealed that one in six people had been subjected to some form of sexual abuse as children (NSPCC, 1995). If young people are to be protected from this they need to know what to protect themselves against and how. Without sex education this cannot be done effectively.

○ Many young people are becoming involved in sexual relationships at increasingly young ages — 12 and 13 is not uncommon. However, their emotional maturity may not be as rapid as their physically maturity, or their level of knowledge. This 'cognitive immaturity' (Stuart-Smith, 1996) means they are unlikely to understand the consequences of their actions and so they are more likely to put themselves at risk. Sexual education and services are therefore essential to minimise the harm they may cause themselves.

○ Family breakdown is widespread and children often lack a stable male or female role model. If young people are to relate properly to people of the same and different genders they need to understand what the differences are between the genders and that both genders deserve equal respect. Good sex education can allow young people to explore these issues and develop an understanding of them.

○ Many parents feel unable to undertake the sex education of their children. They do not feel sufficiently skilled or confident (Allen, 1987). In studies they have welcomed the idea of schools providing sex education, at both primary and secondary level. However, they wish to know what is being taught and how (Health Education Authority, 1994).

All these factors show that children have the right to sexual health promotion. Parents/ carers also have responsibilities in relation to the sexual health of their children. Often parents see this as a duty to 'protect' their children. In reality this responsibility to protect their children can be best served by educating them to protect themselves.

CONCLUSIONS

It is clear that children and adolescents have sexual health needs and sexual health rights. If these needs are to be met and these rights to be protected, good sexual health promotion is essential. Although there are those who argue that promoting the sexual health of young people is immoral and encourages promiscuity, there is good evidence to suggest that good sex education and appropriate service provision actually reduces some of the potential problems of adolescent sexual activity. Countries which are committed to such approaches have lower rates of teenage pregnancy and sexually transmitted diseases, whilst individual programmes of comprehensive sex education combined with accessible services have shown promising results. Young people are sexually aware and sometimes sexually active at early ages, and whilst for some young people this presents no problems, for others there is the risk of physical, mental and emotional ill-health. A plea to chastity and morality appears very unlikely to reduce those risks, especially in a social climate where sex is regularly exhorted and exploited. To ignore the situation serves merely to compound the potential problems. It would appear that the best way forward is a partnership involving parents, schools, communities and service providers, working together to meet young people's sexual health needs and to protect their sexual health rights.

REFERENCES

Aggleton P (1996) *Promoting Young People's Sexual Health*. London: Health Education Authority.

Allen I (1987) *Education in Sex and Personal Relationships*. London: Policy Studies Institute.

Babb P (1993) Teenage conceptions and fertility in England and Wales, 1971–91. *Population Trends* **74**.

Baldo M, Aggleton P, Slutkin G (1995) *Does sex education lead to earlier or increased sexual activity in youth?* Paper presented to the XI International Conference on HIV/AIDS, Berlin.

Bloxham S (1995) *Interagency Sexual Health Activities for Young People in the Morecambe and Lancaster District*. Lancaster: University College of St Martin.

Bridgeman J (1996) Don't tell the children: the department's guidance on the provision of information about contraception to individual pupils. In: Harris N (ed.) *Children, Sex Education and the Law*. London: National Children's Bureau.

Brown L, Savage S (1993) Breaking down the barriers. *Healthlines*, June, 18–19.

Burke T (1995) A healthy approach to partnership. *Young People Now*, March, 20–21.

Craft A, Stewart D (1993) What about us? *Sex Education for Children with Learning Disabilities*. Sheffield: The Home and School Council.

Denman S, Gillies P, Wilson S, Wijewardene K (1994) Sex education in schools: An overview of recommendations. *Public Health* **108**, 251–256.

Department for Education (1993) *Education Act 1993.* London: Department for Education.

Department for Education (1994) *Education Act 1993: Sex Education in Schools* (Circular 5/94). London: Department for Education.

Department of the Environment (1988a) *Local Government Act.* London: Department of the Environment.

Department of the Environment (1988b) *Local Government Act 1988* (Circular 12/88). London: Department of the Environment.

Department of Health (1992a) *The Children Act 1989, An Introductory Guide for the NHS.* London: HMSO.

Department of Health (1992b) *The Health of the Nation.* London: Department of Health.

Department of Health (1993a) *Children Act Report 1992.* London: HMSO.

Department of Health (1993b) *The Health of the Nation, Key Area Handbook, HIV/AIDS and Sexual Health.* London: Department of Health.

Department of Health and Social Security (1980) *Guidance on Family Planning Services to Young People.* London: DHSS.

Downie R, Fyfe C, Tannahill A (1990) *Health Promotion Models and Values.* Oxford: Oxford University Press.

Driscoll J (1993) Detached — that's a sort of house innit? *Youth Clubs,* December.

Effective Health Care (1997) *Effective Health Care,* 3, February. York: NHS Centre for Reviews and Dissemination, University of York.

Family Education Trust (1995) *Publications Catalogue.*

Family Planning Today (1994) American SIECUS visit in November. *Family Planning Today,* 3rd quarter.

Few C, Hicken I, Butterworth T (1996) *Partnerships in Sexual Health and Sex Education.* University of Manchester.

Finn L (1986) Promoting teenage health. *Health Education Journal* 45(2).

Fisher N (1994) *Your Pocket Guide to Sex.* Harmondsworth: Penguin.

Francome C, Walsh J (1995) *Young Teenage Pregnancy.* Middlesex University and The Family Planning Association.

Frost J, Forrest J (1995) Understanding the impact of effective teenage pregnancy prevention programs. *Family Planning Perspectives* 27(5).

Hamilton V (1992) HIV/AIDS — A peer education approach. *Youth and Policy* 36, 27–33.

Hancock C (1994) Schools for scandal. *Health Service Journal,* 28 April, p. 21.

Harris N (1996) The regulation and control of sex education. In: Harris N (ed.) *Children, Sex Education and the Law.* London: National Children's Bureau.

Hayes I (1995) Sex education in the early years. *Health Education,* January.

Health Education Authority (1988) *Teaching about AIDS.* London: Health Education Authority.

Health Education Authority (1994) *Health Update 4 Sexual Health.* London: Health Education Authority.

Health Education Authority (1995) *Health Related Resources for People with Learning Difficulties.* London: Health Education Authority.

Health Education Authority (1996) *Promoting Sexual Health Services to Young People.* London: Health Education Authority.

HMSO (1989) *An Introduction to the Children Act.* London: HMSO.

Howard M, McCabe J (1992) An information and skills approach for younger teens. In: Miller B, Card J, Playoff R, Peterson J (eds) *Preventing Adolescent Pregnancy.* London: Sage.

Jarvis M (1992) HIV, Who Knows Best. *Youth Clubs with the Edge,* June, 28–30.

Kirby D, DiClemente R (1994) School based interventions to prevent unprotected sex and HIV among adolescents. In: DiClemente R, Peterson J (eds) *Preventing AIDS: Theories and Methods of Behavioural Interventions.* New York.

Kirby D, Barth R, Leland N, Fetro J (1991) Reducing the risk: impact of a new curriculum on sexual risk-taking. *Family Planning Perspectives* 23, November/December.

Koo H, Dunteman G, George C, Green Y, Vincent M (1994) Reducing adolescent pregnancy through a school and community based intervention: Denmark, South Carolina, revisited. *Family Planning Perspectives* 26, September/October.

Landman R (1994) *Let's talk about sex? Accessing sex education services for black people with learning difficulties.* East Birmingham Health Promotion Service.

Massey D (1995) *Sex Education Source Book.* London: Family Planning Association.

Mawer C (1995) Knowledge and perceptions of local contraceptive services. *Education and Health* 13(2).

Mellanby A, Phelps F, Crichton N, Tripp J (1995) School sex education: an experimental model with educational and medical benefit. *British Medical Journal* 311, 414–420.

Milburn K (1995) A critical review of peer education with young people, with special reference to sexual health. *Health Education Research* 10, December.

National Curriculum Council (1990) *Curriculum Guidance Five: Health Education.* National Curriculum Council.

NSPCC (1995) *Words into Deeds.* London: NSPCC.

Oakley A, Fullerton D, Holland J, *et al.* (1995) Sexual health education interventions for young people: a methodological review. *British Medical Journal*, 310, 158–162.

Office of Population Censuses and Surveys *OPCS Monitor, Conceptions in England and Wales 1991: Residents of RHAs and DHAs.*

Ray C (1995) Laying the foundations for effective sex education. *Sex Education Matters* (6), 10–11.

Read (1993) Safe haven based on West Side Story. *The Independent*, 15 June.

Riches V (1994) *Sex and Social Engineering.* Oxford: Family Education Trust.

Sex Education Matters (1995) Pet your dog not your date! The US experience of fear-based sex education. *Sex Education Matters*, 10–11.

Smith T (1993) Influence of socio-economic factors on attaining targets for reducing teenage pregnancies. *British Medical Journal* 306, 1232–1235.

Stuart-Smith S (1996) Teenage sex. *British Medical Journal* 312, 390–391.

Tameside & Glossop Health Authority (1992) Primary Health Care Family Planning Service Health Needs Assessment, Tameside & Glossop Health Authority.

Thomson R (1996a) Sex education and the law, working towards good practice. In: Harris N (ed.) *Children, Sex Education and the Law.* London: National Children's Bureau.

Thomson R (1996b) The moral high ground. *Sex Education Matters*, Spring, 6.

United Nations Children's Fund (1995) *The Convention on the Rights of the Child.* UK Committee for UNICEF, London.

Vincent M, Clearie A, Schluchter M (1987) Reducing adolescent pregnancy through school and community based education. *Journal of the American Medical Association* 257, 3382–3386.

Walsall Health Promotion Unit (1992) *Perceptions of Contraception Among Teenagers in Walsall.* Walsall Health Promotion Unit.

West J, Hudson F, Levitas R, Guy W (1995) *Young People and Clinics: Providing for Sexual Health in Avon.* University of Bristol.

Whelan R (1995) *Teaching Sex in Schools – Does it Work?* Oxford: Family Education Trust.

Williams E, Kirkman R, Elstein M (1994) Profile of young persons' advice clinic in reproductive health, 1988–93. *British Medical Journal* 309, 786–78.

Further Reading

General

Department of Health (1993) *The Health of the Nation, Key Area Handbook, HIV/AIDS and Sexual Health.* London: Department of Health.
Gives useful guidance on appropriate and accessible sexual health provision for young people.

Health Education Authority (1994) *Health Update 4 Sexual Health.* London: Health Education Authority.
Comprehensive statistical information on sexual health generally, including useful data on young people.

Johnson AM, Wadsworth J, Field J (1994) *Sexual Attitudes and Lifestyles.* Oxford: Blackwell.
Results of the large-scale, authoritative and comprehensive Wellcome survey on the sexual attitudes and lifestyles of representative cross-sections of British society.

Sex Education

Family Education Trust (1995) *Tried but Untested, Sex Education in Schools.* Oxford: Family Education Trust.
A series of articles from the 'moral majority', which attempt, without success, to show that sex education does not work and moreover is harmful for the moral welfare of young people.

Few C, Hicken I, Butterworth T (1996) *Partnerships in Sexual Health and Sex Education.* University of Manchester.
A study of the school nurse's role in sex education in schools. Provides useful insights into the problems and potentials for school nurses in this area. Includes information on the education and training needs of school nurses and sex education. Contains guidelines on developing a partnership approach to sex education, and co-ordinating strategies for sex education.
See also *Principles and Practices of Sexual Health and Sex Education in Schools – A Framework for Developing Professional Education and Training,* by the same authors.

Massey D (ed.) (1995) *Sex Education Source Book.* London: Family Planning Association.
An update and thought-provoking collection of papers on major aspects of sex education, including gender issues, lesbian and gay issues and the needs of young people with learning difficulties.

(1985) *Sex Education, Some Guidelines for Teachers.*
A comprehensive book on good practice. Primarily aimed at teachers but useful for anyone working on sexual health issues with this group.

Young People with Learning Difficulties

Craft A, Stewart D (1993) *What about us? Sex Education for Children with Disabilities.* Sheffield: The Home and School Council.
A short and easy to read introduction to some of the issues around sexual health for young people with learning disabilities. Aimed at parents but useful for professionals new to the area.
See also their chapter in Massey D (ed.) (1995) *Sex Education Source Book.* London: Family Planning Association.

Legal Aspects

Harris N (ed.) (1996) *Children, Sex Education and the Law.* London: National Children's Bureau.
An excellent collection of papers on the many complex and interesting legal issues relating to sex education and sexual health services for young people. Includes chapters which examine the influence of 5/94, the Department for Education's sex education guidance, the Gillick ruling and Clause 28.

International Approaches

Baldo M, Aggleton P, Slutkin G (1995) *Does sex education lead to earlier or increased sexual activity in youth?* Paper presented to the XI International Conference on HIV/AIDS, Berlin.
A summary of many international sex education programmes which shows that earlier or increased sexual activity did not result from the programmes.

Frost J, Forrest J (1995) Understanding the impact of effective teenage pregnancy prevention programs. *Family Planning Perspectives* 27, September/October.
This article looks at several successful pregnancy prevention programmes and explores the elements within the programmes which may have accounted for their success. Concludes that although the programmes' successes were generally small, they were significant and important.

Miller B, Card J, Pallioff R, Peterson J (eds) (1992) *Preventing Adolescent Pregnancy.* London: Sage.
Papers detailing thoroughly researched and wide-ranging US approaches to sex education.

Services

Health Education Authority (1996) *Promoting Sexual Health Services to Young People.* London: Health Education Authority.
Based on research with young people, these are guidelines for purchasers and providers of sexual health services for young people and detail how such services can be effectively promoted.

Chapter 9

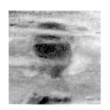

ACQUIRING KNOWLEDGE

MIKE THOMAS RMN BSC RNT CERT ED MA AND
CELIA HYNES RSCN RN RCNT RNT BA

KEY POINTS

- ○ QUANTITATIVE AND QUALITATIVE RESEARCH
- ○ SURVEYS AND INTERVIEWS
- ○ QUALITIES OF INTIMATE RELATIONSHIPS
- ○ EARLY ATTACHMENTS

This chapter aims to provide an overview of approaches to research that we feel have either a direct or indirect bearing on the development of sexuality in children and young people. It will purposely steer away from giving a blow by blow critique of past and present research, as this could prove both repetitive and monotonous and might instil preconceived notions in the reader of such research. Instead, the chapter will discuss the two major schools of research and relate the underlying principles from physiological, psychological and social perspectives. (This is done in the hope that further research in this vital area will be stimulated.)

If, for the sake of developing a theme, it is accepted that sexuality can be defined as three inter-related components, each with its own 'school' of knowledge, then the task of demonstrating research difficulties becomes more manageable. These three 'schools' are, respectively, physiology (gender), psychology (self-image), and sociology (role).

RESEARCH METHODOLOGIES

The first task is to examine briefly the various research methodologies, indicate their similarities and their differences and reach some conclusions regarding their rigour with respect to expanding the knowledge base of sexuality. To examine these differing approaches in great detail is beyond the scope of this chapter – it would take a book (if not several) to convey

---

the complexities of research approaches. There are several texts easily available if the reader desires to explore these issues further. A broad-brush approach is taken in the spirit of encouraging debate. We acknowledge the constraint of such an approach.

Before embarking on a review of the common themes of research, we asked ourselves several questions that we feel are worth a mention here, and we would urge you to do the same. A child's sexuality is of immense importance from the day of conception, when parents consider predictions of the gender of their offspring. The outcome will influence their child's upbringing not only in terms of the treatment received, but also in terms of the overall perceptions and views which people hold about children. Are children fragile beings? Are they able to make decisions and choices?

While many adults and parents would argue that children cannot make decisions, the Children Act (1989) would argue otherwise, and from a health care perspective so would the Children's Charter (1996). A fragile view of children may prevail and it must be recognised that any attempt to acquire knowledge from children pre-puberty will be fraught with difficulties.

In general, research approaches can be divided into two great camps: quantitative and qualitative. Field and Morse (1985) distinguish between these approaches in that the quantitative approach *tests* theories that have already been generated, while the qualitative approach aims to *develop* theory from the data gathered in an inductive way. In other words, each camp has its own group of methodologies and analysis and some subgroups are used by both camps (i.e. quantitative would lay claim to experimental approaches and qualitative to phenomenological approaches yet both would use collecting tools such as questionnaires and correlation tables).

Quantitative Research

In 'classic' quantitative research the most respected and rigorous approach is the experimental method. A phenomenon exists; concepts and principles are developed to define and describe the phenomenon or aspects of it; a theory is presented as to the action/reaction of the study subject; a testable hypothesis is generated and action taken to prove or disprove the hypothesis; and analysis using mathematical formulas (statistics) is used to demonstrate that cause and effect is (or is not) chance.

In order to retain rigour the experimental approach also uses control or baseline measurement, uses a valid measuring system or tool, attains reliable results and attempts to generalise findings into other schools. One of the benefits of experimental research is that it allows the researcher to adjust elements of the environment and measure the differences that result. There is strict control of the adjustments (dependent variables) whilst the environmental factors that cannot be controlled are at the very least acknowledged to exist (independent variables). Obviously the use of the stereotypical white-tiled laboratory with hi-tech equipment and minimum human interference lends itself to a more disciplined research approach as validity, reliability and control of variable are easier to implement.

It follows, then, that some schools of scientific knowledge can adopt the experimental approach much more comfortably than others. Within the discipline of sexuality the same rule applies; some elements of sexuality can be studied using the experimental approach. Biological studies (particularly in the field of gene research) have given, and continue to give, a growing body of knowledge regarding embryonic development. The onset of secondary sexual characteristic (puberty) is also addressed. It could be argued that much attention is given to this area of child development at the expense of others. Medical research within gynaecology, obstetrics and general physiology has allowed us to gain more knowledge of major physiological growth and alteration and in some cases the correct medical interventions. The work of Masters and Johnson (1966), for example, with their use of valid measuring tools, gave us knowledge of physiological changes in both females and males during the human sexual response cycle (of equal importance has been the study of individuals known as hermaphrodites).

Psychology would also qualify (in certain studies at least) as adding to our knowledge of human sexuality with its use of experimental techniques. Hebb (1972), for instance, examined the relationship between the level of emotional arousal and the efficiency of performance. While this research did not primarily concentrate on sexual arousal, it did consider the emotional states which individuals encounter and the responses that occur as a direct result of that emotion. In other words the observation of children's behaviour or the acceptance of verbal feedback cannot be taken as read. We must therefore consider the variety of emotions which children and young people encounter and the effect that this may have on their everyday performance. The fluctuations of feelings are likely to permeate into any research that is being undertaken.

The classic research by Skinner (1938) and also by Watson (1950) outlined the idea that behaviour can be learnt instead of being the result of biological or neurological inheritance. This is an important point when viewing responses of children, young people and adults to sexuality, purely because their expectations and behaviours are likely to be as a result of socialisation, both primary and secondary. Acquiring knowledge in this way is therefore perhaps less valid, as it may not be measuring the 'true' or believed 'true' responses.

Work by Diamond (1965) and Zuger (1970) would support this. Children who were biologically sexually atypical were in essence amenable to environmental influences on their sexual identity. Children with a dual gender identity physiologically were still able and happy to function within the gender identification to which they had been socialised. The experiments by Harlow in 1971, which considered deprivation, served to show that it is not always the predetermined gene processes that influence behaviour. Harlow's study on rhesus monkeys demonstrated the preference shown by the monkeys for bodily contact over food. Harlow asserts that this finding suggests that it is far more important to gain comfort and warmth than it is to satisfy hunger. More importantly, these experiments indicated a direct link between experience and sexual behaviour. The research revealed that failure to make bodily contact by the monkey at an early age led to failure to copulate in adult life. It was thought that as a result of isolation the monkeys had not undergone the natural events of positioning as young offspring, which led to a deficiency of a specific response when mating was expected. This is an interesting point as young children (particularly males) have been known to masturbate from as early an age of 18 months as a source of comfort (Illingworth, 1983). It could therefore be argued, bearing in mind the limitations of transferring animal data to humans, that the more sexually explicit and knowledgeable a young child, the more in control they will be as an adult.

As behaviour is considered by quantitative research as central to development, it is perhaps essential here that we discuss sex typing. We have briefly mentioned this in terms of the atypical child, but must now consider how knowledge surrounding sex roles and sex typing is undertaken. Sex-role stereotyping is basically a belief that each sex behaves in a particular way. Despite the age of liberation and equal opportunity there prevails belief in some predetermined gender-specific behaviour. This would contradict the model of learned responses. There are naturally cultural considerations that would require a degree of understanding in terms of sex-appropriate behaviour. There is even a suggestion that the preconceived ideas of male and female strongly affect the way in which children are viewed. In support of this is the early research by Luria and Rubin (1974) that considers how, under everyday circumstances, it is difficult to distinguish the sex of newborn babies when they are wearing nappies. The research found that adults viewing these babies would describe them in certain ways without knowledge of the sex of the child (i.e. a male to be robust and strong and a female to look soft and fine featured). In support of these studies are others based on similar findings. Condry and Condry (1976) observed reactions of a group of students towards a child's reaction when seeing a 'jack in the box'. Half of the students believed that the child was female, the other half that the child was male. The response to the 'jack in the box' was seen as that of anger if the child was a male, and that of fear if the child was a female. This is an interesting response that may suggest belief in the implicit power and control of males over females.

It takes little foresight to acknowledge that the influence of others and poor perceptions of the various entities will place a subjective slant on the research process. As far back as the 1920s Floyd Allport compared judgements made by those working in groups and those working alone. The more 'extreme' responses to the tasks asked were given by those working alone. This suggested (and subsequently supported) that those working in groups did not want to deviate from what was perceived as the 'presumed central tendency'. This is worth remembering, not just in terms of peer pressure, but also in terms of sex roles and sex stereotyping. To deviate from the perceived norm is likely to bring about conflict and anxiety.

REFLECTION POINT

When you were a child can you recall, in terms of sexuality, gender, fashion, or relationships being influenced by the majority view or 'norm'?

The experimental approach, we would argue, is an extremely important scientific approach in the study of sexuality and should be acknowledged as such. The debate between qualitative and quantitative, hard and soft science and so on is not relevant in this respect. However, the experimental approach has its limits. It begins to crumble and fall apart if the variables cannot be controlled. If the measurement involves human behaviour or perception or interaction, then the results are open to criticism.

Before leaving the experimental approach, one more aspect requires comment. The experimental approach has increased knowledge of human sexuality but it is questionable whether that knowledge has been adequately disseminated. Sex education (with parental consent) takes place in schools that most of the nation's children attend and this education is assimilated into the curriculum at various stages. Yet one television programme discussing sex and sexuality (Marg Clarke, 1996) demonstrated that in one snooker club only one in 50 men could place a pointer on where the clitoris was when shown a diagram of the female vulva. Many men are still ignorant about menstruation and the menopause, whilst many women are not knowledgeable about the function of the prostate gland or why men should carry out testicular examination. It could be argued, of course, that these individuals had received limited sex education and that this knowledge deficit was a direct consequence of that fact. What is perhaps most disturbing is the fact that it was not a priority to know or even to find out! This theme of dissemination will be revisited later, but it is a case in point that knowledge regarding sexuality tends to be circulated amongst the professionals (researchers, psychologists, medical and allied professions, nurses and so on), despite the fact that there is increased attention on sex education in schools. Pappenheim (1995) quotes one young female teenager as stating: 'By the time we had our sex education in school, I was already pregnant', and goes on to discuss why Britain has the highest rate of teenage pregnancy in Western Europe. This is in contrast to the liberal approach of the Dutch to sex and sexuality that provides The Netherlands with one of the lowest teenage pregnancy rates in the world (Thompson, 1993).

Qualitative Research

Returning to the theme of research, if one wishes to investigate a phenomenon that does not easily lend itself to an experimental method, then the researcher is forced to develop new techniques. These techniques must meet at least some of the demands of science. In the jargon, they must be 'positivist' in their stance. Positivism, we would argue, is really just being thorough and involves defining the phenomenon to be investigated and stating why it would be interesting to investigate. It also provides a rationale, aims and objectives and compiles a question (hypothesis), discusses the investigative technique (method) and how the results will be analysed, presented and disseminated.

In the last 30 years such a flexible parameter has led to mushrooming of different qualitative methods, particularly within the phenomenological fields. Phenomenology may be viewed as a way of thinking in terms of the life events encountered by people. The classic work of Husserl (1965) considers the experiences in living an everyday life as an advantage in considering this concept. In other words, data are gathered via a variety of techniques (for example interviews, letters, diaries, etc.) and interpretation made of the same. The influential work of Glaser and Strauss (1967) and the Grounded Theory approach enables the researcher to develop theories that are based in reality. The process of investigation continues until a theory of sufficient detail is developed. What they have in common is the rejection of certain notions that are not positivist. The qualitative approaches do not support the ideas purely because they are traditional (it's always been done that way and therefore it must be the right approach) or because the majority of people agree with something, or on hunches, beliefs or assumptions. Positivism helps qualitative approaches retain scientific rigour.

Whether this scientific rigour is research in the pure sense is obviously debatable. Within the research community life may very well have been academically quieter if social scientists had entitled their approach as social investigation and never used the term qualitative research. The most commonly used qualitative approaches tend to be social surveys, questionnaires, ethnographic studies, social observation (participant/non-participant) and interviews (Oppenheim, 1966). Within sexual research each has its own advantages. Social survey was the tool used by Kinsey *et al.* (1953) in their influential report. Observation (nonparticipant) supplemented by physiological measuring tools was adopted by Masters and Johnson (1966). Interviews and questionnaires are widely used in current research (particularly within psychological studies) and one could accept a certain degree of evidence under this category from the field of counselling and behavioural interventionists. Freud himself in 1905, when writing on the sexual theories of children and infantile sexuality, speaks first of direct observation of 'what children say and do', and second of what adult neurotics consciously recall from their childhood during the process of psychoanalysis. It is clear to see that it is primarily the adult interpretation of the observations made which leads towards the development of Freud's theory surrounding the phallus, which suggests the male child does not believe the female child has a possession which provides pleasurable sensations. The male child believes that the female is lacking in some way.

Wellings *et al.* (1994) extensively researched the issue of first sexual intercourse to establish a pattern in sexual activity. They conclude that there has been (overall) a decrease in the age of engagement in sexual intercourse and discuss several issues regarding why this may be the case. They suggest that it has coincided with a change in attitude towards social disapproval in terms of sex before marriage. However, this research only asked for experiences from the age of 13 years onwards.

Frequently the assessment of young people's sexual health needs are examined by the use of survey and interviews. An example of this is the work by Mackereth and Forder (1996), who used focus group interviews over a period of 1 year. Again there was difficulty in access and subsequently the age group of 11–16 years was concentrated upon (MacDonald, 1988). Within children's nursing there is also a plethora of literature pertaining to adolescents and also to attitudes of nurses towards sexuality (see, for example, Wall-Hass, 1991) but limited information surrounding those under the age of 11. This is an interesting point purely because many children's nursing models address sexuality as part of their identified assessment for care delivery, for example the Manchester Children's Hospital Trust adaptation of Roper, Logan and Tierney's model. It is little wonder, then, that the parts of the documentation pertaining to sexuality are completed with such statements as 'wears appropriate clothes', or 'dresses in pinks/blues'.

It is understandable that under the three subcategories which define sexuality that experimental approaches have concentrated on the physiological area. Qualitative approaches (social investigation) generally speaking concentrate on human interaction and internal perceptions (attitudes, self-esteem, self-concept). The problem with a qualitative approach is the uncontrollable elements (variables) which humans bring into the research environment. In addition, recent findings in political polls appear to indicate that surveys are not particularly reliable because people do not always tell the truth. In essence this is retrospective research that fails to provide a true account of the situation. The problem with reflecting on past events is that it is primarily a voyeuristic journey by the researcher, a subjective chronological narrative that does not allow for objective, valid and reliable data to be collected. If we are asking adults, then we are asking them to access memory and also their unconscious. For all we know the adult could be using this journey as a way of justifying past and present sexual behaviour.

The same argument could apply to social surveys, especially amongst adolescents who are asked about their own sexual activities and who respond to what they perceive as the rather clichéd and hackneyed social norms (young males equal studs while young females equal shy virgins). Questionnaires and surveys also have similar problems as well as suffering from the researcher's own bias. An example of this is the work by Halson (1991). Her research into the sexual harassment and heterosexuality of young women describes instances of females being in the position of gratifying the male, in her words of 'servicing the young men's sexual requirements'. (It must be remembered here that the researcher is female and investigating a sensitive topic area.) There is also the problem with intrusive questions so they tend to be rather safe and bland (or artificially jolly!). There is also the age factor itself; asking children questions about sex and sexuality is a minefield of legal and ethical problems and it is easier therefore to ask adults to recall their own childhood (not a particularly reliable tool) or to ask parents about their children.

The Sexual Offenders Act (1956) clearly stipulates what is permissible by law in terms of gender, age and sexual behaviour. Without reiterating the whole of the guidance of this Act, it discusses limitations surrounding sexual activity of both genders with the same or opposite gender in relation to age in years. The law would view sexual acts in a social and cultural light related to chronological age, age of consent and penetration. The physiologist would recognise the onset of the capability for sexual acts in a physiological framework related to the developments of secondary sex characteristics (age of puberty), whilst social scientists would argue that sexual activity is mature when the person's emotional and psychological participation is voluntary. It must be considered here that if the age of consent for sexual activity is stipulated, then it should also be stipulated for investigation purposes. Researchers have to be both brave and determined to act in what can be a grey area of the law. Even conducting research with teenagers has its difficulties as parents have a right to refuse consent (this could be on religious grounds as well as on grounds of immaturity). Children generally are gaining more autonomy that is upheld by central governing bodies. The United Nations Convention on the Rights of the Child (Article 12), which was agreed and accepted by the UK government, states that children and young people have a right to be consulted, express their views and be involved in making decisions regarding their care and welfare (United Nations Children's Fund, 1995).

In September 1995 the Royal College of Nursing published a report entitled *The Health Needs of School Age Children*. This report is considered by those who produced it as a 'guide' for school nurses and other nurses who work with school age children. While the report covers some of the aforementioned, it also once again focuses specifically on adolescents as having special needs in terms of sex education and exploration to the exclusion of other age ranges.

Interviews, particularly about roles and self-image, can be useful. There has been enough work done to show that interviewing children is now fairly refined and could provide useful data. The skills required in such an approach are not only the interviewing techniques but also the interpretation of information. Kohlberg (1969, 1973), for example, has shown that children move across a developing continuum from a literal world to a symbolic world interpretation as they reach late adolescence. He applied this in particular to moral reasoning. Kohlberg believed that all children experience the stage of their development where they obey rules and conform in order to obtain rewards. They then move onto a stage of conventional morality, where the child conforms to avoid the disapproval of others, before progressing to a stage where it is important to do the right thing in order to avoid guilt feelings. The ultimate stage of morality would be where actions are guided by ethical principles that allow the individual to avoid condemnation. This final stage is expected to occur around the age of 16 years. However, Kohlberg suggests that for many these expectations of morality are never attained and that children develop moral standards for themselves. Other psychologists would disagree, proposing that children do have a sense of right and wrong and that there is a development of a conscience.

This linking of a stage of development to the growth of moral reasoning is paralleled by the changing understanding of the concept of 'love' (in the romantic–erotic sense) as children grow up. Whilst the concepts of 'boy' and 'girl' can be applied to all age groups, the disjunctive concept of 'love' would be a rather different matter. Love is a difficult concept to define. It has been proposed that love is essentially active and that by being active it is therefore giving in nature; unconditional and without the need to receive (Fromm, 1993). There is a belief that all individuals seek out love; that striving for love is a powerful motivating factor while at the same time meeting sexual and affiliative needs (Dion and Berscheid, 1974). Love is an emotion that nearly everyone has experienced at some time in their life. Yet even though this is a familiar concept, researchers still struggle to agree on what constitutes love and how it can be measured. Some common theories of love include attachment styles that are based on the expectations we have of significant others from an early age. These attachments are often categorised in terms of security, anxiety, ambivalence or avoidance (see, for example, Hazan and Shaver, 1987). Other theories are in terms of behaviours or functions and are often broken down into the ability to attract and retain a mate, to reproduce with that mate and to provide a parental investment. There are also varying styles of love that can be found in the work of Lee (1977) and also Hendrick and Hendrick (1986), ranging from Eros (love at first sight) to Agape (a selfless love, caring without self-interest). Sternberg (1988) suggests that love is an accumulation of differing functions corresponding to levels of intimacy, commitment and passion. Adolescents may have some emotional responses to love purely because they may be experiencing sexual attraction from and towards others or have a powerful desire to give and/or receive.

It is not adolescents alone who may seek some comfort in this way, and this is being acknowledged, particularly in the field of sex education. It is therefore the interpretation and understanding of these concepts that are likely to influence the way in which children and young adults behave. Is there, for example, a need to be 'in love' in order to be accepted by peers and possibly to prove some perceived normality for parents and adults? There has been a prevailing concern that to instruct children and young people on sex will lead to a more promiscuous society and increased teenage pregnancy rate. Yet the Family Planning Association (1994) suggests that the provision of sex education and early sexual experience does not encourage teenage sex. Young people wanted more information from authoritative sources. It is quite remarkable that in the 1990s young people continue to rely on friends and schoolyard banter to gain information. Gaining information in this way leaves the individual open to incorrect advice and potential hazards. That is not to suggest that peers are ill-informed, but that they may only be informed from personal experience that could have been unsatisfactory and risky. In contrast to the belief that sexual activity is increased in teenagers, a report in Healthlines (1995) provides an example where the effective sex education programmes in certain schools were actually leading to a decrease in sexual activity.

While there remains a somewhat clinical and medical feel around the material used in delivering information about sex, there have been some recent changes (see for example Harris and Emberley, 1995; Jewitt, 1994). A more 'natural' approach is being taken which discusses issues of positions during sexual activity and also masturbation, which for many young children pre-puberty is a source of comfort. There does, however, remain a lack of emphasis on the pleasurable side of sex and on the desire and the love that may be felt for another person. These feelings are powerful emotions, magnetic in their attractions and at times incapacitating in their response. Young people need to be able to acquire knowledge around these emotive and passionate feelings, to know that it is normal, or that it is acceptable to fall in and out of attraction before finding a mate and having their needs met.

Observations, either participant or non-participant, have points of containment. Watching children and adolescents play, learn, interact or engage in behaviour is obviously useful. Piaget (1951) learnt and differentiated much by interacting with his children. His training as a biologist may have been helpful! However, the parameters involved in the study of sexuality means that observation by its very nature will be confined to social behaviour. In terms of role and sexuality, some elements of self-image and sexual interaction can be observed, but once in the area of intimate behaviour it is a technique out of the question. Masters and Johnson (1966) received criticism for observing sexual activity on the basis that the volunteers being watched were extroverted or exhibitionists and results may not reflect the activities of the introverted individual. By intimate activity one does not even have to mean sexual coupling, but activities such as bathing and proxemics between parents and children.

There are issues such as hygiene activities and proxemics between parents and children. (How many parents, particularly men, desist from bathing with their children now out of fear?) Within this aspect of intimate activity are also issues of attraction and courtship behaviour (particularly language).

Within qualitative approaches (social investigation) the work of some theorists from social psychology and counselling have to be included. Taking an overview of sexuality without taking account of the work of social scientists would leave out too much important data. Social scientists opened new ground for researchers to test new hypotheses. Bowlby (1973) and his work on attachment, for instance, has been taken into the laboratory with some success; it also influences the law that gives mothers custody of children in the majority of separations. The significance of a child's attachment was referred to earlier when considering the response of monkeys in Harlow's experiments, but Bowlby's view of early mental well-being related to attachment and nurture was that it is a biological drive to keep the infant close to a source of protection. As in the findings by Harlow, it could be argued that this mother–child attachment may even influence later sexual behaviour.

Both Winnicot (1970) and Lacan (1992) have suggested that from these early attachments the self emerges as a direct reflection between the baby and the carer. This mirroring leads to a complex game where the baby elicits a response from the significant other and is not unlike the reflection of how the individual sees themselves within the context of their life group. However, Klein (1946) proposes that the child knows the mother/carer only in terms of the bodily contact between them and the sensations created in the child by this contact. These sensations may or may not be pleasurable. This is of importance if only for recognising that children may strive to form relationships that will fulfil them, or relationships that they perceive will fulfil them. These relationships may or may not be satisfying. Early attachments may influence the behaviour of individuals as they form sexual relationships and may lead to specific behaviour patterns.

Fromm (1985) would argue that responses to intimate relationships take on particular qualities. These qualities may take the form of possession, dominance or manipulation. Fromm made a series of statements related to therapeutic view of love and affection. Love itself has a series of core values or attributes whether applied to romantic–erotic love, parental love, sibling love, love for labour (or creativity), and so on in each type of relationship. Whilst accepting the differences in types of love (some of which have been mentioned earlier), they all share four core values, these being the desire to *care* for another, to *trust* another, to have *responsibility* for another and to *know* another. Love reaches a state of contentment when such values are returned. For example, in a parent–child relationship, to *care* includes behaviour such as physical or emotional nurturing and concern about the well-being of the child (over time the child may take over this role as an adult). In this example *trust* means accepting the beliefs and statements of one another, which leads to each having responsibility for the other's feelings. In other words both parent and child behave in a way that does not hurt the other. To *know* one another is based on security in each other's company, curiosity about views and attitudes, and a degree of prediction about what responses would be made in different situations. Underlying these core values is the main motivation of each partner which Fromm states can be split into either *wanting* another or *needing* another. Both occur in all relationships, but he was particularly interested in the main motivator. To need equals insecurity, clinging and so on. To want equals benign pleasure in the other's company. This may raise the question as to what are the effects of a needy mother on a child's emotional development and the effects of a needy child if the mother or father is cold and authoritarian. What if both the child and the parent are needy, and what are the implications of this on sexual development?

A direct influence on acquiring knowledge may have its basis in early life experiences as suggested by the work of eminent psychoanalysts. It has to be admitted that the work of the psychoanalysts is difficult to absorb fully into the scientific domain. The work of Freud and Jung does leave the scientist wondering if they would be more comfortable classified under literature. Take for example Freud's Oedipus complex, which claims that all youngsters have feelings of sexual attraction towards their mothers and feelings of hostility towards their fathers. He suggested that there is a repression of these feelings in order to prevent the difficult consequences of acting out these feelings. Freud's presentation of the ego, superego and id is an example of how science can be limited in its expansion of knowledge. Freud's whole work can be said to be based on the existence of the id, ego and superego, but whether one accepts his view (or not) has to be based on 'belief'. He never explained *where* these entities existed in the anatomical sense. (You could argue that the id might exist in the older lower brain – the limbic system with the hypothalamus and pituitary gland perhaps – but where is the ego? Or the superego? In fact one could bring theories of personality into this discussion because where anatomically is the 'person'?) For the scientist such visionary theorists pose a dialectical problem – there is a concept called ego that may or may not actually exist. The scientist or researcher will prove it does or does not, but how? To date there are no reliable and valid instruments to measure whether the ego exists. It is as ephemeral as the concept of God and must be accepted as a theoretical concept until proven one way or another. Science is unable to help and in fact constrains further debate. It is almost ironic that Freud's work on sexuality and mental defence mechanisms and the early years of a child cannot be proven one way or another. He was after all a qualified doctor and neurologist.

The field of sexuality as a credible area of knowledge started to gain major interest in the 1960s following Masters and Johnson's *Human Sexual Response* (1966). Kinsey's *et al.* (1953) survey was also of immense help. The work of Freud and his contemporaries was not to the taste of most social scientists and psychoanalysis gained repute through media interest in the main. Prior to the 1960s most information could only be found in the fiction literature. One obvious example is DH Lawrence's *Lady Chatterly's Lover* (Penguin Trial 1960), but there were many more authors who wrote in the coded version that Victorian England imposed on social language. Only in later years when biographical details regarding the writers' personal lives emerged did textual double meanings become known. Such fiction would have to be searched if a reader wanted to find references to sexual activities that went further than bland descriptions. This Victorian morality had an effect on published output, with what could be termed 'cultural' publishing open to scrutiny and found in mainstream society, and a growth in 'sub cultural' publishing which could only be accessed with some effort and was often catalogued as 'erotic' work. This sub culture was almost exclusively male-led and involved literature, art, sculpture and so on which was perhaps an attempt to impose some sort of intellectual rationale on the field. Crudity lay elsewhere, in bawdy plays, public houses (comedians and songs), the haunts of prostitutes, clubs, and sea ports. These were considered the interests of the working class male, certainly not art (although theatre did manage to alter its image at the turn of the century). Whilst tolerated by the establishment, such outlets for sexual recreations were often periodically suppressed.

Both these middle class and working class pursuits could possibly be called 'educational' for the adult male, although there is little evidence to indicate they reached a wider audience and retained their exclusivity until the second or third decade of the twentieth century. The emancipation of women, the rise in unemployment, the slow recovery from one war and the decline into European boundary disputes had its effects on the entertainment industry (sub-culturally). The Victorian schism between the males' exposure to sexual issues and the females' exclusion, and the hypocrisy regarding immoral (read dirty) sexual activities and moral (read romantic repression) sexual activities began to be eroded. More and more subcultural issues began to reach mainstream audiences.

The influence of the entertainment industry was truly felt with the advent of 'motion pictures', which led to journals, newspapers and radio shows carrying stories about the new 'stars'. These film stars quickly became role models for social interactions in general society and great lengths were taken to ensure the public were not informed of their real behaviour and attitudes, particularly their sexual mores. To a more insidious extent the advent of the television also led to social modelling. In music the growth of jazz in the 1930s and 1940s, the increasing use of faster and looser beats by the Big Band sound, the influence of black American Blues which led to the poor whites' rock 'n' roll sound, together with the rise in youth involvement as listeners, led to anti-heroes appearing. The adolescents followed the progress of individuals who 'rebelled' against social manners and the attitudes of parental figures. Its a cliché to say it, but nevertheless the 1960s was the most recent historical accumulation and pinnacle of economic, cultural, subcultural and social growth in sexuality. Sexuality in the entertainment sense (movies, television, music, comedy, literature and the media) influenced moral behaviour and allowed a new type of academic freedom (Masters and Johnson's work, the feminist perception such as Germaine Greer's fulminations, Simone de Beauvoir's influential work) which could focus on sexuality itself. Women in particular demanded more information on the effects and risk of the contraceptive pill, child-rearing practices, termination of pregnancy, and so on.

The moral backlash against this movement began in the mid 1970s, against a background of industrial unrest, increasing unemployment and boundary disputes in Europe and else-where (people may forget that the first Falklands claim was in 1978), mirroring to an extent the late 1920s and 1930s. The moral movement was firmly entrenched in the 1980s. The spread of HIV/AIDS perhaps lent the new moralists the weapons of fear and ignorance.

This digression into a broad-brush overview of the last eight decades has served a purpose. Historical searches, archive investigations and biographical studies are all recognised as honourable methods of qualitative research. The general approach taken above is clearly not research, but is used to illuminate how social and cultural progress can provide an insight into sexuality without having to meet the rigour and demands of applied or theoretical research. It is also used to move forward into another area – to show how this overview also provides some real knowledge of the sexuality of adolescents and children. A study of youth culture provides some interesting perceptions, particularly in terms of peer behaviour and attitudes towards authority. A study of parental responses to their young child provides information on gender typing and attachment, whilst a study of play allows some understanding of peer influence and cognitive development. In the last century society has become more open to scrutiny and the area of sexuality has moved into mainstream acceptance. The vestiges of the sexual subculture at the turn of the century which have not grown into the mainstream have most probably continued deeper into what is now termed pornography. This area has nonetheless survived and grown, although its very nature of concealment and secrecy makes research difficult. Still, paedophiles are contactable on the Internet; holiday destinations can be booked purely to cater for sexual encounters with children; institutionalised abuse of children continues to be investigated with disheartening regularity; and the number of adult survivors of familial abuse continue to lead to speculation that they are the 'tip of the iceberg'. Adults (mostly male), in other words, continue to be interested in sexual experiences with adolescents and/or children, but we cannot say with any certainty why this should be the case.

Research is needed in this area, but how should this be carried out? An experimental approach is obviously not acceptable. Surveys and questionnaires will hardly lead to a reliable result. Observations are immoral and illegal. One is left with the anecdotes of survivors, therapeutic interactions, self-reporting, deductive views, criminal charge sheets and police interviews. All rely on a high standard of record keeping. There are worries about validity here as well as the generalisations of conclusions. And what if certain findings are morally opaque (i.e. the child who 'loves' the abuser and learns guilt on growing older, or the incestuous siblings who hide the facts but continue the relationship). Should such studies be censored by the researcher before publication? After all, the reader may damn the investigator and the subject. Even when there is evidence of sexually unacceptable practices continuing, it is extremely hard to carry out the research. As previously mentioned, the freedom to research or theorise often mirrors the current social mores – so one final aspect of scholarly exploration into sexuality involves political influences.

David Steel's Abortion Act (1967) passed into statute during a period of active tolerance and growth of social freedom and responsibility. As Peters (1963) pointed out, freedom without responsibility is totally different. Without communal agreement regarding the boundaries of social behaviour and without the communal acceptance of authority to intervene by setting boundaries via rule setting you have a free-for-all culture. This is almost a form of group sociopathy with the most cunning and strongest gaining the material wealth at the expense of long-term economic growth and social cohesion. The political and business leaders who condone or actively support the removal of 'safety net' legislation inevitably attempt to transfer the burden of responsibility onto the individual citizen or family groups by trumpeting a return to some imaginary past moral basis. It is almost tragically comical that the more communal and more tolerant a society becomes, the more permissive is the expression of freedom, whilst the less communal and less tolerant society relies heavily on moral crusades and a reduction in freedom. This occurs just as much in the sexual field as it does in the political, economic or cultural field. It also appears to influence politicians across the political spectrum.

Edward Heath's Conservative opposition to Harold Wilson's Labour Government of the 1960s and early 1970s did not prevent passage of legislation such as David Steel's abortion bill (1967), or the majority of legislation related to equal pay (1970), employment protection (1975), sex discrimination (1975) and race relations (1976). Whilst no doubt the structure of such legislation and their passage through Parliament would have differed had Heath been in government and Wilson in opposition, it is likely that the Conservatives would have countenanced similar measures. Certainly all three major parties believed (in the main) in consensus government and took utilitarianist or pragmatic rather than ideological stances. In such a political environment research into the sensitive area of sexuality could, and did, flourish.

The government of Margaret Thatcher, faced with a weak opposition, deliberately led an ideological revolution in British political and industrial life. To be reactive was equated with being radical and 'safety net' legislation was quickly abandoned and a 'deregulated' society encouraged. Thatcher's refusal to allow investigation into sexual attitudes and behaviour in the UK is widely known and is here presented as one example of the prevailing political will at that time. The implications for research into aspects of sexuality (during a period when HIV numbers were rising) is self-explanatory.

If an overview of influential legislation since the Second World War were taken it would quickly be seen that some led changes in society, or enforced the communal will, whilst others reacted to events. Atlee's 1945 Government was perhaps the most socially radical (Health Service Act, 1946; nationalisation of steel, coal, railway and universal benefits), whilst the Wilson era responded to the communal will (already mentioned) and Thatcher's period led via deregulation and reacting where required (as in the Children Act, 1989). It can therefore be concluded that a chapter on research issues in sexuality has to take account of political influence and its effects not only on the opportunity for research to take place, but also on the dissemination of results.

To some extent consideration has been given to the importance of gender roles and their place in the process of acquiring knowledge. That is to say that males and females are expected to function and perform in certain ways as both children and adults. Predominantly these expectations are that there will be an engagement in a heterosexual relationship, which will lead to the procreation of children and the perhaps naive belief of sexual fulfilment with a lifelong partner. This naivety also permeates the belief that there is limited knowledge surrounding heterosexual and homosexual relationships. The myth that a person chooses a straight or gay relationship is poorly understood, when research suggests that it is more common for an individual to engage in sexual exploration with both sexes. This is frequently disregarded by adults or simply passed over in the presence of children when children are in some sense more knowledgeable and up-to-date than adults. Knowledge is supplemented by school playground conversations, the media, and general adult gossip or conversations around the home. This information gathering is, however, potentially dangerous if adults are not prepared to discuss all aspects of sexuality with their children. Failure to discuss points will lead to an unbalanced and confusing view of the perceived rights and wrongs. Children need to understand that sexuality is not 'set in stone', that not all girls will have husbands and children, and not all boys will have wives and children. As adults we therefore have a responsibility to be open and honest with children and provide opportunities for discussion from an early age.

The questions that may then be asked is how soon and whose responsibility, and also how do adults overcome their embarrassment surrounding issues of sexuality or discuss the pleasures of engaging in sexual activity and of sharing an intimacy with a significant other of both physical and emotional sensations? Many professionals receive little or no training in dealing with questions surrounding sex and sexuality. Parents receive less.

CASE STUDY

Take as an example Sarah, who as an adult recalls her first experience of menstruation. Sarah remembers feeling different and having a sore stomach. She was 11 years old and found blood in her underwear. Sarah believed that she was seriously ill and called her mother to help. Little was said about the event and her mother placed what seemed a rather obscene pad between Sarahs legs to absorb the 'mess'. It was her sister who reassured her that this was part of normal development. Nothing more was discussed with her mother. Sarah wondered if her father knew and felt ashamed. Her knowledge was increased by reading anything that briefly resembled issues surrounding areas of menstruation, babies, and relationships.

What are your feelings and responses of your first exposure to either menstruation itself or discussions surrounding menstruation?

How might you have dealt with Sarah's embarrassment?

CONCLUSION

This chapter has explored research methodologies in the scientific environment and found both quantitative and qualitative methods useful yet still wanting. The examination of quasi-research methods such as literature searches, therapeutic approaches and cultural history studies provides some interesting points and occasionally some insight, but does not provide sufficient rigour, particularly in reliability. Accepting the influence of political climate is also interesting and salient within the research context and therefore cannot really be excluded. Yet sexuality as a school of human investigation, whether in the physiological, psychological or sociological domain, remains fragmented and disjointed. Each domain calls upon its own favoured investigative techniques and much data is published and fairly easy to obtain. Still, the nagging doubt remains that modern citizens are easily embarrassed by notions of sexuality, that the language of social interaction contains few acceptable words or phrases that can be used in public, and that early sexual experiences are the basis for our education. Later sexual behaviours, attitudes, and the widespread standard of knowledge is poor and may be a consequence of earlier life experiences.

So where should research go from here? Quantitative experimental work will continue in the hard sciences such as genetics, biology, physiology, pharmacology and medicine, but political will is needed to ensure that the findings reach children in an educationally acceptable way.

Interviews, surveys and questionnaires as data-collecting tools need more rigorous screening to exclude bias, misinformation or lies. Otherwise they should not be used at all. Their worth may return as the respondents feel more reassured that it is all right to profess their own individual views irrespective of society's judgement. In other words, a greater degree of tolerance in the wider society may lead to more valid data.

Observational techniques will probably remain in the hands of researchers such as Masters and Johnson or medical staff. It is possible that the response to voyeuristic curiosity which current 'education' videos provide may be a potential tool, albeit inadvertently.

Sexually unacceptable practices such as paedophilia need to be taken more seriously. Research could include the collation of data in a National Register. This could include not just criminal indictments, but also records of the children's statements, therapeutic records, police interviews and so on. Ethical guidelines need to be examined and agreed upon, again on a national basis, providing enough information for social policy-makers.

The use of historical research such as biographies, archive searches or cultural studies are useful. But if the researcher, like the epidemiological statistician, takes a back-calculation in an attempt to build a model even in a qualitative sense, more could be gained in terms of education and good practice.

We have at times felt frustrated in the acknowledgement of the small amount of information and knowledge that pertains to the need for exploration of these issues in relation to children pre-puberty. Perhaps we recognise in ourselves and significant others a need to 'know', in order to alleviate fear and anxiety. Despite the perceived rights of the child there is a definite failing on behalf of children in that they are perhaps unnecessarily wrapped up in cotton wool by adults purely to allow adults to protect themselves.

More research into adult behaviour and into the difficulties that adults encounter in terms of dissemination of information may have to be the starting point if children and young people are to be, first, treated on an mature basis, and second, if research is to go beyond the scope of its existing pattern. Children's nurses may be in a prime position to influence this change. The role of the nurse as advocate considers how best the needs of children and young people can be satisfied. There is an emphasis on health education and dissemination of knowledge, expertise and understanding. There could be more emphasis on the learning process regarding sex and sexuality once the immediate treatment regarding illness has been instigated and providing the child is not acutely ill. Leaflets and booklets are readily displayed regarding such areas as drugs, smoking and so on, yet there is little or no information regarding sex. This could be termed as opportunistic education not purely about contraception or HIV, but simply around how to engage in relationships, begin a sexual experience and recognise that the sex act is not only about procreation but also about pleasure.

REFERENCES

Abortion Act (1969) London: HMSO.
Abortion Law Reform Association (1967) *A guide to the abortion act.* London: Alta.
Bowlby J (1973) *Separation: Attachment and Loss,* vol. 2. New York: Basic Books.
Children Act (1989) Chapter 41. London: HMSO.
Children's Charter (1996) *Services for Children and Young People.* London: Department of Health.
Clarke M (1996) *Good Sex Guide.* Granada Television Series.
Condry J, Condry S (1976) Sex differences: A study in the eye of the beholder. *Child Development* **47,** 812–819.
de Beauvoir S (1988) *The Second Sex.* London: Pan Books.
Diamond M (1965) A critical evaluation of the ontogeny of human sexual behaviour. *Quarterly Review of Biology* **40,** 147–175.
Dion K, Berschied E (1974) Physical attraction and peer perception among children. *Sociometry* **37,** 1–12.
Employment Protection Act (1975) London: HMSO.
Equal Pay Act (1970) London: HMSO.
Family Planning Association (1994) Contraception: teenagers want confidential advice. *Nursing Standard* 8.31.18.
Field PA, Morse JM (1985) *Nursing Research: The Application of Qualitative Approaches.* Rockville: Aspen.
Freud S (1905) *Three Essays on the Theory of Sexuality,* standard edn. London: Hogarth Press.
Fromm E (1985) *The Art of Loving,* 4th edn. London: Unwin Paperbacks.
Glaser BG, Strauss AL (1967) *The Discovery of Grounded Theory.* New York: Adline Publishing Company.
Halson J (1991) *Young women, sexual harassment and heterosexuality: violence, power relations and mixed sex schooling.* In: Abott P, Wallace C (eds) *Gender Power and Sexuality.* Basingstoke: Macmillan.
Harlow HF (1971) *Learning to Love.* San Francisco: Albion.
Harris RH, Emberley M (1995) *Let's Talk about Sex: Growing Up, Changing Bodies, Sex and Sexual Health.* London: Walker Books.
Hazan C, Shaver P (1987) Romantic love conceptualised as an attachment process. *Journal of Personality and Social Psychology* **52,** 511–524.
Health Service Act (1946) London: HMSO.
Healthlines (1995) Sex education does not encourage teenage sex. *Healthlines,* October, 26.5.
Hebb DO (1972) *Textbook of Psychology,* 3rd edn. Philadelphia: WB Saunders.

Hendrick C, Hendrick SS (1986) Theory and method of love. *Journal of Personality and Social Psychology* 30, 392–402.

Husserl E (1965) *Phenomenology and the Crisis of Philosophy.* New York: Harper & Row.

Illingworth RS (1983) *The development of the infant and young child; normal and abnormal.* Edinburgh: Churchill Livingstone.

Jewitt C (1994) *Exploring Healthy Sexuality: A Guide to Sex Education in a Youth Setting.*

Kinsey AC, Pomeroy CE, Martin CE, Gebhard PH (1953) *Sexual Behaviour in the Human Female.* Philadelphia: WB Saunders.

Klein M (1946) Notes on some schizoid mechanisms. *The Writings of Melanie Klein* 3, 1–24.

Kohlberg L (1969) Stage and sequence: the cognitive–developmental approach to socialisation. In: Goslin DA (ed.) *Handbook of Socialisation Theory and Research.* Chicago: Rand McNally.

Kohlberg L (1973) Implications of developmental psychology for education: examples from moral development. *Educational Psychologist* 10, 2–14.

Lacan J (1992) *Ecrits: A Selection.* London: Routledge.

Lee JA (1977) A typology of styles of loving. *Personality and Social Psychology Bulletin* 3, 173–182.

Luria Z, Rubin JZ (1974) The eye of the beholder: Parents' views on sex of newborns. *American Journal of Orthopsychiatry* 44, 512–519.

MacDonald A, Clarke D (1988) Framework for care. *Nursing Times,* 31 August, 84 (35).

Mackereth C, Forder J (1996) Assessing the sexual health needs of young people. *Health Visitor* 69 (4), 144–146.

Masters W, Johnson V (1966) *Human Sexual Response.* London: Churchill.

Oppenheim AN (1966) *Questionnaire Design and Attitude Measurement.* New York: Basic Books Incorporated.

Pappenheim K (1995) Sex – A national taboo. *Midwives,* March.

Peters RS (1963) *Authority, Responsibility and Education.* London: Allen and Unwin.

Piaget J (1951) *The Origins of Intelligence in Children.* New York: International University Press.

Race Relations Act (1976) London: HMSO.

Royal College of Nursing (1995) *Health Needs of School Age Children.* Royal College of Nursing Briefing Paper.

Sex Discrimination Act (1975) London: HMSO.

Sexual Offenders Act (1956) London: HMSO.

Skinner BF (1938) *The Behaviour of Organisms.* New York: Appleton Century Croft.

Sternberg RJ (1988) A triangular theory of love. *Psychological Review* 93, 119–135.

Thompson E (1993) Personal services. *Health Service Journal* 29 April, 30–31.

United Nations Children's Fund (1995) *United Nations Convention on the Rights of the Child* (Article 12).

Wall-Hass CL (1991) Nurses' attitudes toward sexuality in adolescent patients. *Pediatric Nursing* 17(6), 549–555.

Watson JB (1950) *Behaviours.* New York: Norton.

Wellings K, Field J, Johnson AM, Wadsworth J (1994) *Sexual Behaviour in Britain, The National Survey of Sexual Attitudes and Lifestyles.* Harmondsworth: Penguin.

Winnicott DW (1970) Residential care as therapy. In: Winnicott C, Shepherd R, Dais M (eds) *Deprivation and Delinquency.* London: Tavistock.

Zuger B (1970) Gender role determination: a critical review of the evidence from hermaphroditism. *Psychosomatic Medicine* 32, 449–463.

FURTHER READING

Bagley, C, King K (1990) *Child Sexual Abuse: The Search for Healing.* London: Routledge.
A good historical and social overview with interesting cultural perspectives.

Cicchetti D, Carlson V (eds) (1990) *Child Maltreatment: Theory and Research on the Causes and Consequences of Child Abuse and Neglect.* Cambridge: Cambridge University Press.
An historical overview and recent psychological perspectives on consequences of developmental problems.

Faller KC (1990) *Understanding Child Sexual Maltreatment.* London: Sage.
Covers working with statutory bodies and should be read in conjunction with Kahan's book.

Jacobs E, Douglas G (1993) *Child Support and Legislation.* London: HMSO.
Provides guidance on the law and procedures within the field of Child Support.

Kahan B (1989) *Childcare Research Policy & Practice.* Milton Keynes: Open University Press.
A good broad approach to research issues for policy-makers.

Usher JM, Baker DC (1993) *Psychological Perspectives on Sexual Problems — New Directions in Theory and Practice.* London: Routledge.
Interesting views on the development of sexuality and its social/cultural presentations.

Wilson K and James A (1995) *The Child Protection Handbook.* London: Baillière Tindall.
The book covers assessments and current interventions for professionals in this field.

Chapter 10

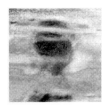

EMPTY BOXES

TONY HARRISON BA RN RSCN RNT

KEY POINTS	
○ CHILD HEALTH NURSING	○ SEXUALITY
○ FAMILY-CENTRED CARE	○ ATTITUDES
○ NURSING MODELS	○ KNOWLEDGE AND SKILL

The organisation of nursing in many areas of the UK revolves around frameworks called models. Many models use, for assessment, questions about activities of daily living, eating, sleeping, etc. which are frequently arranged in a box format for completion. One such activity is 'expressing sexuality'. In my experience this is always an 'empty box' in child health nursing.

Child care which is instinctive, fluid, seamless and natural is more normally called mothering, and care which is seen to be of this nature is more often seen as being maternal in type. It is not surprising that this *maternal* instinct seems to have been elevated from a Darwinian species survival talent into the Judeo–Christian mystic ideal of motherhood as a state of grace. But while this type of care does undoubtedly contain facets of all these images, it remains a complex package of responses, instincts, caring and nurturing, of which the most certain thing we can say is that, in general, it does children good.

Given that most children's nurses would agree that mothering does children good, it is not at all surprising that they frequently see maternal care as the model for nursing sick children. Indeed, this approach does have its advantages. First, it takes evidence from children themselves as to the best care they can imagine, which, of course, is predominantly maternal care. Second, even when the child's evidence is not taken into account child care workers would describe maternal care as being obviously effective. However, there are studies which show that this is not a phenomenon attributed only to biological parents, but that it is also possible for those who adopt the role of parents [Tizzard 1977]. The fact that nurses view themselves (and possibly the law may view them) in parental roles, i.e. *in loco parentis*, only goes to bolster this assumed link between the maternal and nursing care.

But just how far can this analogy be stretched? Nurses are palpably not the parents of the children for whom they provide professional care, and by implication, therefore, they lack the instinctive and historic commitment of the particular parent for a specific child. While it is undoubtedly true that many children's nurses do detail what they describe as 'maternal instincts' towards children in general, and some children more specifically, in my experience this does not seem to be linked to either their gender or whether, in fact, they have themselves parented a child. I would hypothesise that such innate ability actually reflects the paediatric equivalent of Benner's (1984) instinctual expert nurse. I am, however, inclined to think that if this *is* the case, then it is exactly as Benner describes: a mix of nursing knowledge, experience and creative aptitude and based on experiential learning and talent within the science of nursing. If this is the case then its links to the experience of motherhood seem not quite so firm. Motherhood as a model of nursing seems ultimately to resurrect the 'how can you nurse children if you have never had one?' argument which supposes that the current fashion for reflective practice (Coutts-Jarrnan, 1993; Reed and Procter, 1993) in which personal experience is analysed, and learning is identified and generalised to other situations, simply formalises a process that nurses have been doing for many years. This somewhat fatuous argument suggests that all children's nurses who are mothers/fathers have internalised their experiences of parenthood and simply extrapolated from these experiences nursing knowledge which could benefit others. Nurses who are not themselves parents must therefore be inadequate as children's nurses.

REFLECTION POINT

Do you feel that being a parent improves the ability to nurse children? Ask some child health nurses who were nursing children before and after the birth of their own child for their views.

MODELS OF NURSING

If, therefore, nursing is not simply mothering *per se*, then what is it? If, as many would suggest, it is more about empowering, who is to be empowered, the nurse, the parents or the child?

While working as a practitioner I have encountered various 'models' of nursing and would categorise the most common under two distinct headings.

○ *The professional babysitter*   In this 'model' the nurse truly is *in loco parentis*. S/he cares for the child while parents/relatives are absent from the ward. On their return, the child is handed back. Only the briefest of parental contact is made. Once returned, the nurse goes on to care for the next child who has been temporarily 'orphaned'.

○ *Family-centred care*   Arguments continue as to a clear, let alone a concise, definition of 'family-centred care' (Campbell and Summersgill, 1993), Personally, I have always tried to work within a definition which sees the child as the principal duty of care inextricably linked with the effects of the dynamics of the family (positive or negative) on his/her care. This approach is one which ensures a dynamic and hopefully therapeutic relationship, not only with the child but also with the family as a whole.

The professional nursing of children, then, is something different from the care of children by parents. Nursing is, at least in theory, methodical, planned, and based on nursing knowledge, research and theory. Perhaps the most striking indication of this is the use of the nursing process (a systematic approach to care borrowed from experimental research rather than endogenous to nursing) and last, but by no means least, the use of the so-called nursing models. Such approaches epitomise the difference between nursing and mothering. The nurse who, imbued with the spirit of family-centred care or a view of maternal care as perfect, and who would not consider approaching any subject which differs from the family norm, runs two dangers in regard to sexuality issues:

1. She assumes that the parents/family understand the importance of sexuality issues in childhood and so can make judgements on that basis.
2. If the family has a moral framework which prohibits discussion around this issue, then that includes everything to do with the subject entirely.

Professional care requires us to empower families with knowledge and understanding about sexuality issues so that they have the basis on which to make decisions. Collusion in silence serves neither child and family nor the proactive image of nursing. Mothering and nursing when blurred in distinction and view can give rise to collusion of this nature. Professional assessment and intervention as characterised by a model approach help us as carers to refocus.

Nursing models are, at their simplest, representations of reality. They represent one person's nursing approach, the salient points of which can be communicated to other nurses and utilised by them either wholly or with modification. Nursing models have the potential, at least in theory, of allowing the experienced nurse to take one specific approach and communicate it to less experienced nurses who wish to develop the ability to deliver care at a standard which the author of the model attests the approach produces.

The use of models in nursing in the UK is undeniable. The remit of this chapter, however, is not to discuss models *per se*, but rather to focus on how, and indeed if, models address issues pertinent to sexuality and sexual health of children in relation to nursing care. Because there are many models in existence, I have chosen to focus on just one group, often referred to as reductionist models.

The reductionist model most prevalent in the UK is arguably that devised by Roper, Logan and Tierney (1980). This model utilises the activities of daily living (normally an approach attributed to Henderson, 1960) as an assessment schedule and a basis for planning nursing care. Activities of daily living (ADL), as the name suggests, are activities which, when seen together, comprise life, i.e. eating, drinking, sleeping, etc. These authors are not alone in their use of ADLs, with more contemporary model architects such as Casey (1988) also utilising this approach. I must confess, however, that I am far from persuaded as to the validity of an approach which surmises that humans, of any age, are merely the sum of the things that they do. Furthermore, I find it strange, not to say a little alarming, that given their reductionist nature, they have gained such popularity in a profession which espouses holism as a central philosophy.

I would suggest that among the reasons for their popularity are that: they are easy to use; they are easy for clients to understand; lots of hospitals mass printed formats using this model (i.e. habit); nurse education has over-emphasised them; and finally, they have received a great deal of nursing press.

All too often the ADL approach has been utilised only as an assessment structure and not carried through logically into care planning. However, whatever its nature, it is well used and so will provide our exploration of whether sexuality is addressed within nursing care models.

REFLECTION POINT

If your area uses an ADL approach, or if you have encountered it in the past in relation to child care, which 'boxes' (ADLs) were, in your experience, least likely to be filled in on assessment (i.e. empty)?

From my experience, both as a clinician and as a nurse tutor, the two most likely boxes to be empty are those allocated to what Roper *et al.* refer to as 'dying' and 'expressing sexuality', that is, of course, assuming that such titles have been maintained. In some clinical areas the former has been changed to terms such as 'anxiety' or 'perception of illness', whilst the latter has often been reduced to what I will later argue are merely the constituent parts of the original with terms such as 'body image' or 'relationships'.

Although in this context, 'dying' is not part of our remit, the fact that it is consistently the absent bedfellow of sexuality is a very significant area for exploration. From my own clinical practice I have observed that those patients who are expected to die do have this box filled in. At best, however, the information it contains merely details the nurse's assessment of the patient's knowledge of their impending death or their wishes about the same, and at worst, is filled in with some idiot terminology such as 'for tender loving care (TLC)' — presumably to differentiate it from the rather rough, unloving care customarily dished out to those without the good fortune to have a terminal diagnosis!

It would seem that the term 'dying' is seen by many nurses as dealing only with the act of death rather than the anxiety and fear inherent in ill-health. Consequently it is assumed permissible to avoid it altogether, especially if staff themselves have difficulty coping with any discussion of the topic.

I would argue that the same is true when attempting to complete the 'expressing sexuality' box in that many nurses associate this exclusively with sexual acts. It is hardly surprising, therefore, that given such an all too narrow definition, some nurses may experience anxiety even at the possibility of discussing such intimate topics with families and children.

This anxiety may have several roots or variables affecting it.

TERMINOLOGY

The term sexuality, Batcup and Thomas (1994) have argued, has not been satisfactorily defined within the nursing context. Many definitions of the term are given in this text ranging from the purely biological through to the holistic. In my experience, practitioners do tend to associate the term with sexual acts rather than as a holistic concept including self-regard, body image, sexual function, gender significance and relationships. This seems adequately demonstrated by those units which have chosen to supplant the terminology 'expressing sexuality' for others such as body image or relationships, thus replacing the term for the whole with one of its component parts. Furthermore, sexuality defined in terms of genital acts is likely only to be applied to the teenage population. Younger children are, of course, seen as being sexless. Now, this all seems extremely curious from a professional group who, with the possible exception of Health Visitors, receive more education about childhood development, gender socialisation, sexual evolution/activity and relationships than any other. Having, at least in theory, covered such issues within training, how can we fail, so pointedly, to address them in practice? Perhaps the answer lies in just how these issues are actually covered in the pre-registration education programmes – if indeed at all – while in post-registration education you might be hard pressed to find courses or programmes that cover the subject at all!

CASE STUDY

Mary and Geoff, both 26, had been trying for some time to have children. Eventually Mary was treated with fertility drugs, after which she gave birth to quads. At birth one of the children, a girl, died. The three remaining boys, although experiencing some health problems, all survived.

All three boys were treated for various conditions on the same paediatric medical ward, and at times, particularly during the winter months, the boys tended to share coughs and colds and so were sometimes both for social as well as medical reasons admitted on to the ward en masse.

A nurse caring for the boys (all of whom were rather heavy positers) had run out of their own clothes and so resorted to the clothes cupboard to dress the boys after their bath. Unfortunately only pink baby clothes were available. When the mother arrived she became extremely distressed.

Why do you think mother was distressed?

How could this situation have been avoided?

The above story is a real one. The ward in question used an ADLs approach and, as frequently was the case, the admitting nurse had not filled in the 'expressing sexuality' box at all. She explained later that as she felt it was about sexual relationships it had no pertinence to this particular case. The nurse who had been caring for the children on the day in question had referred to the care plan and assessment data prior to delivering care and noted nothing which would explain why the mother became distressed.

Mary and her husband had been deeply saddened by the death of their daughter as they had wanted a girl child. This particular family had long traditions of and valued gender-specific colour coding in relation to their children. When the mother saw her three little boys in pink it reminded her physically and forcibly of her dead daughter and how she would have looked had she survived. This was the cause of this mother's distress. While colour-coding in relation to boys and girls is obviously an issue of gender, in this instance I would argue that it could have been assessed under the heading of 'expressing sexuality', which would have saved both mother and nurse much unnecessary distress. To some, but not to the mother concerned, this may seem a small matter in the run of things, but it is an issue of quality and is about care.

FEAR, TABOO AND TREMOR

At the beginning of 1997 much negative media interest was focused around a review of research on teenage pregnancies produced by the University of York (Dickson *et al.*, 1997). The report concluded that children need to be taught about sex and contraception prior to puberty. The furore which followed the report, largely from the political right, was as vocifer-ous as it was nonsensical. Nurses working in a society, culture and climate which, at least in certain quarters (and sadly those which seem to have most access to the media), insist that any sex education of pre-pubescent children can only bring about harm, are hardly likely to feel at ease encouraging young clients to talk about matters relating to sexuality. The experi-ence of the school nurse in Leeds pilloried in the press for dealing with questions about obscure sexual practices involving chocolate bars can do little to increase the confidence of children's nurses in dealing with the subject. In addition, and more alarmingly, concealed within this stifling approach to children, sex and education by the media there seems also to be the insidious perception of the nurse as a possible abuser. The Allit situation (see Royal College of Nursing, 1994), the Donnelly case (see Long, 1992), and latterly the well-meaning but alarmist advice from the RCN about sexual abuse and children (1996), only help to fos-ter a suspicion in the mind of both the public and the profession that there is something potentially murky whenever sex and childhood collide in the context of nursing. But why should this be?

The writer and humorist Willy Rushton once claimed that Queen Victoria did in fact die in 1961. He was, of course, referring to the British view of sex. The poet Philip Larkin dated the event slightly later when he declared that:

Sexual intercourse began in 1963 ...
Between the end of the Chatterly trial and the Beatles' first LP.

Even as we near the end of the twentieth century, the cultural ethos of Victorian England seems still to have a strange and persuasive stranglehold on our view of sexuality. In the minds of many, including some neophyte nurses, any discussion of sex is seen as lewd and so is best avoided. Yet even the most cursory glance through any of our national newspapers would leave one to suppose that, as a nation, we are completely at ease with even the most bizarre of sexual practices where everything from the sexual peccadillos of the rich and famous to the more instructional journalistic approach which offers advice on how to do it longer, slower and with more feeling compete for our attention. Yet here, too, the tradition of the late Victorians is felt, in particular the seaside post card, where the emphasis on the nudge and the wink still seems to pervade. For the British, it would seem that it is only permissible to talk about sex as long as we do so with tongue in cheek — if you will pardon the expression!

One would have hoped that the process of nurse education would address such pre-existing problems and enhance the student nurse's ability to deal with issues of sexuality. However, some would argue that this is not actually occurring (Van Oolfen and Charnock, 1994: 202–210). This is possibly due to the fact that nurse educationalists themselves rose through a multilayered system in which sexual inhibitions are laid down rather than removed. The nurse tutor who teaches sexual health who is him- or herself sexually repressed, homophobic or a misogynist is sadly not a rarity.

INADEQUACY

My experience of teaching paediatrics at post-registration level has been that many students express feelings of inadequacy about dealing with issues of sexuality. Inadequacy is a very complex emotion and, I would argue, should never be interpreted as simply feeling that a subject is too sensitive to deal with. Inadequacy is dangerous because it is disempowering. Nurses who have confidence in their ability to deal with issues which are raised around sensitive or intimate topic areas are more happy to approach them, sure in the knowledge that they have the ability to make a significant difference.

Billy Connolly once said that God played his most devilish trick on the English when He made humans have sex with the same organs they use to urinate and defaecate. If there is one thing people like talking about less than sex, it is any reference to their toilet habits. Yet bowel function is one area commonly addressed in nursing and, even given the intimate nature of the subject, nurses will and do address the issue of altered bowel function with alacrity because they feel that they have both the skills and the knowledge to deal with any questions which may arise. It is quite acceptable, therefore, for nurses to enquire about bowel motions when the reason for the child's admission has nothing to do with bowel function because they feel confident to give advice on dietary manipulation, etc. which will make them feel effective.

Sex and sexuality, however, remain areas where most 'angels' fear to tread. Even enlightened nurses who have, despite social pressure and possibly their own upbringing, identified that sexuality is a vital area in nursing care may be, and in my experience often are, completely paralysed by a lack of knowledge and skills.

CARE ORGANISATION

Holism has been a concept and word much trumpeted in nursing and most nurses would consider their approach to nursing care to be a holistic one. Holism deals with the whole person as a complete entity rather than seeking to reduce them to their constituent parts. It is even a philosophy eschewed by nurses who predominantly use a reductionist model like the Roper, Logan and Tierney model under discussion. A tenet of holism is that the nurse will assess and plan care to meet all the patient's identified nursing needs regardless of whether these pertain to the reason for admission or not. The child admitted for repair of a squint may also have a dietary problem identified which makes little difference to the surgery, but which is causing the family some concern. The nurse will deal with this problem by getting dietary advice, referring to dieticians, Health Visitors, etc. Most of us would, I feel, like to work and nurse in this comprehensive manner, but is that always feasible, possible or desirable on an organisational level?

As throughput and bed occupancy have become watch-words within hospital environments it must be the case that prioritisation will change. Staff shortages, increased patient load and declining availability of specialist nurses is now leading to a tighter focus of care which may eventually see holism as a luxury and one which is not entirely suited to the modern health care system. In this system, nursing has a tight focus on the presenting problem of the child and family. But while in some scenarios either model may be defendable, selective holism, i.e. missing out the bits with which we may not be comfortable, can never be defended and is never acceptable.

PERSONAL BELIEFS/PROFESSIONAL VALUES

While it is inevitable that there will be many who will not share my particular views, and even a considerable number of individuals whose views are diametrically opposite, the issue at hand is not the variance of opinion but just what the approach of the profession should be as a whole. It is well documented that personal beliefs and values *do* influence the care we give, both negatively and positively, and that it is part of every individual nurse's duty to examine this interplay between the internal personal world and the external professional one in order to ensure that patients and their families receive the best possible care.

John is 14 years old and has Down syndrome. He is admitted to a paediatric medical ward with problems of asthma. The auxiliary nurse finds John masturbating in a cubicalised toilet on the ward and remonstrates with him loudly about how this is bad for him and then makes him wash his hands. You, as the nurse in charge, observe this. What would you do?

The auxiliary nurse in the above scenario obviously believes that masturbation is not a positive thing for John. She may believe this honestly and totally. Given that this is the case, should she not in her conviction try to impress upon John the problem with the activity she has observed? Here we have either a clash of beliefs or one individual imposing their values on another. We as nurses could say that when we are dealing with patients and their families we are there to empower their health by advice and intervention which increases their capacity for sexual health or indeed decreases their risk of disease or other problems. Within this paradigm approach we are stating implicitly that the issue in hand is not what we believe or what we do in relation to our sexuality, but rather enhancing whatever it is the client wants to do or express. However, this client-centred model is also deficient in other serious ways. The teenage boy who discusses the fact that he gets excited at the thought of forcing girls to have sex and would like to know how to protect himself against genitourinary infections is obviously not going to receive approbation from any nurse. In this example, the sexual expression in question, i.e. rape, could be seen as unhealthy and so need correction. But how is that decision made and who actually makes the decision? The auxiliary nurse in the previous example thought that masturbation was an unacceptable activity which was unhealthy. Who is to say that she is not right?

Whilst an agreed definition of expressing sexuality (as advised by Batcup and Thomas) is required for nursing, some agreement is also desirable on just what is and what is not healthy within that expression. While what is socially sanctioned as healthy in terms of sexuality and its expression does obviously change with time, this change is never uniform across society. The de-medicalisation/criminalisation of homosexuality would provide an excellent example of this and highlights the fact that, although many people now see homosexuality as a legitimate sexual expression, there remain many who would strongly and often quite vocally disagree. How, then, as health care providers, are we going to find a consensus view of what is sexually healthy in a society where consensus is so hard to achieve?

It may be that sexual health can only be defined as that which sits most comfortably with the internal reality of the individual, providing that it falls within boundaries of sexual expression that are not harmful or exploitative to others. However, how does this sit with regard to children who may not appreciate harm and who may not recognise exploitation? I would argue that any social definitions of sexual health which revolve around the child being socialised to *fit in* with the family, group or community norm does, in reality, negate any notion of inner harmony in which the child learns to balance its internal and external worlds, except, of course, by force and at cost. Such a definition also denies the positive possibility of the creative tensions so evident in the battle between many teenagers and their parents during puberty.

The WHO definition of sexual health is:

> *A capacity to enjoy and control sexual and reproductive behaviour in accordance with a social and personal ethic. Freedom from fear, shame, guilt, false belief and other psychological factors inhibiting sexual response and impairing sexual relationships and freedom from organic disorders, diseases and deficiencies that interfere with sexual and reproductive functions.*

This definition (WHO Regional Office for Europe, 1986) is certainly comprehensive! A closer reading of this definition does, however, reveal the fact that it seems to have been developed not with children but with adults in mind. The 'personal ethic' mentioned is, in many instances, not personal to the child at all but specific to the adults around it. It is also a personal ethic which may be beyond or even actually denied children, either because of the nature of their particular stage of childhood or, more likely, the nature of the experience of the adults who order their world.

Once defined, however, the professional approach to enhancing sexual development must hinge on that particular definition rather than vacillate with the individual view of each nurse. To do otherwise would be to negate any view of parity of care and equal access to equitable health care, advice and health enhancement.

THE HEALTH PROMOTION ROLE OF THE NURSE

Much has been both made and assumed about the health promotion role of the nurse. Nurses are seen as front line workers for whom the opportunity of both opportunistic and planned health promotion is a reality (Pender, 1987; McBridge, 1995). Health promotion skills are included in most curricula, although on occasion I would argue that the skills actually concentrated on are health education rather than health promotion, which implies an ability to promote behaviour change. This idealised world of health promoters in action can, however, be questioned.

REFLECTION POINT

Sample several care plans in your clinical area and identify how many sections deal with a health promotion issue which was not the primary admitting concern.

The pace of health care, certainly within the acute sector, has forced many health care workers to alter their generally holistic approach to care to one which is more focused on the priorities of care which their particular organisation dictates. The division of health care into semi-autonomous and perpetually competing entities has, for some, produced a work environment populated with goals which are both very specific and specifically short term. Health promotion and indeed health education which neither contribute to 'closed consultant episodes' or which do not bear fruit for some time, when this patient may be in fact some other Trust's problem (particularly true in paediatric practice), are hardly likely to be prioritised. The possibility of skill mix alterations which further reduce the contact of the qualified practitioner and the child does nothing to encourage or validate this significant holistic role. This being increasingly the case, it must fall to the profession to protect, project and enhance the roles which it sees as being part of its armoury of skills.

I would argue that health promotion falls into this category. Politics must meet passion in this debate if this vital role for the nurse is not to be eroded. Within the current debate on evidence-based nursing (and indeed medicine) it seems strange that an excellent example of effective nursing, i.e. health promotion/education, which has been proven to be effective in enhancing health, reducing disease and achieving its goals if accepted by the client, is largely ignored.

There are, it would seem, many problems with addressing sexuality issues as they relate to children in nursing care. The model approach chosen for critique is only one of many and all differ significantly – even radically – one from another. It would, however, be unfair to single out this, albeit reductionist model, for singular criticism. In its favour it does, at least in its original form, actually highlight *expressing sexuality* as an issue. In addition, it does have a component part which asks the nurse to correlate the activities of living with a developmental and independence/dependence continuum scale. In this, the authors of this reductionist model and others like it have also highlighted the area (in Roper, Logan and Tierney's case explaining in some depth what they think should be considered under this ADL in their model) within the context of nursing. Users of other more symbolic or interactionist models may, at this point, be feeling just a little smug. However, it must be remembered that these models actually give no prompts at all and that it is only the individual nurse who has already identified this area as being important to nursing care who will probably ever actually address the issue. This then brings us back to the need for addressing sexuality and of the skills needed in order to incorporate it into care. Given that the ADLs do specifically address this issue of sexuality, the tool should not at this stage be blamed for the users' deficiencies.

It is important to make clear the premise on which this author would encourage all nurses caring for children and families to address issues of sexuality in care. Being a fan of holism and health promotion, I would always advocate a holistic health assessment for any child/family accessing nursing care at any point (an issue which may yet be a political battle for the future). However, this is not to suggest that nurses should become intrusive, voyeuristic or obsessive. I would argue that, as with diet, sleep, development and play, all families have a right to be offered, with clear explanation, the opportunity to voice health-related concerns about any area of life and to receive appropriate intervention and assistance.

What is at issue is more the offer than the response. I would anticipate that most, when offered the opportunity to discuss any problems relating to sexuality, sex or gender issues, would actually say that they had none. Maybe this is because nurses are themselves unclear, unsure and under-confident in this area and that when on the rare occasion an offer to discuss problems relating to sexuality is made, the nature of the subject under discussion is not actually clarified. The parent/child may not fully understand the nature of the enquiry and this may make them seem antagonistic, which indeed may be another reason why the nurse may have been anxious about approaching the issue in the first place. In my experience, any family, when asked questions of a personal nature which they cannot fully understand, is likely to respond negatively. For example, when I have asked about a patient's living conditions, families have often responded negatively. On reflection, this was because I had not clearly identified with these families either the nature or the reason for the enquiry, i.e. if a child has asthma, the nature of home heating levels, carpeting, etc. may be significant in relation to the child's care (dust allergy). Once explained, however, I have never encountered any problems. The same applies equally to explaining the holistic nature of a nursing assessment and the construction of a nursing care plan. Having adequately explained the approach and what each activity stands for, including *expressing sexuality*, again, I have had few problems.

The issue then is one of quality. True, some parents and indeed their children may suggest that they have no health concerns in this area, and for many of them that will be true. Some may have difficulty in discussing such issues at any level because they reflect a previous social response (and current one if some debates are to be considered) of sexual repression, which has left them unable to address such issues without embarrassment. This then becomes an issue not only of quality, but also of trust.

The solution, I would argue, must rest with education. Educating nurses to see health promotion as their role, educating nurses to be confident to deal with this role in all its aspects and educating nurses about the vital necessity of dealing with these issues. Education of the public and education of decision-makers must also follow. A role not valued is quickly lost within our health care system and nurses must be proactive in retaining their holistic health promotion role rather than, in the name of short-term efficiency gain, having it rationalised into a role which is predicated by a 'sometime, but only if you've got the time' credo.

REFLECTION POINT

What can you do to alter the situation in your own practice so that all children and families receive both the offer of help on issues of sexuality and the explanation and information on what these are?

REFERENCES

Batcup D, Thomas B (1994) Mixing the genders. An ethical dilemma. How nursing theory has dealt with sexuality and gender. *Nursing Ethics* 1(1), 43–52.
Benner P (1984) *From Novice to Expert. Clinical Excellence in Nursing Practice.* Berkely, CA: Addison-Wesley.

Campbell S, Summersgill P (1993) Keeping it in the family. Defining and developing family centred care. *Child Health* 1(1), 17–28.

Casey A (1988) A partnership with child and family. *Senior Nurse* 8(4) 8–9.

Coutts-Jarrnan J (1993) Using reflection and experience in nursing education. *British Journal of Nursing* 2(1), 77–80.

Dickson R, Fullerton D, Eastwood A, Sheldon T, Sharp F (1997) Preventing and reducing the adverse effects of unintended teenage pregnancies. *Effective Health Care* 3(1). NHS Centre for Reviews and Dissemination, University of York. Plymouth: Churchill Livingstone.

Henderson V (1960) *Basic Principles of Nursing Care*. London: International Council of Nurses.

Long T (1992) To protect the public and ensure justice is done: An examination of the Philip Donnelly case. *Journal of Advanced Nursing* 17, 5–9.

McBridge AS (1995) *Health Promotion in Hospital*. London: Scutari.

Pender N (1987) *Health Promotion in Nursing Practice*. Stamford: Appleton & Lang.

Reed J, Procter S (1993) *Nurse Education: A Reflective Approach*. London: Edward Arnold.

Roper N, Logan W, Tierney A (1980) *The Elements of Nursing*. Edinburgh: Churchill Livingstone.

Royal College of Nursing (1994) *The Care of Sick Children. A Review of the Guidelines in the Wake of the Allit Enquiry*. London: Royal College of Nursing.

Royal College of Nursing (1996) *Protection of Nurses Working with Children and Young People*, Issues in Nursing and Health no. 39. London: Royal College of Nursing.

Tizzard B (1977) *Adoption. A Second Chance*. London: Open Books.

Van Oolfen E, Charnock A (1994) *Sexuality and Patient Care. A Guide for Nurses and Teachers*. London: Chapman & Hall.

WHO Regional Office for Europe (1986) *Concepts for Sexual Health*. Copenhagen: WHO.

FURTHER READING

Foster RL, Hunsberger MM, Anderson JJT (1989) *Family Centred Nursing Care of Children*. Philadelphia: WB Saunders.
An excellent overview section on promoting healthy sexuality. (1989 version only.)

Igoe JB (1993) Healthier children through empowerment. In: Wilson-Barnett J, MacLeod-Clark J (eds) *Research in Health Promotion and Nursing*. Hampshire: Macmillan.
An excellent discussion re the topic in question.

Phillips T (1994) Children and power. In: Lindsay B (ed.) *The Child and Family. Contemporary Nursing Issues in Child Health and Care*. London: Ballière Tindall.
This chapter looks at the changes in the power base of children in general and sexually over history.

Savage J (1987) *Nurses, Gender and Sexuality*. London: Heinemann.
Excellent chapter critique on the Roper, Logan and Tierney model in relation to sexuality.

INDEX

Location references in **bold** indicate figures and tables

Thatcher, Margaret and research into sexuality, 213
Therapeutic behaviour, 3
Transexualism, 62
Transvestitism, 62
True hermaphroditism, 103
Turner's syndrome, 95–97

U
Undescended testes, 109–111
Unilateral cryptorchidism, 109, 111
United Nations Convention on the Rights of the
    Child, 184–185, 206–207
USA, sexual health promotion programmes, 180–181
    abstinence-based, 172, 182–183

V
Vaginal
    atresia, 107

development, 91, **92**, 106–107
    malformations, 106–107
Verbal attack, 84
Victorian morality
    attitudes towards sexuality, 225
    and literature, 211
    pornography, origins, 212

W
Wardship, concept, 14
WHO definition, sexual health, 228
Women, sexual abuse of children, 148, 151
Woodehouse Park Clinic, Manchester, 192

Y
Young people's rights, 183–188